SADLIER

VOCABULARY WORKSHOP®

ACHIEVE

Level E

Jerome Shostak

Senior Series Consultant

Vicki A. Jacobs, Ed.D.
Director, Teacher Education Program
Harvard Graduate School of Education
Cambridge, Massachusetts

Series Consultants

Louis P. De Angelo, Ed.D.
Superintendent of Schools
Diocese of Wilmington
Wilmington, Delaware

John Heath, Ph.D.
Professor of Classics
Santa Clara University
Santa Clara, California

Sarah Ressler Wright,
   M.A. English Ed, NBCT
Head Librarian
Rutherford B. Hayes High School
Delaware, Ohio

Carolyn E. Waters, J.D., Ed.S.
Georgia Dept. of Education (Ret.)
English Language Arts Consultant
Woodstock, Georgia

Reviewers

The publisher wishes to thank for their comments and suggestions the following teachers and administrators, who read portions of the series prior to publication.

Sr. Maureen Lawrence McDermott, IHM, PhD
Superintendent, Secondary Schools
Archdiocese of Philadelphia Schools
Philadelphia, PA

Aidan T. Brett
Teacher, Language Arts
Springfield High School
Springfield, PA

Kristy L. Raymond
English Teacher, Dept. Chair
Livermore High School
Livermore, CA

Audrey G. Silverman
National Board Certified English Teacher
Dr. Michael Krop Senior High School
Miami, FL

Dawn S. Wolfe
Teacher, English Department
Walnut Hills High School
Cincinnati, OH

Cover: Concept/Art and Design: MK Advertising, Studio Montage and William H. Sadlier, Inc. Cover pencil: Shutterstock.com/VikaSuh.
Photo Credits: akg-images: 57, 125 *top*; RIA Nowosti: 212 *top*. Alamy Stock Photo: 13 *background*; Photos 12: 144 *right*; Mark Boulton: 24 *left*; Alistair Heap: 113 *top*; Jill Hunter: 168; Geraint Lewis: 13 *inset*, 196; Jochen Tack: 36 *top*; A.F. Archive: 28, 120; Archive Images: 68 *top*; Dinodia Photos: 208; Image Source: 37 *center*; imageBROKER/Norbert Michalke: 81 *top right*; Ivy Close Images: 76; MARKA: 29; Mary Evans Picture Library: 12 *right*, 25 *bottom*, 100 *top*, 164; Moviestore Collection Ltd: 40; Pictorial Press Ltd: 128; Trinity Mirror/Mirrorpix: 100 *bottom*. Art Resource/Mingei International Museum: 169 *center*; Nick Saunders/Barbara Heller Photo Library, London: 169 *bottom*; Nimatallah: 200 *top*; Vanni: 17; Alfredo dagli Orti: 172; DeA Picture Library: 200 *bottom*, 201 *bottom*; Réunion des Musées Nationaux: 56 *top*; Scala: 56 *bottom*; Scala/White Images: 69 *top*, 188 *left*; The New York Public Library: 44. Associated Press: 80-81 *top left*. Bridgeman Images/The Worst of all Losses, (oil on cavas), Brooks, Robin (Contemporary Artist)/ Private Collection: 188; Ken Welsh/Portrait of William Shakespeare (1564-1616) (engraving), English School, (19th century)/Private Collection: 12 *left*; Manufacturing 'Tyrian Purple', illustration from 'Hutchinson's History of the Nations', c.1910-15 (litho), Dudley, Robert Ambrose (1867-1951)/ Private Collection/The Stapleton Collection: 24 *right*; The Singer Chenard, as a Sans-Culotte, 1792 (oil on panel), Boilly, Louis Leopold (1761-1845)/Musee de la Ville de Paris, Musee Carnavalet, Paris, France: 25 *top*. Everett Collection, Inc.: 84. Getty Images: 192; DEA/G. DAGLI ORTI: 124 *top*; Mitchell Funk: 176; Chris Hellier: 216; Julie Lemberger: 156 *inset*; Spencer Platt: 112; Petr Svarc: 125 *bottom*; Bettmann: 101 *background*, 104, 108, 116; Bridgeman Images: 124 *bottom*; Congressional Quarterly/ Scott J. Ferrell: 157 *top*; Photodisc: 145 *inset*. The Granger Collection: 60. The Image Works, Inc./James Marshal: 113 *bottom*; Lebrecht: 212 *bottom*; Museum of London/HIP: 101 *inset*; TopFoto/Fortean: 160. iStockphoto.com/monkeybusinessimages: 10. Lebrecht Music & Arts: 132, 213. Mary Evans Picture Library: 68 *bottom*; Classic Stock/C.P. Cushing: 152. Masterfile/ImageBROKER/ Norbert Michalke: 81 *bottom right*. NASA: 72. Newscom/CQ Roll Call/Tom Williams: 220. Photodisc: 13 *background*, 56 *inset*, 113 *background*, 144 *background*, 144 *inset*, 156 *top*, 188 *inset*. PhotoEdit/Michelle D. Bridwell: 157 *bottom*. Pierre Gildesgame Maccabi Sports Museum, Ramat-Gan, Israel/The Joseph Yekutieli Maccabi Sports Archive: 144 *center*. Punchstock/Photodisc: 13 *inset*. Science Source/John Eastcott & Yva Momatiuk: 64; Patrick Landmann: 36 *bottom*; Biology Pics: 201 *top*. Shutterstock.com/Booka: 37 *top*; Fedorov Oleksiy: 68; Ice-Storm: 100 *background*; Janika: 100 *top*; MustafaNC: 100 *top*; Myotis: 37 *bottom*; nadi555: 144 *inset*; Saranai: 57 *inset*; zhu difeng: 24 *background*; Kaspars Grinvalds: 113 *top*; Alexey Laputin: 204; Fedorov Oleksiy: 69 *top*; Olena Zaskochenko: 80 *background*; NASA/AridOcean: 169 *top right*. Sport Club Hakoah, Vienna: 144 *left*, 145. Superstock/Minden Pictures/BIA/Chris Romeiks: 148. Wikimedia Commons/Smithsonian National Postal Museum: 16; The Metropolitan Museum of Art/Napoleon Sarony: 88.I

S® and **VOCABULARY WORKSHOP**® are registered trademarks of William H. Sadlier, Inc.

Printed in the United States of America.
ISBN: 978-1-4217-8510-3
5 6 7 8 9 10 11 BRR 23 22 21 20 19

For additional online resources, go to SadlierConnect.com.

CONTENTS

iWords Audio Program is available at **SadlierConnect.com**.

PROGRAM FEATURES

For more than five decades, VOCABULARY WORKSHOP has proven to be a highly successful tool for vocabulary growth and the development of vocabulary skills. It has also been shown to help students prepare for standardized tests. VOCABULARY WORKSHOP ACHIEVE maintains that tradition in a newly designed format.

Each of VOCABULARY WORKSHOP ACHIEVE's 15 Units introduces 20 words in two 10-word lists—**Set A** and **Set B**. Both Set A and Set B contain exercises to help you develop deeper understanding of the 10 words in each set. Combined Sets A and B then provide practice with all 20 of the words in the Unit. Review and Word Study activities follow Units 3, 6, 9, 12, and 15 and offer practice with the 60 vocabulary words in the preceding three Units.

Each level of VOCABULARY WORKSHOP ACHIEVE introduces and provides practice with 300 vocabulary words and contains features such as reading passages, writing prompts, vocabulary in context, evidence-based questions, and word study that will help you to master these new vocabulary words and succeed in using skills to comprehend unfamiliar words.

Each Unit in VOCABULARY WORKSHOP ACHIEVE consists of the following sections for **Set A** and **Set B**: an introductory **Reading Passage** that shows how vocabulary words are used in context, **Definitions** that include sentences that give examples of how to use the words, **Using**

Context, Choosing the Right Word, and **Completing the Sentence**—activities that provide practice with the vocabulary words. Each introductory **Reading Passage** is a nonfiction text that includes most of the vocabulary words from the Unit to which it belongs. In addition, **Synonyms**, **Antonyms**, and **Vocabulary in Context** in combined Sets A and B round out each Unit with practice with all 20 Unit words.

The five Review sections cover all 60 words from their corresponding Units. **Vocabulary for Comprehension** is modeled on the reading sections of college entrance exams. It presents reading comprehension questions, including vocabulary-related items and evidence-based items that are based on the reading passages.

Word Study sections that contain activities on **Idioms**, **Denotation and Connotation**, and **Classical Roots** follow the Review. These sections will help you develop your understanding of figurative language and practice skills that will help you to determine the meaning of new and unfamiliar vocabulary.

The Final Mastery Test assesses a selection of words from the year and allows you to see the growth you have made in acquiring new vocabulary words and in mastering the comprehension skills you need to understand unfamiliar words.

ONLINE RESOURCES
SadlierConnect.com

Go to **SadlierConnect.com** to find iWords, an audio program that provides pronunciations, definitions, and examples of usage for all of the vocabulary words presented in this level of VOCABULARY WORKSHOP ACHIEVE. You can listen to the entire **Reading Passage** and the 20 Unit vocabulary words one word at a time, or download all of the words in any given Unit.

At **SadlierConnect.com** you will also find interactive vocabulary quizzes, flash cards, and interactive games and puzzles that will help reinforce and enrich your understanding of the vocabulary words in this level of VOCABULARY WORKSHOP ACHIEVE.

VOCABULARY IN CONTEXT

The context of a word is the printed text of which that word is part. By studying a word's context, we may find clues to its meaning. We might find a clue in the immediate or adjoining sentence or phrase in which the word appears; in the topic or subject matter of the passage; or in the physical features—such as photographs, illustrations, charts, graphs, captions, and headings—of a page itself.

The **Reading Passages** as well as the **Using Context**, **Choosing the Right Word**, **Vocabulary in Context**, and **Vocabulary for Comprehension** exercises that appear in the Units, the Reviews, and the Final Mastery Test provide practice in using context to decode and to determine the meaning of unfamiliar words.

Three types of context clues appear in the exercises in this book.

A **restatement clue** consists of a synonym for or a definition of the missing word. For example:

Faithfully reading a weekly newsmagazine not only broadens my knowledge of current events and world or national affairs but also _____ my vocabulary.

a. decreases   **b.** fragments   **c.** increases   **d.** contains

In this sentence, *broadens* is a synonym of the missing word, *increases*, and acts as a restatement clue for it.

A **contrast clue** consists of an antonym for or a phase that means the opposite of the missing word. For example:

"My view of the situation may be far too rosy," I admitted. "On the other hand, yours may be a bit (**optimistic, bleak**)."

In this sentence, *rosy* is an antonym of the missing word, *bleak*. This is confirmed by the presence of the phrase *on the other hand*, which indicates that the answer must be the opposite of *rosy*.

An **inference clue** implies but does not directly state the meaning of the missing word or words. For example:

"A treat for all ages," the review read, "this wonderful novel combines the _____ of a scholar with the skill and artistry of an expert _____."

a. ignorance . . . painter   **c.** wealth . . . surgeon

b. wisdom . . . beginner   **d.** knowledge . . . storyteller

In this sentence, there are several inference clues: (a) the word *scholar* suggests knowledge; (b) the words *novel*, *artistry*, and *skill* suggest the word *storyteller*. These words are inference clues because they suggest or imply, but do not directly state, the missing word or words.

VOCABULARY AND READING

There is a strong connection between vocabulary knowledge and reading comprehension. Although comprehension is much more than recognizing words and knowing their meanings, comprehension is nearly impossible if you do not know an adequate number of words in the text you are reading or have the vocabulary skills to figure out their meaning.

The **Reading Passages** in this level provide extra practice with vocabulary words. Vocabulary words are in boldface to draw your attention to their uses and contexts. Context clues embedded in the passages encourage you to figure out the meanings of words before you read the definitions provided on the pages directly following the passages.

Test Prep

Your knowledge of word meanings and your ability to think carefully about what you read will help you succeed in school and on standardized tests, including the SAT® and ACT® exams.

The **Vocabulary for Comprehension** exercises in each Review consist of a reading passage followed by comprehension questions. The passages and questions are similar to those that you are likely to find on standardized tests.

Types of Questions

You are likely to encounter the following types of questions in VOCABULARY WORKSHOP ACHIEVE and on standardized tests.

Main Idea Questions generally ask what the passage as a whole is about. Often, but not always, the main idea is stated in the first paragraph of the passage. You may also be asked the main idea of a specific paragraph. Questions about the main idea may begin like this:

- The primary or main purpose of the passage is . . .

- The author's primary or main purpose in the passage is to . . .

- Which of the following statements most nearly paraphrases the author's main idea in the ninth paragraph (lines 77–88)?

- The main purpose of the fourth paragraph (lines 16–25) is to . . .

Detail Questions focus on important information that is explicitly stated in the passage. Often, however, the correct answer choices do not use the exact language of the passage. They are instead restatements, or paraphrases, of the text.

Vocabulary in Context Questions check your ability to use context to identify a word's meaning. For example:

- As it is used in paragraph 2, "adherents" most nearly means . . .

Use the word's context in a passage to select the best answer, particularly when the vocabulary word has more than one meaning. The answer choices may contain two (or more) correct meanings of the word in question. Choose the meaning that best fits the context.

Inference Questions ask you to make inferences or draw conclusions from the passage. These questions often begin like this:

- It can be most reasonably inferred from the information in the fifth paragraph (lines 53–69) that . . .
- The passage clearly implies that . . .

The inferences you make and the conclusions you draw must be based on the information in the passage. Using the facts you learn from the passage in addition to the knowledge and reasoning you already have helps you understand what is implied and reach conclusions that are logical.

Evidence-Based Questions ask you to provide evidence from the passage that will support the answer you provided to a previous question. These questions often begin like this:

- Which choice provides the best evidence for the answer to the previous question?
- Which statement is the best evidence for the answer to the previous question?

Questions About Tone show your understanding of the author's attitude toward the topic of the passage. To determine the tone, pay attention to the author's word choice. The author's attitude may be positive (respectful), negative (scornful), or neutral (distant). These are typical questions:

- The author's primary purpose in the passage is to . . .
- Which word best describes the author's tone?

Questions About Author's Technique focus on the way a text is organized and the language the author uses. These questions ask you to think about structure and function. For example:

- In the context of the passage, the primary function of the fourth paragraph (lines 30–37) is to . . .
- The organizational structure of the passage is best described as . . .

To answer the questions, you must demonstrate an understanding of the way the author presents information and develops ideas.

VOCABULARY AND WRITING

The **Writing: Words in Action** prompt provides you with an opportunity to practice using text evidence to respond to a prompt about the introductory **Reading Passage**. You will have the opportunity to demonstrate your understanding of the Unit words by incorporating the new vocabulary you have learned into your own writing.

WORD STUDY

Word Study helps build word knowledge with strategies to help you look closely at words for meanings. Word Study instruction and practice include **Idioms**, **Denotation and Connotation**, and **Classical Roots**.

Idioms

Three Word Study sections feature instruction on and practice with idioms. An idiom is an informal expression whose literal meaning does not help the reader or listener understand what the expression means, such as "raining cats and dogs," "the apple of my eye," or "a dark horse." While every language has its own idioms, English is particularly rich in idioms and idiomatic expressions. Developing a clear understanding of idioms will help you better understand the figurative language that authors use in their writing.

Denotation and Connotation

Instruction in **Denotation and Connotation** and practice with connotations is included in two of the Word Study sections. Understanding a word's connotation will develop your skills as a reader, writer, and speaker.

Understanding the difference between denotation and connotation is important to understanding definitions and how concepts are used, as well as in choosing the right word. In these exercises, practice choosing the correct word by determining the emotional association of the word.

Classical Roots

Each Word Study includes a **Classical Roots** exercise that provides instruction in and practice with Greek and Latin roots. Developing a useful, transferable technique to make sense out of unfamiliar words through Greek and Latin roots will help you unlock the meanings of thousands of words. An example word drawn from the vocabulary words in the previous Units is referenced at the top of the page and serves as a guide to help you complete the exercise.

PRONUNCIATION KEY

The pronunciation is indicated for every basic word in this book. The pronunciation symbols used are similar to those used in most recent standard dictionaries. The author has primarily consulted *Webster's Third New International Dictionary* and *The Random House Dictionary of the English Language* (*Unabridged*). Many English words have multiple accepted pronunciations. The author has given one pronunciation when such words occur in this book except when the pronunciation changes according to the part of speech. For example, the verb *project* is pronounced **prə jekt'**, and the noun form is pronounced **präj' ekt**.

Vowels	ā	lake	e	stress	ü	loot, new
	a	mat	ī	knife	u̇	foot, pull
	â	care	i	sit	ə	jump, broken
	ä	bark, bottle	ō	flow	ər	bird, better
	au̇	doubt	ô	all, cord		
	ē	beat, wordy	oi	oil		

Consonants	ch	child, lecture	s	cellar	wh	what
	g	give	sh	shun	y	yearn
	j	gentle, bridge	th	thank	z	is
	ŋ	sing	th̶	those	zh	measure

All other consonants are sounded as in the alphabet.

| **Stress** | The accent mark follows the syllable receiving the major stress: en rich'. |

Abbreviations	*adj.*	adjective	*n.*	noun	*prep.*	preposition
	adv.	adverb	*part.*	participle	*v.*	verb
	int.	interjection	*pl.*	plural		

*Read the following passage, taking note of the **boldface** words and their contexts. These words are among those you will be studying in Unit 1. It may help you to complete the exercises in this Unit if you refer to the way the words are used below.*

The Globe Theatre: Then and Now
<Historical Nonfiction>

Do you laugh and **gape** at the antics of TV reality-show stars? Chances are you would have done more than that at a performance at the Globe Theatre, circa 1600. Today's dubious celebrities have nothing on the old Globe's daring actors and their raucous, rowdy audiences. In Elizabethan London, many in the ruling class viewed theatrical productions as dangerous. They thought theaters—and actors themselves— threatened the common good. That's why theaters were banished to the city's seedier neighborhoods. Built on the south banks of the River Thames in 1599, the Globe was one of the more famous theaters of its day. It was part-owned by William Shakespeare, and aristocrats and commoners alike came to see his plays. If these playgoers were lucky, they might also see Shakespeare himself.

The open-roofed Globe could hold up to 3,000 people. At the base of the apron stage (a raised platform with the audience on three sides), there was a pit where people—called "groundlings"— would stand and watch the play for a penny. Those who paid slightly more to sit in the stadium-style seats had to tread **warily**, or risk falling into the pit. The actors were almost always men, playing both male and female parts. Audience members were both **unkempt** and unruly, so actors had to endure the insults, taunts, and **gibes** of the rambunctious crowd—and often had to dodge the rotten produce hurled at them.

The Globe continued to thrive even after Shakespeare's death in 1616. It remained a lively and exciting place, but the **dour, stolid** Puritans in power disapproved of playacting. Their strict, joyless views on life contrasted with the Globe's **opulent**, rollicking productions, which were considered **insidious** and corrupting. So in

William Shakespeare,
1564–1616
Background: The original
Globe Theatre

1642, Parliament ordered the Globe and all other London theaters closed. Constables were **deployed** to enforce the rule, actors were punished and even jailed, and anyone caught attending a play was fined. The building was dismantled, and those long-ago theater lovers were left **bereft**.

More than three centuries later, the American actor and director Sam Wanamaker went looking for the remains of this historic theater. He was appalled to find only a dirty plaque that read, "This is on or around where Shakespeare had his Globe." Wanamaker started the Shakespeare Globe Trust in 1970 to raise funds to rebuild Shakespeare's historic theater. Not everyone was convinced of his vision. Early support was **tentative**. What some called a replica of the Globe, others dismissed as a theme park that would **adulterate** Shakespeare's legacy. But Wanamaker's **fortitude** and perseverance paid off: In 1997, Shakespeare's Globe officially opened near the site of the original. The modern Globe has proven the doubters wrong—if anything, it **augments** Shakespeare's reputation as the greatest playwright of all time.

Today, the new Globe plays to packed houses. While most seasons emphasize the works of Shakespeare, often performed **verbatim**, contemporary plays are also featured. The Bard, renowned for his love of mischief, might have approved of a recent production of *Much Ado About Nothing*, one featuring an all-female cast in the **guise** of princes, lords, and soldiers. Shakespeare's Globe transports us back to the experience of theater as it was 400 years ago. Yet occasional hints of modern life, such as jets flying overhead during performances, remind us that the Globe Theatre is part of twenty-first century London—and not just a footnote in history books.

Inset: Eamonn Walker in *Othello*;
Background: The reconstructed Globe Theatre

Audio

For iWords and audio passages, go to SadlierConnect.com.

Definitions

Note the spelling, pronunciation, part(s) of speech, and definition(s) of each of the following words. Then write the appropriate form of the word in the blank space in the illustrative sentence(s) following.

1. **ambidextrous**
(am bi dek' strəs)

(*adj.*) able to use both hands equally well; very skillful; deceitful, hypocritical

Occasionally a teacher will come across a child who displays _____ abilities when taught to write.

2. **augment**
(ôg ment')

(*v.*) to make larger, increase

Many couples have to _____ their income in order to pay the mortgage on a new home.

3. **deploy**
(di ploi')

(*v.*) to position or arrange; to utilize; to form up

A bugle call is a signal used to _____ troops for inspection, parade, or battle.

4. **gibe**
(jīb)

(*v.*) to utter taunting words; (*n.*) an expression of scorn

The recruits rushed into battle so that no one could _____ at them for cowardice.

Voters may reject a candidate who resorts to personal _____ instead of discussing the issues.

5. **intimation**
(in tə mā' shən)

(*n.*) a hint, indirect suggestion

They were too proud to give any _____ of their financial difficulties.

6. **opulent**
(äp' yə lənt)

(*adj.*) wealthy, luxurious; ample; grandiose

The tour guide showed us the _____ living quarters of the royal family.

7. **reiterate**
(rē it' ə rāt)

(*v.*) to say again, repeat

Effective speakers often _____ an important statement for emphasis.

8. **stolid**
(stäl' id)

(*adj.*) not easily moved mentally or emotionally; dull, unresponsive

_____ people can generally be expected to take most things in stride.

9. **tentative**
(ten′ tə tiv)

(*adj.*) experimental in nature; uncertain, hesitant

Negotiators have come up with a _____ agreement that will keep both sides at the bargaining table past the strike deadline.

10. **unkempt**
(ən kempt′)

(*adj.*) not combed; untidy; not properly maintained; unpolished, rude

According to my parents, the latest fashions make me and my friends look _____.

Using Context

*For each item, determine whether the **boldface** word from pages 14–15 makes sense in the context of the sentence. Circle the item numbers next to the six sentences in which the words are used correctly.*

1. Today the museum director announced that the Asian art department will **augment** a rare statue for its collection.

2. The electric company will **deploy** repair crews in case of a severe storm or other emergency that affects the power supply.

3. I decided to **reiterate** my offer to help my brother with his Spanish homework in hopes that this time he will accept.

4. The **opulent** home has two bedrooms, a living room, a small kitchen, a backyard, and a one-car garage.

5. In our area, the appearance of tiny white flowers known as snowdrops is a welcome **intimation** of spring.

6. The security guard's **stolid** expression suggested that he would not be likely to engage in friendly chitchat with the people who went in and out of the lobby.

7. The movie's ending was so cleverly **unkempt** that many people in the audience gasped in surprise.

8. Despite the **gibe** it received from the critic for being silly and far-fetched, the television show became a huge success and has been running for seven years now.

9. My cousin is **ambidextrous**, so she is comfortable using these left-handed scissors.

10. The late-night silence was broken by the loud, **tentative** screech of an owl.

Choosing the Right Word

*Select the **boldface** word that better completes each sentence. You might refer to the passage on pages 12–13 to see how most of these words are used in context. Note that the choices might be related forms of the Unit words.*

1. The librarian hoped to (**deploy**, **augment**) the rare book collection by purchasing a first edition of Walt Whitman's book of poetry, *Leaves of Grass*.

2. Have you heard the joke about the (**ambidextrous**, **opulent**) loafer who was equally adept at not working with either hand?

3. The proctor (**intimated**, **reiterated**) the directions for the test before we began.

4. The young prince, who much preferred blue jeans, had to dress in the (**stolid**, **opulent**) robes designed for the coronation.

5. A sort of heaviness in the air and an eerie silence were the first real (**reiterations**, **intimations**) of the approaching cyclone.

6. Because the situation is changing so rapidly, any plans we make to deal with the emergency can be no more than (**ambidextrous**, **tentative**).

7. The speaker (**deployed**, **gibed**) all the facts and figures at her command to buttress her argument.

8. By studying the reactions of simpler life forms, researchers have greatly (**reiterated**, **augmented**) our knowledge of human behavior.

9. Let us not forget that the early fighters for women's rights were greeted with the (**gibes**, **opulence**) of the unthinking mob.

10. In this scene of wild jubilation, my (**stolid**, **tentative**) roommate continued to eat her peanut butter sandwich as though nothing had happened.

11. How annoying to hear the same silly advertising slogans (**gibed**, **reiterated**) endlessly on television!

12. One of the chief reasons for your dateless weekends is undoubtedly your (**opulent**, **unkempt**) appearance.

Completing the Sentence

Choose the word from the word bank that best completes each of the following sentences. Write the correct word or form of the word in the space provided.

~~ambidextrous~~	~~deploy~~	~~intimation~~	~~reiterate~~	~~tentative~~
~~augment~~	~~gibe~~	~~opulent~~	~~stolid~~	~~unkempt~~

1. Since my acceptance of the invitation was only **tentative**, the host may be one guest short at the dinner party.

2. Why would someone who is usually so neat and well-dressed appear in public in such a(n) **Unkempt** state?

3. Perhaps I would be bored with the **Opulent** lifestyle of a millionaire, but I'm willing to try it.

4. An experienced baseball manager **deploys** his outfielders according to the strengths and weaknesses of the opposing batters.

5. Her unchanging facial features and controlled voice as she received the news gave no **intimation** of her true feelings.

6. Why should I be the object of all those **gibes** just because I'm wearing a three-piece suit on campus?

7. Many ballplayers can bat from either side of the plate, but they cannot throw well with each hand unless they are **ambidextrous**.

8. At the risk of being boring, let me **reiterate** my warning against careless driving.

9. The company commander called his troops together and asked for more volunteers to **augment** the strength of the raiding party.

10. We learned that beneath her **stolid** exterior there was a sensitive, highly subtle, and perceptive mind.

Definitions

Note the spelling, pronunciation, part(s) of speech, and definition(s) of each of the following words. Then write the appropriate form of the word in the blank space in the illustrative sentence(s) following.

1. **adulterate**
(ə dəl' tə rāt)

(*v.*) to corrupt, make worse by the addition of something of lesser value
Hospitals take strict precautions to assure that nothing _____ the blood supply.

2. **bereft**
(bi reft')

(*adj., part.*) deprived of; made unhappy through a loss
Individuals who live to be very old may eventually find themselves completely _____ of friends and family.

3. **dour**
(daủr)

(*adj.*) stern, unyielding, gloomy, ill-humored
Dickens's Mr. Gradgrind in the novel *Hard Times* is an example of a character with a _____ and sullen disposition.

4. **fortitude**
(fôr' ti tüd)

(*n.*) courage in facing difficulties
The residents of the Mississippi delta showed remarkable _____ during and after the flood that destroyed their homes and businesses.

5. **gape**
(gāp)

(*v.*) to stare with open mouth; to open the mouth wide; to open wide
First-time visitors to Niagara Falls can be expected to _____ at the spectacular sights nature has provided for them.

6. **guise**
(gīz)

(*n.*) an external appearance, cover, mask
The thieves gained entry to the home by presenting themselves in the _____ of police officers.

7. **insidious**
(in sid' ē əs)

(*adj.*) intended to deceive or entrap; sly, treacherous
The investigators uncovered an _____ scheme to rob people of their life savings.

8. **pliable**
(plī' ə bəl)

(*adj.*) easily bent, flexible; easily influenced
Spools of _____ copper wire are standard equipment for many kinds of maintenance workers, including electricians.

9. **verbatim**
(vər bā′ təm)

(*adj., adv.*) word for word; exactly as written or spoken

Newspapers often publish the _____ text of an important political speech.

At the swearing-in ceremony, the Chief Justice reads each line of the Oath of Office, and the new President repeats the oath _____.

10. **warily**
(wâr′ ə lē)

(*adv.*) cautiously, with great care

The hikers made their way _____ up the steep and rocky trail.

Using Context

*For each item, determine whether the **boldface** word from pages 18–19 makes sense in the context of the sentence. Circle the item numbers next to the six sentences in which the words are used correctly.*

1. The students, who were as **pliable** as soft putty and truly eager to acquire new skills and knowledge, proved a joy to the new teacher.

2. He is chairman of an **insidious** society that is concerned with helping the less fortunate.

3. The organic foods company looked for ways to make tasty treats without having to **adulterate** them with sugar and corn syrup.

4. As the years passed, her increasingly **dour** and forbidding personality alienated all who knew her, even those who had once been her bosom buddies.

5. People paused to **gape** at the damage created by the water main rupture.

6. The committee had no chairperson **verbatim**, but the members worked together so well that none was really necessary.

7. Great wealth often means that a person is **bereft** and never without what he or she needs.

8. Although the protestors shouted angry threats, their intimidation was powerless against the unyielding strength and **fortitude** of the candidate.

9. Some suggest that hikers approach wild animals **warily** and watchfully, but I say it is much wiser not to approach them at all.

10. An evening **guise** at her friend's house for supper was just what my aunt needed to unwind after a hectic day.

Choosing the Right Word

*Select the **boldface** word that better completes each sentence. You might refer to the passage on pages 12–13 to see how most of these words are used in context. Note that the choices might be related forms of the Unit words.*

1. Cassius, Brutus, and the other conspirators against Julius Caesar had developed a(n) (**pliable, insidious**) plot to assassinate the Roman dictator on the Senate floor.

2. There we were at the very edge of the cliff, with our front wheels about to plunge into a(n) (**gaping, adulterating**) ravine!

3. To make beaded jewelry, it is essential that the materials you use to thread the beads, such as fine gauge wire, silk, leather, or cord, be (**pliable, verbatim**) and easy to work with.

4. Though all hope of victory had faded, the remaining troops continued to resist the enemy with a (**bereft, dour**) tenacity.

5. The ticking grew louder as the bomb squad (**warily, pliably**) opened the package found on the grounds of the governor's residence.

6. Before the spies could begin their mission, each of them had to repeat (**dourly, verbatim**) every word of the secret codebook.

7. Do you expect me to listen to a lot of tired old ideas dressed up in the (**fortitude, guise**) of brilliant new insights?

8. When the famous pop star appeared at a local restaurant and began playing her guitar, it was difficult for the patrons not to (**gape, adulterate**).

9. What they call their "(**insidious, pliable**) outlook on life" seems to be simply a lack of any firm moral standards.

10. Do you believe that the curriculum has been (**gaped, adulterated**) by the inclusion of courses on aspects of popular culture?

11. I must have been (**bereft, pliable**) of my senses when I bought that old car!

12. Recruits who complain of the cold should try to show a little more (**fortitude, wariness**) in facing the elements.

Completing the Sentence

Choose the word from the word bank that best completes each of the following sentences. Write the correct word or form of the word in the space provided.

adulterate	dour	gape	insidious	verbatim
bereft	fortitude	guise	pliable	warily

1. To this day, historians are still debating whether or not Aaron Burr was guilty of a(n) __insidious__ plot to break up the United States.

2. Having learned to respect the power in his opponent's fists, the boxer moved __warily__ around the center of the ring.

3. The __dour__ expressions on the jurors' faces as they grimly filed back into the courtroom did not bode well for the defendant.

4. I recorded the speaker's presentation, but now I wish I had a software program that could help me transcribe the speech __verbatim__ so that I can find appropriate quotations to use in my report.

5. The twigs that were to be woven into the basket were soaked in water to make them more __pliable__.

6. America's earliest settlers faced the hardships of life on the frontier with faith and __fortitude__.

7. How can you tell whether the chopped-meat patty you ate for lunch had been __adulterated__ with artificial coloring and other foreign substances?

8. In Shakespeare's famous tragedy *Othello*, Iago comes to Othello in the __guise__ of a friend but proves to be a deadly enemy.

9. As the magician's assistant seemed to vanish into thin air, the entire audience __gaped__ in amazement.

10. What a tragedy that in the twilight of her life the unfortunate woman should be __bereft__ of all her loved ones!

Synonyms

*Choose the word or form of the word from this Unit that is the same or most nearly the same in meaning as the **boldface** word or expression in the phrase. Write that word on the line. Use a dictionary if necessary.*

1. **gawk** at the huge jaws of the crocodile   _____

2. gave no **indication** of being nervous   _____

3. **rehash** the same old theories   _____

4. **post** the remaining guards at the exits   _____

5. showed great **strength** in standing up for her rights   _____

6. need to **enlarge** the computer's memory   _____

7. an **underhanded** attack on my good name   _____

8. quoted the lines from the movie **exactly**   _____

9. the **unemotional** judge's ruling   _____

10. disregarded her **sloppy** appearance   _____

11. a **gloomy** expression   _____

12. threw out the **contaminated** lab sample   _____

13. **skillful** handling of the tools   _____

14. **stripped** of his fortune   _____

15. the **appearance** of caring friends   _____

Antonyms

*Choose the word or form of the word from this Unit that is most nearly opposite in meaning to the **boldface** word or expression in the phrase. Write that word on the line. Use a dictionary if necessary.*

1. a person with a **rigid** viewpoint   _____

2. **boldly** crossed the narrow bridge   _____

3. a **definite** date for the party   _____

4. **praised** her for her efforts   _____

5. decorated in a **very simple** style   _____

Writing: Words in Action

Write a brief essay in which you compare and contrast watching a live performance to watching a show on television or on your computer. Use examples from your reading (refer to pages 12–13), personal experiences, and prior knowledge to support your points of comparison. Use three or more words from this Unit.

Vocabulary in Context

*Some of the words you have studied in this Unit appear in **boldface** type. Read the passage below, and then circle the letter of the correct answer for each word as it is used in context.*

Hamlet is Shakespeare's most performed play. More than 100 movie and television versions have been produced, the earliest a silent black-and-white French film in 1907. *Hamlet* is so familiar that many students can recite verbatim Hamlet's "To be or not to be" soliloquy. Many of the world's finest actors have interpreted Hamlet's complex role. Even Disney's 1994 animated movie *The Lion King* includes **intimations** of the *Hamlet* story.

Shakespeare's play opens at night on a platform before Elsinore castle, where watchmen encounter a ghost in the guise of the recently buried King Hamlet. The next night the ghost urges Prince Hamlet to seek revenge for the king's cruel murder. The young, innocent Ophelia, whom Prince Hamlet loves, becomes part of the collateral damage as Hamlet pursues his quest.

In Act 3, Scene 1 (sometimes called the "Nunnery Scene"), **pliable** Ophelia obeys her father's order to return Hamlet's love letters and gifts. Feigning madness, Hamlet asks Ophelia if she is honest and fair. (The pun on *fair*, which means both "just" and "beautiful," is one of many rhetorical devices Shakespeare uses throughout the play.) Ophelia responds, "Could beauty, my lord, have better commerce than with honesty?" Throughout this scene **ambidextrous** Hamlet **gibes** at Ophelia, saying he once loved her, then telling her he never loved her. He denounces marriage and **reiterates**, "Get thee to a nunnery!"

Much discussion of the four-hour play focuses on why Hamlet delays in avenging his father's murder. Is he simply weak, lacking the **fortitude** to murder his uncle? Or does he seek to verify the ghost's accusation? Read the play and decide for yourself what makes Hamlet tick and why the play remains so powerful more than 400 years after Shakespeare wrote it.

---

1. Intimations are
  a. statements
  b. hints
  c. secrets
  d. concerns

2. A person who is **pliable**, as Ophelia is said to be, is usually
  a. easily influenced
  b. extremely brave
  c. very strong
  d. difficult to frighten

3. Hamlet is **ambidextrous** because he is
  a. clever
  b. romantic
  c. two-handed
  d. deceptive

4. A person who **gibes** at another is
  a. complimenting
  b. criticizing
  c. reprimanding
  d. taunting

5. The word **reiterates** most nearly means
  a. forbids
  b. hollers
  c. restates
  d. commands

6. To lack **fortitude** is to lack
  a. courage
  b. ambition
  c. cunning
  d. motive

Read the following passage, taking note of the **boldface** words and their contexts. These words are among those you will be studying in Unit 2. It may help you to complete the exercises in this Unit if you refer to the way the words are used below.

Fashion Victims
<Informational Essay>

Some people spend a lot of time **scrutinizing** the image their clothes project. As the saying goes, "Clothes make the man." Some outfits are practical, **impervious** to rain or wind or sun or biting insects, while other outfits are chosen to express the **quintessence** of the wearer. People may not always be aware of it, but clothes offer hints about wealth, status, and even political standing. For as long as humans have worn clothes, **adroit** observers have discerned these clues.

Color

The color of clothes often tells a story. For millennia, societies around the world **extolled** the color purple. It came to represent royalty, wealth, and power because dyeing cloth purple required expensive ingredients. Ancient Greek writers were **meticulous** when describing the recipe for purple dye, a product derived from mollusks. For one gram of dye, the Greeks needed nearly 10,000 shellfish. Thus, obtaining purple clothing was not **feasible** for any but the wealthiest

people. Chinese officials in the Tang Dynasty also favored purple robes, which were dyed with ingredients from a different mollusk. With the expansion of the Spanish empire in the sixteenth century, purple found a near rival in a deep, bright crimson, which came from a dye made of crushed cochineal insects found in Central and South America. After the British army adopted red, the soldiers sent into battle came to be known as the **belligerent** army of Redcoats.

White, in many cultures, suggests purity and spirituality. In the African countries of Nigeria and Zambia, people wear white for good luck at joyous occasions, but it is the color of bereavement in India and Asia. In Europe and the United States today, black is the color of mourning. Dyers in days gone by saturated cloth many times to ensure the darkest possible color. Because the dyeing process was labor intensive and thus expensive, only wealthy Europeans could afford black cloth.

Tyrians made purple dye from the murex shellfish.

Social and Political Status

Throughout the world, rulers historically passed laws that controlled their subjects' consumption of certain foods, building materials, and clothing. Rule breakers put their freedoms in **jeopardy**. In ancient Rome, only citizens could wear togas—and usually only in the natural off-white color of wool. Citizens running for public office could bleach their togas white, so even a **cursory** glance told the observer who was running for office. These Romans came to be known as *candidati*, or "extra white" men. In Revolutionary-era France, in the late 1700s, the *sans culottes* became a political force and participants in the country's revolution. *Sans culottes* means "without breeches." Wealthy people rode horseback and so wore breeches. The *sans culottes* were working class and wore trousers.

Eventually, laws that restricted consumption disappeared in every area but fashion, but this was not the result of the edicts of **benevolent** rulers. The **impetus** that drove such laws had been the desire to segregate people into visible, hierarchical categories. Regulations on fashions

The *sans culottes* were French Revolutionaries.

were designed to penalize **duplicity** among commoners, who might try to get ahead by dressing like aristocrats. For years, rulers believed that people who dressed as they wished would not be **amicable** subjects. Yet even as support for these laws turned **tepid** and they fell into disuse, purple remained the prerogative of the wellborn and wealthy until 1856. That's when an 18-year-old Englishman named William Perkin developed an inexpensive artificial dye of intense purple, which made the color, like fashion itself, accessible to all.

Audio

For iWords and audio passages, go to SadlierConnect.com.

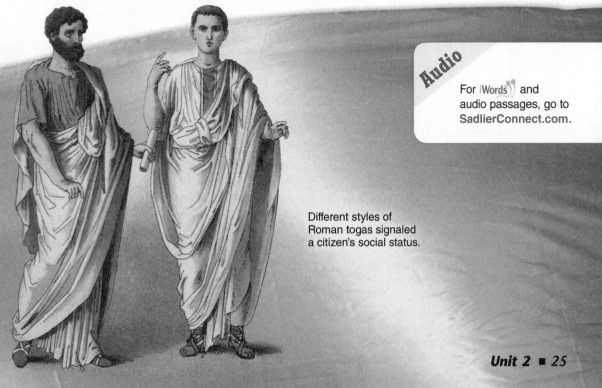

Different styles of Roman togas signaled a citizen's social status.

Definitions

Note the spelling, pronunciation, part(s) of speech, and definition(s) of each of the following words. Then write the appropriate form of the word in the blank space in the illustrative sentence(s) following.

1. adroit
(ə droit′)

(*adj.*) skillful, expert in the use of the hands or mind

Many rodeo performers are ___adroit___ at twirling a rope while on horseback.

2. benevolent
(bə nev′ ə lənt)

(*adj.*) kindly, charitable

The newcomers had nothing but ___benevolent___ feelings toward all their neighbors.

3. cursory
(ker′ sə rē)

(*adj.*) hasty, not thorough

The mayor gave a final ___cursory___ glance at the text of her speech before mounting the podium.

4. duplicity
(dü plis′ ə tē)

(*n.*) treachery, deceitfulness

We found it difficult to believe that our good friend could be capable of such ___duplicity___.

5. feasible
(fē′ zə bəl)

(*adj.*) possible, able to be done

Our city needs to develop a ___feasible___ plan of action for dealing with storms and other emergencies.

6. grimace
(grim′ əs)

(*n.*) a wry face, facial distortion; (*v.*) to make a wry face

The ___grimace___ of the refugee in the photograph reveals the pain of homelessness.

Most people ___grimace___ at the mere sound of the dentist's drill.

7. holocaust
(häl′ ə kôst)

(*n.*) a large-scale destruction, especially by fire; a vast slaughter; a burnt offering

Journalists at the time were eager to interview survivors of the Chicago ___holocaust___.

8. meticulous
(mə tik′ yə ləs)

(*adj.*) extremely careful; particular about details

If you have a full-time job outside the home, you may find it exceedingly difficult to be a ___meticulous___ housekeeper.

9. quintessence
(kwin tes′ əns)

(*n.*) the purest essence or form of something; the most typical example

Risking one's own life to save the lives of others is considered the ___quintessence___ of selfless valor.

10. scrutinize
(skrüt′ ə nīz)

(*v.*) to examine closely

Lawyers are paid to ___scrutinize___ legal papers and explain the fine print to their clients.

Using Context

*For each item, determine whether the **boldface** word from pages 26–27 makes sense in the context of the sentence. Circle the item numbers next to the six sentences in which the words are used correctly.*

1. Thanks to several **benevolent** donors, the university will be able to build a new science library.

2. The phrases *a famous celebrity* and *basic fundamentals* are both examples of **duplicity**.

3. If you are hoping to play one of the three eerie witches from the first scene of *Macbeth,* you should practice making a **grimace**.

4. The engineers decided not to widen the roadway because it would be too **feasible** and too expensive.

5. At first I felt very clumsy, but the more I practiced juggling, the more **adroit** at it I became.

6. The chapter in the textbook began with a **cursory** explanation of the topic followed by a detailed, in-depth discussion.

7. Despite being eighty years old, the car is in **meticulous** condition and is even driven during parades and other special occasions.

8. The sun reaches its **quintessence** at noon each day and then begins to move across the western part of the sky.

9. Why don't you quickly **scrutinize** this novel and decide if you want to read it after me?

10. The goal of the peace talks was to reduce the number of missiles the countries produced and prevent any possibility of nuclear **holocaust**.

Choosing the Right Word

Select the **boldface** word that better completes each sentence. You might refer to the passage on pages 24–25 to see how most of these words are used in context. Note that the choices might be related forms of the Unit words.

1. In the Sherlock Holmes stories, we read of the evil Professor Moriarty, whose (**duplicity**, **quintessence**) was almost a match for Holmes's genius.

2. On the morning of the picnic, the sky was gray and overcast, but suddenly the sun came out and smiled on us (**benevolently**, **adroitly**).

3. It was rude of you to (**scrutinize**, **grimace**) so obviously when the speaker mispronounced words and made grammatical errors.

4. The lawyer's (**adroit**, **feasible**) questioning slowly but surely revealed the weaknesses in his opponent's case.

5. Though it may appear rather ordinary to the casual reader, Lincoln's Gettysburg Address is to me the (**duplicity**, **quintessence**) of eloquence.

6. The nightmare that continues to haunt all thoughtful people is a nuclear (**benevolence**, **holocaust**) in which our civilization might be destroyed.

7. Some civil engineers believe that someday it may be (**feasible**, **cursory**) to derive a large part of our energy directly from the sun.

8. It made me very uncomfortable to see the suspicion with which the wary customs officer (**scrutinized**, **grimaced**) my passport.

9. Do you think you are being fair in passing judgment on my poem after such a(n) (**cursory**, **adroit**) reading?

10. I knew you would be (**feasible**, **meticulous**) in caring for my plants, but I did not expect you to water them with a medicine dropper!

11. The mayor says that the (**duplicity**, **feasibility**) of renovating the municipal buildings is certain now that a federal grant and donations will fund the project.

12. Because her statement showed ignorance of the key facts, we knew that she had completed only a (**benevolent**, **cursory**) review of our report.

Completing the Sentence

Choose the word from the word bank that best completes each of the following sentences. Write the correct word or form of the word in the space provided.

adroit	cursory	feasible	holocaust	quintessence
benevolent	duplicity	grimace	meticulous	scrutinize

1. Only when we learned that the embezzler had tried to cast suspicion on his innocent partner did we realize the extent of his __duplicity__.

2. A(n) __cursory__ examination of my luggage was enough to show me that someone had been tampering with it.

3. If, as you claim, you really like raw oysters, why do you make such an eloquent __grimace__ every time you swallow one?

4. The accountant's records—neat, accurate, and complete in every respect—show that she is a most __meticulous__ worker.

5. We must not forget the millions of people who were ruthlessly slaughtered by the Nazis in the __holocaust__ of World War II.

6. An expert from the museum __scrutinize__ the painting, looking for telltale signs that would prove it to be genuine or expose it as a forgery.

7. No one doubted the __benevolent__ intentions of the program for community improvement, but it was ruined by mismanagement.

8. A triple reverse looks mighty impressive on the chalkboard, but I doubt that the play will prove __feasible__ on the football field.

9. King Arthur's Knights of the Round Table were the __quintessence__ of chivalry.

10. Although he shows no particular talent as a worker, he is exceptionally __adroit__ at finding excuses for not doing his job.

Definitions

Note the spelling, pronunciation, part(s) of speech, and definition(s) of each of the following words. Then write the appropriate form of the word in the blank space in the illustrative sentence(s) following.

1. amicable
(am' ə kə bəl)

(*adj.*) peaceable, friendly
Sometimes mediation by a neutral individual can lead to an ___amicable___ settlement of a dispute.

2. averse
(ə vərs')

(*adj.*) having a deep-seated distaste; opposed, unwilling
You are not likely to become a marathon runner if you are ___averse___ to strenuous exercise.

3. belligerent
(bə lij' ə rənt)

(*adj.*) given to fighting, warlike; combative, aggressive; (*n.*) one at war, one engaged in war
I did not expect such a ___belligerent___ answer to my request for directions.
After each ___belligerent___ signed the peace treaty, the war was declared officially over.

4. extol
(ek stōl')

(*v.*) to praise extravagantly
Many inspiring stories and plays have been written that ___extol___ the heroic deeds of Joan of Arc.

5. impervious
(im pər' vē əs)

(*adj.*) not affected or hurt by; admitting of no passage or entrance
It is best to store flour in a container with a plastic cover that is ___impervious___ to moisture.

6. impetus
(im' pə təs)

(*n.*) a moving force, impulse, stimulus
The coming of winter gave a new ___impetus___ to the appeals for food and clothing for needy families.

7. jeopardy
(jep' ər dē)

(*n.*) danger
Experienced mountaineers know that a single mistake can put an entire expedition in serious ___jeopardy___.

8. nostalgia
(nä stal' jə)

(*n.*) a longing for something past; homesickness
Looking at old scrapbooks and reading old letters can bring on a vague sense of ___nostalgia___ for days gone by and friends no longer near.

9. retrogress
(re trə gres')

(*v.*) to move backward; to return to an earlier condition

In the novel, the survivors of a nuclear explosion _____*retrogress*_____ into a state of barbarism and anarchy.

10. tepid
(tep' id)

(*adj.*) lukewarm; unenthusiastic, marked by an absence of interest

A cup of _____*tepid*_____ tea will not warm you up on a chilly morning.

Using Context

*For each item, determine whether the **boldface** word from pages 30–31 makes sense in the context of the sentence. Circle the item numbers next to the six sentences in which the words are used correctly.*

(**1.**) I had become proficient at speaking Spanish during the school year, but my skills began to **retrogress** when I neglected to practice over the summer.

2. Group projects can often be productive, but there is sometimes at least one member who acts as an **impetus** to getting work done.

(**3.**) Even if my best friend and I disagree on certain issues, we're still able to have **amicable** discussions to explain our points of view.

(**4.**) The glass of **tepid** water was exactly what I needed to quench my thirst on such a hot summer day.

5. The **belligerent** question posed by an audience member caused the speaker to request that all attendees mind their manners going forward.

(**6.**) I didn't consider myself a science fiction fan until my friend decided to **extol** me to read *1984* by George Orwell, which is now one of my favorites.

7. Although I have spoken in front of crowds many times, I still find myself so **impervious** to my nerves that my hands shake as I walk up to the podium.

(**8.**) Those who are allergic to cats are often **averse** to the idea of having them as pets.

(**9.**) My doctor reminded me that failing to eat enough fruits and vegetables would put my long-term health in **jeopardy**.

(**10.**) Hearing songs that were popular when I was a child always fills me with a deep sense of **nostalgia**.

Choosing the Right Word

*Select the **boldface** word that better completes each sentence. You might refer to the passage on pages 24–25 to see how most of these words are used in context. Note that the choices might be related forms of the Unit words.*

1. Because I was not even born when The Beatles were at the height of their popularity, their albums do not fill me with (**impetus, nostalgia**).

2. Those who are (**amicable, averse**) to seafood may enjoy the many other menu options.

3. News of famine in various parts of the world has given added (**nostalgia, impetus**) to the drive to increase food production.

4. How many people actually enjoy drinking (**impervious, tepid**) milk before bedtime even though it is highly recommended to ease digestion?

5. Providing a powerful defense force for our nation does not mean that we are taking a(n) (**belligerent, amicable**) attitude toward any other nation.

6. Though the peace talks began with an exchange of lofty sentiments, they soon (**extolled, retrogressed**) into petty squabbling and backbiting.

7. His parents tried to encourage an interest in literature, music, and art, but he seemed (**nostalgic, impervious**) to such influences.

8. Carelessness in even minor details may (**extol, jeopardize**) the success of a major theatrical production.

9. After shouting at each other rather angrily, the participants in the roundtable discussion calmed down and parted (**imperviously, amicably**).

10. Many people become (**nostalgic, averse**) when they watch black-and-white movies and old serial reruns on television.

11. After the dictator walked out of the peace talks, the visiting diplomat tried to carry on (**amicable, belligerent**) negotiations between the two nations.

12. (**Extolling, Retrogressing**) other people's achievements is fine, but it is no substitute for doing something remarkable of your own.

Completing the Sentence

Choose the word from the word bank that best completes each of the following sentences. Write the correct word or form of the word in the space provided.

amicable	belligerent	impervious	jeopardy	retrogress
averse	extol	impetus	nostalgia	tepid

1. What good is a plastic raincoat that is __impervious__ to water if it also prevents any body heat from escaping?

2. My teacher counseled me to keep up my studies, or my performance in class might once again __retrogress__ into mediocrity.

3. Because I was looking forward to a hot bath, I was disappointed at the feeble stream of __tepid__ water that flowed into the tub.

4. Our physical education instructor __extrols__ the virtues of regular exercise.

5. As the old soldier watched the parade, he was suddenly overcome with __nostalgia__ for the youthful years he spent in the army.

6. When I heard you speaking French so fluently, my determination to master that language received a fresh __impetus__.

7. When I realized how bad the brakes of the old car were, I feared that our lives were in __jeopardy__.

8. For centuries, Switzerland has avoided becoming a(n) __belligerent__ in the conflicts that have scarred the rest of Europe.

9. If you are __averse__ to hard study and intensive reading, how do you expect to get through law school?

10. Although the ranchers and miners had been feuding over water rights for years, the sheriff tried to maintain __amicable__ relations with both parties.

Synonyms

*Choose the word or form of the word from this Unit that is the same or most nearly the same in meaning as the **boldface** word or expression in the phrase. Write that word on the line. Use a dictionary if necessary.*

1. remain **unaffected** when insulted — Impervious
2. **imperilment** caused by risky behavior — Jeopardy
3. a brief spell of **yearning** — Nostalgia
4. a **charitable** donor — Benevolent
5. a shocking case of **fraud** — Duplicity
6. the **stimulus** to move forward with the project — Impetus
7. her **antipathetic** response to the homeless man — Averse
8. **hail** the benefits of drinking water — Extol
9. the intimidating **scowl** on his face — Grimace
10. not **practicable** during the winter months — Feasible
11. respond with a **confrontational** voice — Belligerent
12. **exemplar** of good manners — Quintessence
13. staged a **painstaking** re-creation of a famous battle — Meticulous
14. **relapse** to a pattern of self-destructive behavior — Retrogress
15. rescued dozens of people from the **blazing inferno** — Holocaust

Antonyms

*Choose the word or form of the word from this Unit that is most nearly opposite in meaning to the **boldface** word or expression in the phrase. Write that word on the line. Use a dictionary if necessary.*

1. resulted in the **hostile** separation — Amicable
2. gave it a **thorough** inspection — Cursory
3. his **enthusiastic** response — Tepid
4. a **clumsy** maneuver on the balance beam — Adroit
5. **glance at** the bill before paying — Scrutinize

Writing: Words in Action

In a brief essay, discuss the advantages and disadvantages of school uniforms. Use specific examples from your own observations, studies, reading (refer to pages 24–25), or personal experience. Write at least three paragraphs, and use three or more words from this Unit to support your analysis.

Vocabulary in Context

*Some of the words you have studied in this Unit appear in **boldface** type. Read the passage below, and then circle the letter of the correct answer for each word as it is used in context.*

Any **nostalgia** that people might have for the 1950s would probably have to include memories of polyester. This synthetic fabric made its American debut in 1951 and rapidly became the country's favorite fiber. Polyester is derived from coal, air, water, and petroleum, and it has a remarkably broad range of applications in home goods and construction, with products ranging from carpets to electrical insulation. Highly durable, wrinkle-resistant, and stain-resistant, polyester also proved popular for garments, bed sheets, and quilting.

Manufacturers soon found that building hollow fibers into a polyester jacket helped to keep the wearer's body warm in cold weather. Polyester thus became the material of choice for outerwear on the ski slopes. It was also a perfect fabric for the application of fire-resistant finishes. Polyester clothing might not keep the wearer safe in a **holocaust**, but many people felt reassured that the fabric was less likely to catch fire than others.

Despite all its virtues, however, polyester has suffered from an image problem for some years now. Buyers somehow seem **averse** to the material, especially when it is evaluated against natural fibers such as cotton, silk, and wool, and its popularity began to **retrogress**. It is hard to explain why a fabric that is **impervious** to wrinkles, stains, flames, and cold would encounter such a fate, but the truth is many people **grimace** when they find out clothing is made of polyester. Some designers, though, have proved determined to give polyester a second lease on life. A more luxurious variation of polyester called microfiber fabric began to appear in clothes during the 1990s. The texture of microfiber fabric competed with that of silk. In addition, a second wave of experimentation aims at upgrading polyester's already formidable strength so that it may be able to rival the superfiber used in helmets and bulletproof vests.

---

1. **Nostalgia** typically involves feelings of
   a. anger
   b. shame
   c. hilarity
   d. longing

2. A **holocaust** might also be called a
   a. deluge
   b. skirmish
   c. large destructive fire
   d. forewarning

3. The word **averse** most nearly means
   a. indifferent
   b. resigned
   c. opposed
   d. attracted

4. To **retrogress** is to
   a. move backward
   b. shrink backward
   c. delay
   d. avoid

5. The word **impervious** most nearly means
   a. resistant
   b. hostile
   c. responsive
   d. calibrated

6. If you **grimace**, your expression is
   a. happy
   b. wry
   c. amiable
   d. arrogant

*Read the following passage, taking note of the **boldface** words and their contexts. These words are among those you will be studying in Unit 3. It may help you to complete the exercises in this Unit if you refer to the way the words are used below.*

Finding the Facts: Techniques of Modern Crime-Scene Investigation

<Expository Essay>

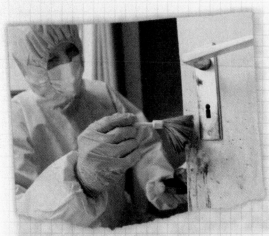

Crime scene investigators use a special powder to "dust" for fingerprints.

Centuries ago, it was common for criminals to escape a **punitive** fate. If there were no witnesses to a crime and if the **craven** wrongdoer had run off and could not be found or could not be **coerced** into confessing, investigators had to rely on both careful reasoning and observation of the crime scene. Yet it was not enough for early investigators to examine a crime scene and then withdraw in order to **muse** on what they had seen: they needed to find actual evidence to convict the criminal. Following the **precedent** set by detectives in the past, today's crime scene sleuths **perpetuate** law-enforcement's reliance on reasoning and observation. But they also use powerful modern techniques made possible by the progress of science.

A well-known method of modern crime-scene investigation is the use of fingerprints to identify criminals. Fingerprints are left behind when a person's hands touch an object, but such fingerprints are usually invisible to the naked eye. To find such evidence at a crime scene, investigators rely on **artifice**: They use special powders to "dust for fingerprints" on walls, doorknobs, or other surfaces. They apply powder to the surface and brush it away. If a fingerprint is in the area, some of the powder will stick to it and reveal its unique pattern. The investigators "lift" the fingerprint with sticky tape and send the tape to a crime lab, along with other objects that may contain invisible fingerprints, such as articles of clothing, knives or other **culinary** tools, or handguns. At the lab, scientists use computers to compare the new fingerprints with others they have on file. When the scientists find a match, this evidence can help prove that a suspect was at the crime

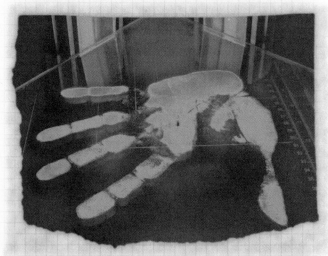

A chemical called luminol exposes blood that can't be seen after it has been washed away.

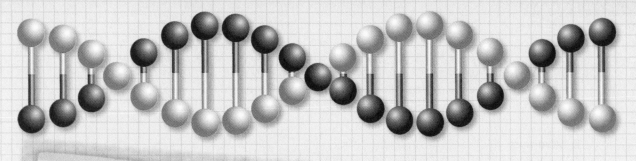

Using DNA analysis, investigators can find traces of skin or blood from a victim or criminal.

scratched the attacker, leaving the skin of the **adversary** under his or her fingernails. Clothing, weapons, or other objects may carry traces of blood, even if they have been cleaned or left outdoors in **inclement** weather. Even minute samples of skin, hair, or blood that once would have been considered **negligible** are now removed from the crime scene and sent to the lab to be tested for DNA. Like fingerprints, DNA testing can provide evidence connecting a suspect to the crime.

While criminals may hope to get away with their crimes, investigators continue their important work. These detectives are **exhilarated** by every scientific development that advances their ability to solve crimes. The tools of modern crime scene investigation make it harder for criminals to avoid punishment. These tools also make it more likely that the wrongs committed by those who unfairly **harass** or harm other people will be **redressed** in a court of law. Then it is up to the judge and jury to ensure the punishment fits the crime.

scene or that he or she handled a weapon used in the crime.

Another technique of modern crime detection is the use of chemicals like luminol to find blood at the scene. Even if a criminal has cleaned up the blood after the victim's **demise**, bloodstains are often left behind that are difficult to remove entirely. Because these bloodstains can be invisible to the naked eye, investigators use luminol to reveal their location. The investigators mix luminol powder into a liquid solution and spray it evenly onto a surface. If there are traces of blood in the sprayed area, the liquid will glow bright blue. The pattern of the bloodstain can help investigators figure out how the crime was committed, and a sample of the blood that is found is sent to the crime lab for further testing.

A more recently developed practice is the use of DNA analysis. The victim of a crime may have

Audio

For iWords and audio passages, go to SadlierConnect.com.

Definitions

Note the spelling, pronunciation, part(s) of speech, and definition(s) of each of the following words. Then write the appropriate form of the word in the blank space in the illustrative sentence(s) following.

---

1. adversary
(ad′ vər ser ē)

(*n.*) an enemy, opponent
A best friend off the tennis court can also be a
fierce _____ on it.

2. coerce
(kō ərs′)

(*v.*) to compel, force
Dictators try to _____ their subjects into
obedience by threatening them or their families with punishment.

3. culinary
(kyü′ lə ner ē)

(*adj.*) of or related to cooking or the kitchen
Cooking shows on television have helped many people
to master the secrets of the _____ arts.

4. demise
(di mīz′)

(*n.*) a death, especially of a person in a lofty position
Traditionally, the tolling of church bells has announced
the _____ of a monarch.

5. fallow
(fal′ ō)

(*adj.*) plowed but not seeded; inactive; reddish-yellow; (*n.*)
land left unseeded; (*v.*) to plow but not seed
After a month without a date, I decided that my social
life was definitely in a _____ period.
In the drought-stricken region, there were millions of
acres of _____.
Farmers often _____ a third of their fields
each year to restore the chemical balance of the soil.

6. liquidate
(lik′ wi dāt′)

(*v.*) to pay a debt, settle an account; to eliminate
After a profitable year, the business was able to
_____ its loan.

7. perpetuate
(pər pech′ ü āt)

(*v.*) to make permanent or long lasting
In most cultures, people try to _____
the customs of their ancestors.

8. punitive
(pyü′ nə tiv)

(*adj.*) inflicting or aiming at punishment
The general led a _____ expedition
against the rebel forces.

| 9. **redress**
(rē dres') | (v.) to set right, remedy; (n.) relief from wrong or injury

An apology can go a long way to _____ the hurt feelings caused by an insensitive comment or a thoughtless act.

The accident victims will seek _____ for the injuries they suffered in the train crash. |
| 10. **urbane**
(ər bān') | (adj.) refined in manner or style, suave

An _____ host puts guests at ease by appearing totally confident and unruffled no matter what happens. |

Using Context

*For each item, determine whether the **boldface** word from pages 38–39 makes sense in the context of the sentence. Circle the item numbers next to the six sentences in which the words are used correctly.*

1. As more people move to the area, it is becoming **urbane** and in need of transportation.

2. Julia Child, the famous American television chef and cookbook writer, attended **culinary** school in Paris in the late 1940s.

3. My brother would love to earn the extra money, so no one has to **coerce** him into working this weekend.

4. Hundreds of fans turned out for the **demise** of the new movie, many dressed in costumes representing their favorite characters.

5. Some readers consider the Joker to be Batman's most ruthless **adversary** because he has great strength and seems to be unbeatable.

6. It is an ancient farming practice to let a field lie **fallow** so that the nutrients in the soil can be restored rather than depleted by constant planting.

7. Since people often **perpetuate** rumors that are completely untrue, it is never a good idea to take gossip seriously.

8. Many fans felt that the quarterback's suspension was excessively harsh and **punitive**.

9. Working to **redress** the newly restored exhibit is a team of conservators and museum artists.

10. This blender will **liquidate** fruits and vegetables into tasty and highly nutritious drinks.

Choosing the Right Word

*Select the **boldface** word that better completes each sentence. You might refer to the passage on pages 36–37 to see how most of these words are used in context. Note that the choices might be related forms of the Unit words.*

1. The critics unanimously praised the actor for the (**urbane, punitive**) charm with which he played the well-bred English gentleman.

2. After several months of losing money, the furniture store held a huge sale, hoping to (**liquidate, redress**) its entire inventory.

3. Do you really expect me to believe that your friends (**coerced, perpetuated**) you into cutting class to go to the movies?

4. To rid your aquarium of parasites, allow the tank to remain (**urbane, fallow**) for several weeks, and keep your fish in a separate tank.

5. Only when the attempt to get the British government to (**redress, perpetuate**) injustices proved unsuccessful did the American colonists resort to arms.

6. May I remind you that the (**urbane, punitive**) action we are authorized to take does not include physical force of any kind?

7. The story takes place in a foreign country where a rogue government agent accepts a mission to (**liquidate, coerce**) an evil dictator.

8. After a long (**urbane, fallow**) period during which she scarcely touched her brushes, the painter suddenly produced a series of major canvases.

9. Our history shows how the (**demise, adversary**) of one political party provides an opportunity for the formation of a new one.

10. If we do not take steps now to clear their names, we will be (**perpetuating, liquidating**) an injustice that has already lasted far too long.

11. When she blocked my jump shot, took the rebound, drove down the court, and scored, I realized that I was facing a worthy (**demise, adversary**).

12. And now I want you all to try my (**fallow, culinary**) masterpiece—a salami soufflé, garnished with sour cream.

Completing the Sentence

Choose the word from the word bank that best completes each of the following sentences. Write the correct word or form of the word in the space provided.

adversary	culinary	fallow	perpetuate	redress
coerce	demise	liquidate	punitive	urbane

1. If we continue to elect unworthy people to public office, we will simply _____ the evils that we have tried so hard to correct.

2. His charmingly _____ manner and keen wit made him a much sought-after guest at social gatherings.

3. The deserted buildings and the land lying _____ hinted at the troubles the farmers in the area were experiencing.

4. I advise you to _____ all of your assets and negotiate with creditors before declaring bankruptcy.

5. There are far more subtle ways of _____ a person into doing what you want than twisting his or her arm.

6. When citizens feel that something is wrong, they have a right under the First Amendment to ask their government for a(n) _____ of grievances.

7. The full extent of my _____ skill is preparing scrambled eggs on toast.

8. The coach took me off the starting team as a(n) _____ measure for missing two days of practice.

9. The _____ of an administration in the United States is never a crisis because a newly elected administration is waiting to take over.

10. In 1858, Abraham Lincoln held a series of debates with Stephen Douglas, his _____ in the contest for U.S. Senator from Illinois.

Definitions

Note the spelling, pronunciation, part(s) of speech, and definition(s) of each of the following words. Then write the appropriate form of the word in the blank space in the illustrative sentence(s) following.

1. **alienate**
(ā′ lē ə nāt)

(*v.*) to turn away; to make indifferent or hostile; to transfer, convey
Gossiping and backbiting are bad habits that are bound to _____ friends.

2. **artifice**
(är′ tə fis)

(*n.*) a skillful or ingenious device; a clever trick; a clever skill; trickery
Even the most renowned art experts were completely taken in by the forger's _____.

3. **craven**
(krā′ vən)

(*adj.*) cowardly; (*n.*) a coward
Those who urged Great Britain to make peace with Hitler were criticized for their _____ attitude.
It is a mistake to assume that everyone who refuses to go to war is a _____ who lacks patriotism.

4. **exhilarate**
(eg zil′ ə rāt)

(*v.*) to enliven, cheer, give spirit or liveliness to
The first landing on the moon, in the summer of 1969, _____ the nation.

5. **harass**
(hə ras′)

(*v.*) to disturb, worry; to trouble by repeated attacks
The judge repeatedly cautioned the prosecuting attorney not to _____ the witness.

6. **inclement**
(in klem′ ənt)

(*adj.*) stormy, harsh; severe in attitude or action
During an _____ New England winter, heavy snowfalls may bring highway traffic to a standstill.

7. **muse**
(myüz)

(*v.*) to think about in a dreamy way, ponder
Philosophers have always _____ on the meaning of life.

8. **negligible**
(neg′ lə jə bəl)

(*adj.*) so unimportant that it can be disregarded
After taxes are deducted, a small raise in salary may result in a _____ increase in take-home pay.

9. **precedent**
(pres' ə dənt)

(*n.*) an example that may serve as a basis for imitation or later action

We hope that students at other schools in our city will follow our _____ in volunteer work and charitable contributions.

10. **sojourn**
(sō' jərn)

(*n.*) a temporary stay; (*v.*) to stay for a time

No matter how short your _____ in Paris, you must take time to go to the Louvre.

Many American graduates _____ abroad before they begin working full-time at home.

Using Context

*For each item, determine whether the **boldface** word from pages 42–43 makes sense in the context of the sentence. Circle the item numbers next to the six sentences in which the words are used correctly.*

1. The **craven** treatment of animals is something I cannot bear to watch.

2. If I'm feeling sluggish in the afternoon, a good workout never fails to **exhilarate** me.

3. As I stood in the field, a bee started to **harass** me, and I worried about getting stung.

4. The **negligible** amount of time that you devote to studying physics will be obvious when you take your final exam.

5. I look forward to the **inclement** greeting of my cousins, who try to contain their excitement.

6. The most popular teacher in the school always attempts to **alienate** her students on the first day by learning something personal about them.

7. I suggested using **artifice** during the scavenger hunt to lead the opposing team astray, but my teammates insisted on retaining integrity.

8. As the oldest child, I try to set a **precedent** for how to behave so that my brothers and sisters know what is expected of them.

9. We decided to make the **sojourn** from the east coast to the west coast by car, so that we could see all the sights along the way.

10. I sometimes **muse** on what my life would be like if I were a movie star, but at some point it's always necessary to come back to reality.

Choosing the Right Word

*Select the **boldface** word that better completes each sentence. You might refer to the passage on pages 36–37 to see how most of these words are used in context. Note that the choices might be related forms of the Unit words.*

1. When Washington refused to serve a third term as President, he set a(n) (**artifice, precedent**) that was to last for 150 years.

2. Did the other journalists (**alienate, sojourn**) the young writer after she expressed some political views with which they disagreed?

3. We need a supervisor who can maintain good discipline in the shop without (**harassing, exhilarating**) the workers.

4. The coach ran the risk of (**musing, alienating**) influential graduates of the school when he suspended a star player who had broken training.

5. Because of the severe sentences she often handed down, she gained the reputation of being an extremely (**negligible, inclement**) judge.

6. Our city government needs basic reforms; clever little (**sojourns, artifices**) will not solve our problems.

7. It is all very well to (**muse, exhilarate**) on what might have been, but it is far better to take action to make good things happen.

8. Since we are making (**craven, negligible**) progress in our fight against pollution, the time has come for us to adopt completely new methods.

9. I admit that we did some foolish things after the game, but you must remember how (**alienated, exhilarated**) we were by the victory.

10. The artist took a (**precedent, sojourn**) to the mountains, hoping to relieve his stress and renew his creativity.

11. We must reject the (**craven, negligible**) advice of those who feel we can solve social problems by abandoning our democratic freedoms.

12. The highlight of my trip to Europe came when I (**sojourned, harassed**) in the birthplace of my ancestors.

Completing the Sentence

Choose the word from the word bank that best completes each of the following sentences. Write the correct word or form of the word in the space provided.

alienate	craven	harass	muse	precedent
artifice	exhilarate	inclement	negligible	sojourn

1. At first we watched the game with relatively little emotion, but we became so _____ by our team's strong comeback that we began to cheer loudly.

2. Magicians rely on sleight of hand and other forms of _____ to deceive their unsuspecting audiences.

3. When Grandfather stubbornly refused to eat his vegetables, he set a(n) _____ that was immediately followed by the children.

4. When planning our trip to the Southwest, we made sure to set aside two days for a(n) _____ at the Grand Canyon.

5. The coach emphasized that the way to stop our opponents' passing game was to _____ their receivers and blitz their quarterback.

6. When the snowstorm lasted into a second day, we listened attentively to the radio to find out if our school was among those closed because of the _____ weather.

7. Since both cars had virtually come to a halt by the time their bumpers met, the damage was _____.

8. Their _____ behavior at the first sign of danger was a disgrace to the uniform they wore.

9. As I lay under the old apple tree, I began to _____ on the strange twists of fate that had led to the present situation.

10. Their bad manners and insufferable conceit _____ even those who were most inclined to judge them favorably.

Synonyms

Choose the word or form of the word from this Unit that is the same or most nearly the same in meaning as the **boldface** word or expression in the phrase. Write that word on the line. Use a dictionary if necessary.

1. their **pretense** used to fool unwary customers _____

2. **pressured** into confessing _____

3. a **castigatory** campaign against a political rival _____

4. to **sell off** poor stock investments _____

5. that **unproductive** phase in the artist's long career _____

6. **pestered** by flies and mosquitoes _____

7. was a **model** for future innovations _____

8. postponed due to **blustery** weather _____

9. a relaxing **stopover** on a tropical island _____

10. an attempt to **rectify** past mistakes _____

11. accepted into **cooking** school _____

12. your **polished** manner that puts people at ease _____

13. **isolated** from society _____

14. a dangerous **rival** who will stop at nothing _____

15. **daydream** about the future _____

Antonyms

Choose the word or form of the word from this Unit that is most nearly opposite in meaning to the **boldface** word or expression in the phrase. Write that word on the line. Use a dictionary if necessary.

1. a **significant** difference in price _____

2. **discontinue** the family traditions _____

3. a **courageous** act _____

4. the **birth** of a corrupt nation _____

5. **discouraged** by the fans' reactions _____

Writing: Words in Action

Write a compare-and-contrast essay about the modern techniques of crime scene investigation and explain which one you believe provides the most effective evidence for identifying and ultimately prosecuting criminals. Use at least two details from the passage (pages 36–37) and three or more Unit words to support your view.

Vocabulary in Context

*Some of the words you have studied in this Unit appear in **boldface** type. Read the passage below, and then circle the letter of the correct answer for each word as it is used in context.*

Many crime scene television shows highlight the methodical techniques that **urbane** forensic scientists and crime scene investigators use to catch each adversary. Some popular storylines involve investigators searching for the cause of a famous person's demise. Other episodes focus on investigators getting so involved in a case that they **alienate** everyone else while the case is ongoing. Although many of the storylines are fictional, the science behind them is not.

Forensic science is defined as the application of science to legal matters. For example, forensic accountants investigate assets **liquidated** in the commission of a crime, and forensic toxicologists study the effects of chemicals on the body. Many forensic scientists who work for police precincts work close to home, but forensic scientists who work for the federal government have to **sojourn** wherever they are needed.

One forensic science profession that is crucial in crime scene investigation is forensic anthropology. Forensic anthropologists sometimes begin their work during a **fallow** period when physical evidence is scarce. These anthropologists use skeletal fragments to identify the race, gender, and unique physical features of a person; they can even use these bones to ascertain the cause of death.

Another forensic science profession is forensic odontology, also known as forensic dentistry. Like forensic anthropologists, forensic odontologists use small pieces of evidence—teeth—to help solve crimes. Forensic odontologists use isotopic carbon analysis to determine a victim's exact age and information about his or her geographic origin. DNA can also be extracted from molars to help identify the victim of a crime. In many cases, forensic anthropologists and odontologists collaborate to help solve crimes. A satisfying outcome of these collaboration is when **craven** offenders receive their adequate punitive sentences.

---

1. A person who is **urbane** is
   a. analytical
   b. wise
   c. refined in manner
   d. follows the evidence

2. To **alienate** people is to make them
   a. hostile
   b. friendly
   c. fearful
   d. distant

3. Liquidated assets are assets that have been
   a. transfered
   b. deposited
   c. spent
   d. eliminated

4. To **sojourn** to solve a case is to
   a. return to a place
   b. travel to a place
   c. stay for a time
   d. stay forever

5. A **fallow** period is
   a. difficult
   b. inactive
   c. crucial
   d. lengthy

6. The word **craven** most nearly means
   a. cowardly
   b. aggressive
   c. busy
   d. remorseful

Vocabulary for Comprehension

Part 1

*Read this passage, which contains words in **boldface** that appear in Units 1–3. Then choose the best answer to each question based on what is stated or implied in the passage. You may refer to the passage as often as necessary.*

Questions 1–10 are based on the following passage.

Thomas Paine was 37 when he arrived in Philadelphia in November 1774 and became co-editor of a magazine. His writing was the **quintessence** of plain
(5) English, without the flourishes and urbane Latin words that made political writing so difficult to understand.

Paine's best-selling *Common Sense* appeared in January 1776, a fifty-page
(10) argument for declaring independence from Britain. He published it anonymously, and in just a few months, half a million copies sold.

In *Common Sense*, Paine lays out a
(15) **meticulous** case of "simple facts, plain arguments, and common sense." Paine sees no **amicable** resolution to the conflict with Britain. He argues that the **belligerent** King George III has, by the
(20) shots fired at Lexington and Concord, shown himself unwilling to compromise or to **redress** wrongs done to the Colonists. "Every quiet method for peace has been ineffectual," he writes, and he adds that
(25) it is absurd to think that a small island can rule a whole continent.

Paine argues that the thirteen colonies are not a British nation, for the colonists come from nations all over Europe. Nor
(30) are the colonists being protected by Britain; they are being made to fight Britain's wars. Except for Britain, he writes, "we should be at peace with France and Spain." He also muses, "Our plan
(35) is commerce, and that, attended to, will secure us the peace and friendship of all Europe; because it is in the interest of all Europe to have America a free port. Her trade will always be a protection, and
(40) her barrenness of gold and silver secure her from invaders."

Finally, if Britain seeks to govern under the **guise** of a "parent country," she should feel ashamed for treating the
(45) colonies as an adversary. These reasons, Paine deduces, are the **impetus** for the colonists to declare their independence.

Colonists everywhere **scrutinized** *Common Sense*, read it aloud in taverns,
(50) and hotly debated Paine's argument. Loyalists (those loyal to the king) opposed Paine's views, believing it was morally wrong to sever ties with Britain and that only the British Parliament could legally
(55) make changes. The Loyalists condemned the Patriots for acts of violence, and fearing that punitive mob rule might put their lives in **jeopardy**, many left for Canada as soon as independence
(60) was declared.

In December 1776 Paine began writing a series of sixteen pamphlets called "The American Crisis." The Crisis Number 1 begins with these memorable lines:

(65) These are the times that try men's souls: The summer soldier and the sunshine patriot will, in this crisis, shrink from the service of their country; but he that stands it now, deserves the love and thanks of man
(70) and woman. Tyranny . . . is not easily conquered; yet we have this consolation with us, that the harder the conflict, the more glorious the triumph. What we obtain too cheap, we esteem too lightly: it is
(75) dearness only that gives everything its value.

1. The primary purpose of the passage is to
   A) give details about how the Revolutionary War began.
   B) provide biographical details about Paine.
   C) inform the reader of Paine's important role during the pre-Revolutionary period.
   D) inform the reader about the Battles of Lexington and Concord.

2. The author quotes from two of Paine's works to
   A) give a sample of Paine's writing and writing style.
   B) refute Paine's argument for independence from Britain.
   C) reveal Paine's personality.
   D) provide biographical information.

3. As it is used in line 15, "meticulous" most nearly means
   A) exceedingly clean.
   B) carefully constructed.
   C) exactly measured.
   D) entirely believable.

4. As it is used in line 19, "belligerent" most nearly means
   A) stubborn.
   B) royal.
   C) peaceful.
   D) combative.

5. Lines 14–26 summarize Paine's
   A) reasons for emigrating to America.
   B) speech to the Continental Congress.
   C) discussion of commerce.
   D) argument in *Common Sense*.

6. According to Paine, why is America safe from invaders?
   A) Britain is defending it.
   B) America has free ports.
   C) America has no gold or silver.
   D) America has a strong navy.

7. Which choice provides the best evidence for the answer to the previous question?
   A) Lines 27–29 ("Paine argues...Europe")
   B) Lines 29–34 ("Nor are . . . Spain")
   C) Lines 34–38 ("Our plan . . . port")
   D) Line 39 ("Her trade . . . protection")

8. As it is used in line 48, "scrutinized" most nearly means
   A) examined.
   B) read.
   C) discussed.
   D) agreed with.

9. What point is the author making by including the sixth paragraph (lines 48–60)?
   A) Most colonists supported Paine's ideas.
   B) Most Canadians disagreed with Paine's ideas.
   C) Paine's ideas were controversial.
   D) Paine's ideas caused riots.

10. Paine's "sunshine patriot" in lines 66–67 is a metaphor for colonists who
   A) live in the South.
   B) are patriotic all the time.
   C) are patriotic only in good times.
   D) serve their country in good times and bad times.

Vocabulary for Comprehension
Part 2

*Read this passage, which contains words in **boldface** that appear in Units 1–3. Then choose the best answer to each question based on what is stated or implied in the passage. You may refer to the passage as often as necessary.*

Questions 1–10 are based on the following passage.

King John I of England (r. 1199–1216) was reckless, needy, and unpopular. His country was impoverished by costly crusades, and he imposed taxes to pay for
(5) unpopular, **opulent** and unsuccessful wars with France. When many of his barons objected to his foreign **"sojourns"** and refused him military support, he **harassed** them with **belligerent** demands for
(10) "scutage"—payments in lieu of military service. When they refused, civil war broke out. On June 15, 1215, a tired and **unkempt** King John was forced to accept peace terms dictated by his rebel barons.
(15) By June 19 those terms had been revised, and the document John signed at Runnymede, west of London, would be known as the Magna Carta (Great Charter). Most of the document's 63 clauses
(20) protected the barons from unjust taxation, but some of them would have a profound influence on English law and on the Constitution of the United States. The words of the Magna Carta may sound familiar to
(25) Americans even if they have never read it.
By stating that the monarch could only levy taxes with his subjects' consent, the Magna Carta ruled that no king was above the law. Clause 39 states "no free man shall
(30) be . . . imprisoned or dispossessed except by the lawful judgment of his peers or by the law of the land."
Three hundred years after the Magna Carta was signed, Clause 39 was invoked
(35) in another struggle against tyranny. In 1628, the English Parliament issued the Petition of Right to protect English citizens against the illegal powers of arrest and imprisonment

adopted by Charles I (r. 1625–1649),
(40) who was **nostalgic** for the days when kings were **extolled** and ruled without parliaments. One of Parliament's leaders, Sir Edward Coke, asserted his insistence that the King could only rule by consent
(45) by proclaiming that the "Magna Carta . . . will have no sovereign."
Coke's **benevolent** spirit illuminates the seventeenth-century charter for the American colonies. It guaranteed subjects
(50) "all the rights and immunities of free and natural subjects—among them immunity of citizens under the Habeas Corpus Act (1679) to being held without charge, a right established in the Magna Carta: "To no one
(55) will we sell, and to no one will we deny or delay right or justice."
King George III of Britain (r. 1760–1820) was reckless, needy, and unpopular, too. After the **demise** of George II, he inherited a
(60) country impoverished by the Seven Years' War (1756–63), and his parliament sought to pay for keeping British troops in America by taxing the colonists. The Stamp Act (1765) was levied without the colonists' consent.
(65) Their resistance was inspired by their knowledge of Coke and the Magna Carta.
When in 1774 the **dour** Sir Thomas Gage was appointed military governor of Massachusetts in the wake of the Boston
(70) Tea Party—itself a protest against unjust taxation—his suspension of Habeas Corpus and use of military courts were interpreted as further violations of the Magna Carta and the principles of Sir Edward Coke.
(75) Gage's authority ended in 1775, and Paul Revere engraved a new seal for Massachusetts. It depicted a militiaman carrying a sword in one hand and the

Magna Carta in the other. The seal's Latin
(80) motto means "By the sword we seek
peace, but peace only under liberty." The
revolutionary symbolism is clear, and the
significance of the rights ensured by the
Magna Carta was clear to Americans as
(85) they fought for liberty. Many of the rights
that the colonists should have enjoyed
under the Magna Carta were included in
the Constitution and the Bill of Rights.

1. In line 7, the word "sojourns" is used
   A) literally.
   B) angrily.
   C) ironically.
   D) imprecisely.

2. As it is used in line 8, "harassed"
   most nearly means
   A) asked.
   B) threatened.
   C) humiliated.
   D) pestered.

3. Which choice best summarizes the
   second paragraph (lines 15–25)?
   A) Most of the 63 clauses were irrelevant to
   the American Constitution.
   B) Some of the 63 clauses had a lasting
   influence in Britain, and later in America.
   C) The Magna Carta would have more
   impact in America than in England.
   D) The Magna Carta protected citizens'
   rights in Britain and the colonies.

4. As it is used in line 40, "nostalgic"
   most nearly means
   A) envious.
   B) pining.
   C) desperate.
   D) optimistic.

5. It can reasonably be inferred that when
   Coke says "Magna Carta . . . will have no
   sovereign," (lines 45–46) he means
   A) no rule is higher than the rule of law.
   B) the Magna Carta deposed King John.
   C) the nation does not need a king.
   D) King Charles I is worse than King John.

6. As it is used in line 59, "demise"
   most nearly means
   A) abdication.
   B) reign.
   C) death.
   D) deposition.

7. The colonists objected to the Stamp Act
   A) because it was unjust.
   B) because it was illegal.
   C) because they could not afford to pay it.
   D) because they rejected Gage's authority.

8. Which choice provides the best evidence
   for the answer to the previous question?
   A) Lines 26–29 ("By stating . . . the law")
   B) Lines 42–46 ("One . . . sovereign'")
   C) Lines 47–56 ("Coke's . . . justice")
   D) Lines 57–63 ("King . . . colonists")

9. What point does the author make in
   lines 81–82 when he writes, **"The
   revolutionary symbolism is clear"**?
   A) Every militiaman carried a sword
   and a copy of the Magna Carta.
   B) The Magna Carta is the militiaman's
   sword of liberty.
   C) The militiaman will defend with his
   sword the liberties enshrined in the
   Magna Carta.
   D) The militiaman is prepared to use
   his sword to slay tyrants.

10. The primary purpose of the passage is to
   A) demonstrate that if Britain had obeyed
   its own laws the revolution could have
   been avoided.
   B) show how laws contained in the Magna
   Carta inspired the colonists' struggle
   for liberty against tyranny.
   C) indicate the major part that Sir Edward
   Coke played in keeping the Magna
   Carta relevant in changing times.
   D) use parallels in history to demonstrate
   the point that different periods offer
   important similarities.

Synonyms

*From the word bank below, choose the word that has the same or nearly the same meaning as the **boldface** word in each sentence and write it on the line. You will not use all of the words.*

ambidextrous	gape	holocaust	opulent
culinary	gibe	impetus	pliable
demise	grimace	inclement	punitive
fallow	harass	nostalgia	sojourn

1. Schools, libraries, and government offices have now been closed for two days because of **stormy** weather. _____

2. Because people are ignoring the "No Parking" signs, the town will impose fines and other **penalizing** measures to deal with the situation. _____

3. It is good for our brains if we make an effort to be **flexible**; for example, if we usually brush our teeth using our right hand, we should sometimes use our left hand instead. _____

4. It is too soon to declare the **decline** of the vinyl record album, since these plastic discs have suddenly become popular again. _____

5. The frugal sisters enjoy meeting in the expensive hotel's **rich** and elegant dining room to have tea from time to time. _____

6. The glee club is giving several concerts to raise money for its upcoming **visit** to Spain and Italy. _____

7. This year, three-quarters of the land on our farm will be seeded, and one-quarter will be left **dormant**. _____

8. Seeing the karate class's impressive demonstration last year gave me the **impulse** to start studying the martial art. _____

9. The appearance of the mother sea lion feeding its pups caused everyone at the beach to stop and **ogle**. _____

10. I don't mean to **annoy** you, but I'm just reminding you once more that I will need my tennis racket back by this weekend. _____

11. Professional wrestling matches are entertaining when opponents play exaggerated roles and dramatically **jeer** at each other. _____

12. Every country in the world shares the responsibility of preventing nuclear **devastation**, but countries that have nuclear arms bear a special obligation to do so. _____

Two-Word Completions

Select the pair of words that best completes the meaning of each of the following sentences.

1. I have _____ chosen an excerpt from the President's inaugural address that I'd like to use in my report. Unfortunately, the passage is far too long to reproduce _____.
a. meticulously . . . reiterate
b. stolidly . . . coerce
c. feasibly . . . liquidate
d. tentatively . . . verbatim

2. Because the course of the disease was so _____, we didn't notice at first that the patient's condition was no longer improving but in fact had begun to _____.
a. adroit . . . redress
b. insidious . . . retrogress
c. tentative . . . adulterate
d. averse . . . perpetuate

3. Tony's general attitude toward people is so _____ that he has _____ absolutely everybody who knows him. If he didn't walk around with such a huge chip on his shoulder, he would have a few friends.
a. impervious . . . exhilarated
b. benevolent . . . deployed
c. amicable . . . redressed
d. belligerent . . . alienated

4. Although I now have a very _____ relationship with my older sister, she recalls that we used to fight over everything, viewing each other as _____.
a. amicable . . . adversaries
b. insidious . . . bereft
c. cursory . . . negligible
d. adulterated . . . dour

5. Some people always stick up their noses at food they're not accustomed to, but I'm not at all _____ to trying something new. Still, experience has taught me to be _____ of such dubious delicacies as chocolate-covered ants, and I usually look before I leap, so to speak.
a. impervious . . . craven
b. averse . . . wary
c. tepid . . . negligible
d. amicable . . . bereft

6. My first _____ of Nelson's double-dealing came when I discovered him whispering with my opponent. Prior to that, I had no inkling of my so-called friend's _____.
a. redress . . . coercion
b. precedent . . . artifice
c. intimation . . . duplicity
d. scrutiny . . . fortitude

7. "I haven't yet had time to give your latest sales report more than a _____ glance," my boss told me. "However, I plan to _____ it carefully before we sit down to discuss it in detail."
a. meticulous . . . augment
b. tentative . . . redress
c. verbatim . . . reiterate
d. cursory . . . scrutinize

Idioms

In the passage "The Globe Theatre: Then and Now" (see pages 12–13), the author says that the Globe Theatre is "not just a footnote in history books."

"Just a footnote" is an idiom that means "of relative insignificance." **Idioms** are colorful expressions that mean something different from their literal meanings. There are thousands of idioms in the English language. Because idioms often "play" with language and are not literal, you can seldom figure out what they mean by analyzing the meaning of each word. For this reason, idioms often do not make sense when they are translated into another language, and they can be difficult to learn.

Choosing the Right Idiom

Read each sentence. Use context clues to figure out the meaning of each idiom in **boldface**. *Then write the letter of the definition for the idiom in the sentence.*

1. If you want people here to trust you, you have to obey the rules and **keep your nose clean.** _____

2. If we **put our heads together**, maybe we can figure out this math problem. _____

3. If you would only **get off my back**, I could concentrate and get this finished more quickly. _____

4. The best espresso machines from Italy cost **an arm and a leg**, so our café will have to survive without one. _____

5. Don't **turn your back on** them now, when they need your help the most. _____

6. I wanted to tell her that I thought she should dress up more for the party, but I **held my tongue.** _____

7. Joe offered to **lend a hand** to the neighbors, who were moving some heavy furniture into storage. _____

8. The butler maintained his formal, detached manner, refusing to **let his hair down.** _____

9. Vickie, who always **keeps an ear to the ground**, knew about the corporate takeover long before it was announced. _____

10. The swindler was so convincing and seemed so honest that he really **pulled the wool over our eyes.** _____

a. help someone complete a job

b. pays close attention to clues about what will happen

c. kept silent

d. work together to think through a problem

e. relax; have fun

f. ignore; refuse to offer help

g. a large amount of money

h. stay out of trouble

i. deceived us

j. stop pestering or annoying me

Classical Roots

mis, miss, mit—to send

The root *mis* appears in **demise** (page 38). The literal meaning is "a sending down," but the word now suggests a death, especially of a person in an elevated position. Some other words based on the same root are listed below.

commissary	**emit**	**missile**	**premise**
emissary	**manumit**	**permit**	**remission**

From the list of words above, choose the one that corresponds to each of the brief definitions below. Write the word in the blank space in the illustrative sentence below the definition. Use an online or print dictionary if necessary.

1. to consent to formally; to authorize; to allow

The law _____ a person convicted of a crime to file an appeal.

2. an object to be thrown or shot

The new fighter plane can fire a(n) _____ with deadly accuracy.

3. to free from slavery or bondage

In some ancient societies, it was the custom to _____ all children born into slavery.

4. a messenger, agent (*"one sent out"*)

The President sent a special _____ to discuss the drafting of a peace agreement.

5. a statement or idea upon which a conclusion is based (*"that which is sent before"*)

Some members of Congress argued that the budget proposal was based on a false _____ .

6. a place where supplies are distributed; a lunchroom

Campers and counselors eat their meals at the _____.

7. a letup, abatement; a relief from suffering

Immediately after undergoing major surgery, a patient may need some medication for the _____ of pain.

8. to release or send forth (*"send out"*)

Crickets _____ a shrill chirp by rubbing their wings together.

*Read the following passage, taking note of the **boldface** words and their contexts. These words are among those you will be studying in Unit 4. It may help you to complete the exercises in this Unit if you refer to the way the words are used below.*

Patronage of the Arts: Help or Hindrance?
<Narrative Nonfiction>

" Is not a patron, my lord, one who looks with unconcern on a man struggling for life in the water, and when he has reached ground, encumbers him with help?" So wrote the British author Samuel Johnson to Lord Chesterfield in 1755. In his letter, Johnson bitterly protested the **supercilious** tone of Chesterfield's belated offer of patronage. Having lived in near-poverty while creating the first dictionary of the English language, Johnson got the last laugh: In his book, he defined *patron* as "a wretch who supports with insolence and is paid in flattery."

A **cogent** and convincing account of patronage of the arts would have to acknowledge its long, productive history. Beginning with the European Renaissance, the period from the fourteenth to seventeenth centuries, art patronage—financial support of an artist by wealthy noblemen, members of the aristocracy, and the papacy—flourished. While this system kept artists employed, the artists had to make whatever their patron wanted, whether a flattering portrait of the patron's wife or a statue of the patron in the role of a biblical figure. Artists composed poems, plays, operas, and symphonies—and hoped their patron liked the results.

The patronage system **bequeathed** countless masterpieces to future generations. Scholars have **ascertained** numerous instances in which the needs of patron and artist **converged**: in a quest for glory, on the one hand, and for funds on the other. Two such cases are shown in the careers of Jean Racine, a French playwright, and George Frideric Handel, a music composer in England.

Louis XIV, king of France from 1643 to 1715, was an important patron of the arts. *Portrait by Charles Le Brun*

Lorenzo de Medici

Young Mozart at the court of Empress Maria Theresa

Jean Racine (1639–1699) was born into a middle-class family and orphaned before the age of four. By an **uncanny** stroke of good fortune, he was privileged to attend the school of Port-Royal near Paris. There, he acquired such a mastery of classical literature as to make him seem virtually **omniscient** on the subject. By the age of twenty, Racine's literary **attainments** had won the young writer considerable **esteem**. Later, Racine produced a play on the life of Alexander the Great, conveying a **scrupulous** parallel to the reign of Louis XIV, well known as a patron of the arts. Racine's goal was transparent: He wished to be **affiliated** with the royal court. Royal patronage, however, did not free even a talent like Racine from criticism. Many contemporaries regarded him as France's greatest tragic playwright, but **malevolent** rivals attacked him and called his work historically inaccurate and without drama.

In Germany, the young George Frideric Handel (1685–1759) was growing up in the town of Halle. Like Racine, Handel, a music composer, showed phenomenal talent at an early age. After three years of travel in Italy, he made his first visit to England in 1710. Within three years, he had won royal patronage at the court of Queen Anne. He spent most of his long life in England, achieving success writing many musical forms: opera, oratorio, orchestral overtures, choral anthems, and chamber music. Much of his work might not have been produced without the financial support of patronage.

Artists have always had to walk a straight line to keep their patronage. Even minor, **venial** offenses might disenchant a patron. Yet it is hard to imagine how artists such as Mozart or Michelangelo might have fared without patronage. Would their works ever have been created and widely **dispersed**? In the end, while art patronage influenced the works of some of history's greatest creators, it has also produced an infinitely rich heritage that has proved **invulnerable** to the passage of time.

Audio

For iWords and audio passages, go to SadlierConnect.com.

Definitions

Note the spelling, pronunciation, part(s) of speech, and definition(s) of each of the following words. Then write the appropriate form of the word in the blank space in the illustrative sentence(s) following.

1. **affiliated**
   (ə fil′ ē āt əd)

   (*adj., part.*) associated, connected

   Being _____ with a well-known law firm is often an important first step on the way to a successful political career.

2. **attainment**
   (ə tān′ mənt)

   (*n.*) an accomplishment, the act of achieving

   In addition to his abilities as a leader, Abraham Lincoln was a man of high literary _____.

3. **bequeath**
   (bi kwēth′)

   (*v.*) to give or pass on as an inheritance

   Few people will make enough money in their lifetimes to be in a position to _____ a fortune to their heirs.

4. **disperse**
   (di spərs′)

   (*v.*) to scatter, spread far and wide

   When a scuffle broke out, the commissioner ordered the police to _____ the crowd.

5. **esteem**
   (es tēm′)

   (*v.*) to regard highly; (*n.*) a highly favorable opinion or judgment

   In many of the world's cultures, young people are taught to _____ their ancestors.

   The Chief Justice of the Supreme Court should be someone whom all parties hold in high _____.

6. **invulnerable**
   (in vəl′ nər ə bəl)

   (*adj.*) not able to be wounded or hurt; shielded against attack

   Medieval lords did everything possible to make their castles _____ fortresses.

7. **malevolent**
   (mə lev′ ə lənt)

   (*adj.*) spiteful, showing ill will

   While pretending to be a loyal friend, Iago told Othello _____ lies.

8. **panacea**
   (pan ə sē′ ə)

   (*n.*) a remedy for all ills; cure-all; an answer to all problems

   You are mistaken if you think that getting more money will be a _____ for all your troubles.

9. **scrupulous**
(skrü′ pyə ləs)

(*adj.*) exact, careful, attending thoroughly to details; having high moral standards, principled

Scientists are trained to record their observations with _____ accuracy.

10. **venial**
(vē′ nē əl)

(*adj.*) easily excused; pardonable

Someone whose offense is deemed by the judge to be _____ may be ordered to perform community service.

Using Context

*For each item, determine whether the **boldface** word from pages 58–59 makes sense in the context of the sentence. Circle the item numbers next to the six sentences in which the words are used correctly.*

1. Ducks have a natural **esteem** for water and will begin swimming when they are just a few days old.

2. Returning a library book a week late is a **venial** misdeed, whereas defacing a book is a more serious one.

3. After taking a required class and passing a test, you can become **affiliated** as a lifeguard.

4. My grandmother decided to **bequeath** her engagement ring to her grandson so that he could give it to his future wife.

5. An animal with plant seeds tangled in its fur can help **disperse** the seeds when it carries them to new sites.

6. Even the most complex project is not **invulnerable** if you break it up into a set of small, doable tasks.

7. The entire country rejoiced at the team's **attainment** of the Olympic gold medal.

8. According to the famous Greek myth, the opening of Pandora's box released chaos and **panacea** into the world.

9. Harry Potter is a well-known example of a hero who struggles against **malevolent** forces; so is Luke Skywalker from the *Star Wars* movies.

10. Whoever turned this diamond ring in to the lost and found was certainly a **scrupulous** person.

Choosing the Right Word

*Select the **boldface** word that better completes each sentence. You might refer to the passage on pages 56–57 to see how most of these words are used in context. Note that the choices might be related forms of the Unit words.*

1. The class of 1956 must have been overjoyed when their college invited the (**invulnerable, esteemed**) poet, Robert Frost, to speak at commencement.

2. Though you forgot my birthday, and I did not receive a gift or card, it was a (**venial, scrupulous**) mistake and I shall forgive you.

3. Her bright, optimistic manner did much to (**bequeath, disperse**) the atmosphere of gloom that had settled over the meeting.

4. Nothing he may (**esteem, bequeath**) to the next generation can be more precious than the memory of his long life of honorable public service.

5. When I found myself flushed with anger, I realized that I was not so (**scrupulous, invulnerable**) to their bitter sarcasm as I had thought I was!

6. She is the kind of person who has many (**attainments, panaceas**) but seems unable to put them to any practical use.

7. Lincoln said, "If you once forfeit the confidence of your fellow citizens, you can never regain their respect and (**esteem, attainment**)."

8. As a member of the grand jury, it is your duty to be (**scrupulous, affiliated**) in weighing every bit of evidence.

9. There are so many different factors involved in an energy crisis that no single measure can be expected to serve as a(n) (**panacea, attainment**).

10. Instead of blaming a(n) (**malevolent, invulnerable**) fate for your failures, why not look for the causes within yourself?

11. The newspaper revealed that the city's chief building inspector was (**dispersed, affiliated**) with a large construction company.

12. The critic recognized the book's faults but dismissed them as (**malevolent, venial**) in view of the author's overall achievement.

Completing the Sentence

Choose the word from the word bank that best completes each of the following sentences. Write the correct word or form of the word in the space provided.

affiliated	bequeath	esteem	malevolent	scrupulous
attainment	disperse	invulnerable	panacea	venial

1. Only by paying _____ attention to innumerable details were the investigators able to piece together the cause of the accident.

2. When I saw the pain he caused others and the pleasure he took in doing so, I realized he was a truly _____ person.

3. The screening committee investigated not only the candidates themselves but also the organizations with which they were _____.

4. I knew the dean would accept my apology when she characterized my behavior as thoughtless but _____.

5. Isn't it remarkable how quickly a throng of sunbathers will pick up their belongings and _____ when a few drops of rain fall?

6. So long as we remained indoors, we were _____ to the arctic blasts that swept down on our snowbound cabin.

7. Her election to Congress was the _____ of a lifelong ambition.

8. When the candidate admitted openly that he had been mistaken in some of his earlier policies, we _____ him more highly than ever.

9. Antibiotics were once considered wonder drugs, but we now know that they are not _____ for all our physical ailments.

10. If only parents could _____ their hard-won practical wisdom and experience to their children!

Definitions

Note the spelling, pronunciation, part(s) of speech, and definition(s) of each of the following words. Then write the appropriate form of the word in the blank space in the illustrative sentence(s) following.

1. **ascertain**
(as ər tān′)

(*v.*) to find out

We need to _____ what it will cost to remodel our kitchen.

2. **cogent**
(kō′ jint)

(*adj.*) forceful, convincing; relevant, to the point

A group of legal scholars held a press conference to present a _____ plea for reform of the state's prison system.

3. **converge**
(kən verj′)

(*v.*) to move toward one point, approach nearer together

The television coverage resumed as soon as the delegates _____ on the hall to hear the keynote speaker's address.

4. **expunge**
(ik spənj′)

(*v.*) to erase, obliterate, destroy

The judge ordered the remarks _____ from the court record.

5. **finite**
(fī′ nīt)

(*adj.*) having limits; lasting for a limited time

There are only a _____ number of possible answers to a multiple-choice question.

6. **nonchalant**
(nän shə lant′)

(*adj.*) cool and confident, unconcerned

The elegantly dressed couple strolled down the boulevard with a _____ air.

7. **omniscient**
(äm nish′ ənt)

(*adj.*) knowing everything; having unlimited awareness or understanding

Scientists today have so much specialized knowledge that they sometimes seem _____.

8. **skulk**
(skəlk)

(*v.*) to move about stealthily; to lie in hiding

The burglar _____ in the alley looking for a way to get into the darkened jewelry store without attracting the attention of anyone who might be nearby.

9. supercilious
(sü pər sil' ē əs)

(*adj.*) proud and contemptuous; showing scorn because of a feeling of superiority

Their _____ attitude toward their servants was extremely offensive.

10. uncanny
(ən kan' ē)

(*adj.*) strange, mysterious, weird, beyond explanation

It is highly unusual for a beginner to display such an _____ skill at playing bridge.

Using Context

*For each item, determine whether the **boldface** word from pages 62–63 makes sense in the context of the sentence. Circle the item numbers next to the six sentences in which the words are used correctly.*

1. My parents, sticklers for cleanliness, always try to **expunge** the house before we have guests over.

2. Her memory of the smallest details is so **uncanny** that I often think she's making them up.

3. That song is so **omniscient** that I can't even go an hour without hearing it on the radio.

4. You made some persuasive points in the debate, but you often brought up **cogent** remarks that did not pertain to the matter at hand.

5. The first step in the hiring process is usually a phone interview to **ascertain** some general details on an applicant.

6. The reporter expected the famous actress to be haughty, but she was surprisingly **supercilious** and graciously discussed her new project.

7. Since there is only a **finite** number of days in the summer, I try to take advantage of the warm weather and spend as much time as possible outside.

8. The security guard watched the shoplifter **skulk** through the aisles of the clothing store as he tried to remain under the radar.

9. In certain climates, warm winds that **converge** with cold winds can cause a tornado.

10. I don't understand how anyone can be **nonchalant** and at ease before going to the dentist, an experience I always find unpleasant.

Choosing the Right Word

*Select the **boldface** word that better completes each sentence. You might refer to the passage on pages 56–57 to see how most of these words are used in context. Note that the choices might be related forms of the Unit words.*

1. Scientists have concluded that a sudden catastrophe (**expunged, converged**) dinosaurs from the face of the earth.

2. I found your criticism of my conduct unpleasant, but I had to admit that your remarks were (**nonchalant, cogent**).

3. It seems unimaginable that when I look at the night sky, the number of stars is actually (**finite, omniscient**).

4. A large crowd (**ascertained, converged**) on the mall to buy the latest gadget.

5. Is it true that some dogs have a(n) (**uncanny, nonchalant**) sense of the approach of death?

6. Though the journey seemed interminable, I knew that it was (**cogent, finite**) and that I would soon be home.

7. When I walked into the abandoned house, I had this (**supercilious, uncanny**) feeling that someone was watching me.

8. Instead of making an informed guess, why not (**ascertain, expunge**) exactly how many students are going on the trip to Washington?

9. Though the couple have spent years studying African history, they do not claim to be (**omniscient, cogent**) in that field.

10. Vast wealth, elegant clothes, and a (**finite, supercilious**) manner may make a snob, but they do not of themselves make a person a true gentleman or lady.

11. When I splattered paint on my art teacher, I tried to appear (**nonchalant, uncanny**) but succeeded only in looking horrified.

12. The reform candidate vowed to root out the corruption that (**skulked, ascertained**) through the corridors of City Hall.

Completing the Sentence

Choose the word from the word bank that best completes each of the following sentences. Write the correct word or form of the word in the space provided.

ascertain	converge	finite	omniscient	supercilious
cogent	expunge	nonchalant	skulk	uncanny

1. Our representative offered one simple but _____ argument against the proposal: It would raise the cost of living.

2. Though I wanted to "let bygones be bygones," I found that I could not wholly _____ the bitter memory of their behavior from my mind.

3. In a situation that would have left me all but helpless with embarrassment, he remained cool and _____.

4. Your ability to guess what I am thinking about at any given time is nothing short of _____.

5. Before making our final plans, we should _____ exactly how much money we will have for expenses.

6. In the opening scene of the horror film, a shadowy figure dressed in black _____ through the graveyard in the moonlight.

7. Because our natural resources are _____ and by no means inexhaustible, we must learn to conserve them.

8. The more knowledge and wisdom people acquire, the more keenly they become aware that no one is _____.

9. As we stood on the railway tracks looking off into the distance, the rails seemed to _____ and meet at some far-off point.

10. Is there anyone in the world as _____ as a senior who attends a mere sophomore class dance?

Synonyms

*Choose the word or form of the word from this Unit that is the same or most nearly the same in meaning as the **boldface** word or expression in the phrase. Write that word on the line. Use a dictionary if necessary.*

1. a **quantifiable** amount of rainfall _____
2. needed to **delete** out-of-date files _____
3. an **eerie** tale of the supernatural _____
4. an **all-knowing** spiritual leader _____
5. shrugged her shoulders **indifferently** _____
6. hold the Nobel Prize winner in high **regard** _____
7. the **realization** of a cherished dream _____
8. the villain's **sinister** thoughts _____
9. **crept around** in the shadows of the old warehouse _____
10. where two lines **intersect** _____
11. **resistant** to normal wear and tear _____
12. **associated** with the state university _____
13. no **easy solution** for the problems of aging _____
14. must **determine** who is responsible _____
15. **handed down** their knowledge to their apprentices _____

Antonyms

*Choose the word or form of the word from this Unit that is most nearly opposite in meaning to the **boldface** word or expression in the phrase. Write that word on the line. Use a dictionary if necessary.*

1. **gather** the seeds _____
2. **careless** in verifying the contents of the document _____
3. the **unconvincing** analysis _____
4. the **unpardonable** mistake of his teenage years _____
5. a **deferential** young starlet _____

Writing: Words in Action

Do you believe that when an artist accepts a patron he or she sacrifices self-expression in favor of the patron's taste? Does patronage support culture and the arts or dictate it? Write a brief essay exploring these questions. Use at least two details from the passage (pages 56–57) and three or more words from this Unit.

Vocabulary in Context

*Some of the words you have studied in this Unit appear in **boldface** type. Read the passage below, and then circle the letter of the correct answer for each word as it is used in context.*

Antico, for the entrance to our camerino we want something created by your hand. . . . We request that you accept the commission willingly and that you start working immediately, since you will gain honor and advantage by it, and we will be grateful.
27 March 1500

"Antico" was the nickname of sculptor Pier Jacopo Alari Bonacolsi (c.1460–1528). His patron, Isabella d'Este, Marchesa of Mantua (1474–1529), is asking him in her letter to make one of his ornate 12– to 16–inch miniature copies of ancient statues to decorate her *camerino* ("little room"). Also known as her *studiolo*, this was a private chambers; the other was her *grotta* ("cave"), where she displayed works by artists she supported as patron, as well as her treasured collection of antiquities. Isabella did not **skulk** unseen behind their genius or seek to **expunge** her name from the list of those involved in the creative process. These rooms defined Isabella, displayed her taste, and demonstrated her power to command the creation of beautiful things. They became the cultural and political center of the court of Mantua, and even her most eminent guests felt honored to be invited into her *studiolo* and *grotta*.

Isabella's request is haughty, but complimentary. The tone is familiar, but formal. It is **nonchalant** in its authority. Many of the greatest artists of the period knew her well: Andrea Mantegna (1431–1506), Titian (c.1485–1576), Giovanni Bellini (c.1430–1516), Pietro Perugino (c.1450–1523), and Leonardo da Vinci (1452–1519) all benefited from Isabella's patronage. Patronage was not, however, a **panacea**. Funds at the court of Mantua were **finite**, but the honor of having work exhibited in her uniquely brilliant and exclusive private gallery was immense. Isabella **esteemed** loyalty, and she rewarded her artists with bejeweled gold medals that carried her likeness and these words: *Benemerentium ergo*—"Well deserved."

---

1. A person who **skulks** is
   a. lying
   b. afraid
   c. hiding
   d. unhappy

2. To **expunge** something is to
   a. erase it
   b. disbelieve it
   c. steal it
   d. spoil it

3. A person who is **nonchalant**, as Isabella is said to be, is
   a. uncaring
   b. wealthy
   c. haughty
   d. confident

4. A **panacea**
   a. fails
   b. is good to eat
   c. cures everything
   d. is a guarantee

5. Resources that are **finite**
   a. never fail
   b. run out
   c. are renewable
   d. are unavailable

6. The word **esteem** most nearly means
   a. disdain
   b. dismiss
   c. promote widely
   d. value highly

*Read the following passage, taking note of the **boldface** words and their contexts. These words are among those you will be studying in Unit 5. It may help you to complete the exercises in this Unit if you refer to the way the words are used below.*

Democracy: From Athens to America
<Speech>

As your student body president, it is my pleasure to address you during this celebration of the anniversary of Abraham Lincoln's Gettysburg Address. Lincoln spoke with **unfeigned** love for democracy when he delivered his magnificent speech. Today, we not only honor that momentous event, but also acknowledge the history behind it that reaches back over 3,000 years.

Lincoln at Gettysburg

Lincoln's United States was a fledgling democracy—an experiment, really, or perhaps a stage in a long, **plodding** journey—that our forebears had boldly **embarked** upon. But in 1863, the country was divided by the Civil War. So when Lincoln stated that ours was a "government by the people, for the people," he expressed his **indomitable** belief in democracy.

What is democracy? It is a form of government in which political authority rests with the people and is conducted by and with their **assent**, or agreement. In a democracy, all citizens are entitled to equal opportunity and equality before the law. Furthermore, democracies are committed to the idea of majority rule. Although in practice democracy is not **infallible**, it is the most natural form of government we know. For as the ancient Greek philosopher Aristotle asserted, man is by nature a political animal.

The roots of our democracy go back to ancient Greek city-states. These entities were small, fortified, independent communities made up of a city and the surrounding countryside. Athens was the most populous—and the one where democracy first took hold. It was ruled by its citizens rather than by monarchs or aristocrats. But at a time when **diffident** and obedient populations ruled by tyrants or kings were the norm, democratic ideas did not take

hold overnight; rather, they emerged over time to the point we are at today in this country.

But democratic ideas did take hold eventually—after their early start some 2,600 years ago, when the aristocrat Draco gave Athens a written code of laws. These laws were harsh but clear, and though they favored the nobility, they became a foundation. Democratic ideas built on these laws a generation later, thanks to the **altruistic** and generous reformer Solon. He repealed many of Draco's harsh laws and replaced them with ones allowing for **clemency**. He also gave citizens a greater voice by establishing a lawmaking assembly. But it was under the leadership of Pericles that ancient democracy peaked and Athens entered its Golden Age. Pericles believed in citizen participation in government, and he had the **temerity** to give all citizens the right to criticize their leaders and generals. At a time when there was a **dearth** of individual rights, the forerunner of the modern democratic state had arrived. And with it came the first politicians, for Athenians prized the skills of oratory and persuasion.

While we must praise the Athenians for introducing democratic ideals to the world, we would be **remiss** not to recognize the **discrepancies** between their form of democracy and ours. Ours is a representative government, while theirs was a limited, direct form in which only Athenian men participated. Indeed, only men who owned land were entitled to citizenship

Solon of Athens

then. And only they could get an education or participate in cultural festivities. Women shared none of those rights. Neither did slaves, though they made up one-fourth of the population. That said, I believe it would be **facile** and insincere of me to condemn outright the shortcomings of the world's first democracy. Out of it developed the country that Abraham Lincoln was trying to unite and preserve on the day he dedicated a cemetery for the **repose** of the Civil War soldiers at Gettysburg. The gifts handed down to this country from ancient Greece and defended by our citizens and our leaders through the ages are something we should all cherish.

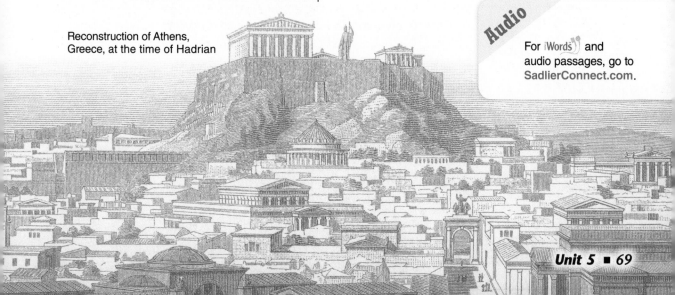

Reconstruction of Athens, Greece, at the time of Hadrian

Audio

For iWords and audio passages, go to SadlierConnect.com.

Definitions

Note the spelling, pronunciation, part(s) of speech, and definition(s) of each of the following words. Then write the appropriate form of the word in the blank space in the illustrative sentence(s) following.

1. **altruistic**
   (al trü is' tik)

   (*adj.*) unselfish, concerned with the welfare of others

   Most people support _____ programs to help the less fortunate of this world.

2. **benefactor**
   (ben' ə fak tər)

   (*n.*) one who does good to others

   Without the help of many _____, most charities would be unable to carry out their work.

3. **dearth**
   (dərth)

   (*n.*) a lack, scarcity, inadequate supply; a famine

   An employer may complain of a _____ of qualified applicants for available jobs.

4. **embark**
   (em bärk')

   (*v.*) to go aboard; to make a start; to invest

   Columbus spent years raising money before he was able to _____ on his perilous ocean voyage in search of a passage to the Far East.

5. **facile**
   (fas' əl)

   (*adj.*) easily done or attained; superficial; ready, fluent; easily shown but not sincerely felt

   Writing is a _____ process for some authors but a laborious task for others.

6. **infallible**
   (in fal' ə bəl)

   (*adj.*) free from error; absolutely dependable

   Some critics seem convinced that their expert knowledge makes them _____ judges of the quality of an artist's work.

7. **pungent**
   (pən' jənt)

   (*adj.*) causing a sharp sensation; stinging, biting

   The kitchen of the French restaurant was filled with the _____ aroma of onion soup.

8. **repose**
   (rē pōz')

   (*v.*) to rest; lie; place; (*n.*) relaxation, peace of mind, calmness

   The mortal remains of thousands who fell in America's wars _____ in Arlington National Cemetery.

   After spending all day with others, you may wish for a period of _____ before dinner.

9. **truculent**
(trək′ yə lənt)

(*adj.*) fierce and cruel; aggressive; deadly, destructive; scathingly harsh

People with _____ dispositions can make life miserable for those who have to work with them.

10. **unfeigned**
(ən fānd′)

(*adj.*) sincere, real, without pretense

The novelist won high praise for her ability to portray the _____ emotions of children.

Using Context

*For each item, determine whether the **boldface** word from pages 70–71 makes sense in the context of the sentence. Circle the item numbers next to the six sentences in which the words are used correctly.*

1. In the days of New England's whaling ships, crew members would **embark** on voyages that lasted for months or even years.

2. People who mock others or engage in name-calling exhibit inexcusable and **facile** behavior.

3. At many colleges, the library is named after the **benefactor** who helped to provide the funds or other resources needed to build it.

4. When there is a **dearth** of tomatoes in late summer, people try to make as much use of them as possible in soups, sauces, and salads.

5. At one time, reaching Jupiter's orbit by spacecraft seemed like an **infallible** goal, yet scientists are now in the midst of a second mission to the gas giant.

6. A referee in a professional sports event such as a tennis or boxing match should be unbiased and **truculent**.

7. It was **altruistic** of you to give up your spot on the canoe trip so that someone who's never had a chance to go can take your place.

8. Limburger cheese has a **pungent** smell that some people find appealing and others find distasteful.

9. The brochures and Web site for the island resort promised visitors a week of fun and **repose**.

10. The fact that he had a slight fever and an ear infection indicated that his illness was completely **unfeigned**.

Choosing the Right Word

*Select the **boldface** word that better completes each sentence. You might refer to the passage on pages 68–69 to see how most of these words are used in context. Note that the choices might be related forms of the Unit words.*

1. Planet Earth is a sort of spaceship on which billions of human beings have (**reposed, embarked**) on a lifelong voyage.

2. The recipe for my great-grandfather's spaghetti sauce, (**pungent, facile**) with bay leaves and other herbs, has been passed down for several generations.

3. Great political leaders know how to appeal to people not only through self-interest but also through their sense of (**benefactor, altruism**).

4. You will surely win more support for your view by quiet discussion than by (**truculent, infallible**) attacks on your opponents.

5. I admired the speaker's (**pungent, facile**) flow of words, but they failed to convince me that she had practical ideas to help solve our problems.

6. She is a popular young woman because people realize that her interest in them is sympathetic and (**truculent, unfeigned**).

7. American Presidents often point to one of their schoolteachers as the (**repose, benefactor**) who helped shape their character and ideas.

8. How do you account for the (**infallibility, dearth**) of doctors who are general practitioners rather than specialists?

9. The critic's (**pungent, facile**) comments during the television panel show were not only amusing but also very much to the point.

10. He is not too well informed on most matters; but when it comes to big-league baseball, he is all but (**altruistic, infallible**).

11. We breathed a sigh of relief when we saw the supposedly missing set of keys (**embarking, reposing**) in the desk drawer.

12. I regretted taking a four-day vacation with a person whose (**altruistic, truculent**) personality made every experience difficult and contentious.

Completing the Sentence

Choose the word from the word bank that best completes each of the following sentences. Write the correct word or form of the word in the space provided.

altruistic	dearth	facile	pungent	truculent
benefactor	embark	infallible	repose	unfeigned

1. As soon as the last passenger had _____, the captain ordered the ship to get under way.

2. In view of the many able people in public life today, I do not agree that we are suffering from a(n) _____ of capable leaders.

3. We were all impressed by your _____ use of unusual words and expressions that you had learned only a few hours before.

4. Humor should be clever and amusing but never so _____ that it hurts the feelings of other people.

5. The custom of putting erasers on pencils is one way of recognizing the fact that no one is _____.

6. I did not realize how beautiful the twins were until they fell asleep and I saw their faces in complete _____.

7. He is not merely unpleasant but actually dangerous whenever he gets into one of his _____ moods.

8. Your _____ joy when it was announced that I had won the scholarship meant more to me than all the polite congratulations I received.

9. What good are _____ principles if no real attempt is made to help people by putting those principles into practice?

10. History tells us that many men and women regarded as failures in their own lifetimes were actually major _____ of humanity.

End Set A

Definitions

Note the spelling, pronunciation, part(s) of speech, and definition(s) of each of the following words. Then write the appropriate form of the word in the blank space in the illustrative sentence(s) following.

1. assent
(ə sent')

(*v.*) to express agreement; (*n.*) agreement
Workers hope that the threat of a long strike will force management to _____ to their demands.
Romeo and Juliet knew they would never gain their feuding families' _____ to marry.

2. chivalrous
(shiv' əl rəs)

(*adj.*) marked by honor, courtesy, and courage; knightly
In today's busy world, where people are often heedless of others, a _____ act is admired by all.

3. clemency
(klem' ən sē)

(*n.*) mercy, humaneness; mildness, moderateness
Many judges are willing to show _____ to first offenders who express regret for their wrongdoing.

4. diffident
(dif' ə dənt)

(*adj.*) shy, lacking self-confidence; modest, reserved
Many a _____ suitor has lost his beloved to a bold rival.

5. discrepancy
(dis krep' ən sē)

(*n.*) a difference; a lack of agreement
_____ in the testimony of witnesses to a crime can have a decisive impact on the outcome of a trial.

6. indomitable
(in däm' ət ə bəl)

(*adj.*) unconquerable, refusing to yield
All who hear of the remarkable deeds of Harriet Tubman admire her _____ courage in the face of grave danger.

7. plod
(pläd)

(*v.*) to walk heavily or slowly; to work slowly
After the blizzard, we had to _____ through deep snowdrifts to reach the nearest stores.

8. remiss
(rē mis')

(*adj.*) neglectful in performance of one's duty, careless
When I am _____ in doing daily chores, I have to spend a big part of the weekend catching up.

9. temerity (tə mer′ ə tē)	(*n.*) rashness, boldness Few of his subordinates had the _____ to answer the general back.	
10. virulent (vir′ yə lənt)	(*adj.*) extremely poisonous; full of malice; spiteful The First Amendment protects the right of free speech for everyone, even those with _____ views that are repugnant to most people.	

Using Context

*For each item, determine whether the **boldface** word from pages 74–75 makes sense in the context of the sentence. Circle the item numbers next to the six sentences in which the words are used correctly.*

1. Everyone was relieved when the two parties reached a **discrepancy** and therefore would avoid a trial.

2. Whenever I feel like giving up on my goals, I read stories about **indomitable** people who inspire me to keep working hard.

3. Instead of punishing me when I had stayed out slightly later than my curfew, my parents granted me **clemency** and reminded me to call if I'm running late.

4. Her **diffident** attitude leads her to make new friends wherever she goes.

5. I would be **remiss** if I did not remind guests to take off their shoes before entering the house, as the host is strict about keeping the floors clean.

6. The inexperienced troops looked for guidance from their **virulent** captain, who had never let them down.

7. My brother will not **assent** to drive me anywhere unless I also do a favor for him.

8. After hiking the winding trails and steep hills, we had to muster the energy to **plod** back to the visitors' center.

9. I realized I had forgotten my umbrella when it started to storm, but luckily a **chivalrous** stranger let me share hers.

10. Although the toddler normally liked dogs, when he met the huge Great Dane he displayed great **temerity** and wouldn't go near it.

Choosing the Right Word

*Select the **boldface** word that better completes each sentence. You might refer to the passage on pages 68–69 to see how most of these words are used in context. Note that the choices might be related forms of the Unit words.*

1. By 1781, George Washington's green recruits of a few years earlier had been forged into a(n) (**chivalrous, indomitable**) army.

2. In a grim old joke, a man found guilty of murdering his parents appeals for (**clemency, assent**) because he is an orphan.

3. Given the glaring (**temerities, discrepancies**) between the applicant's résumé and her actual experience, she did not receive the job.

4. After the hurricane destroyed the city, the people of New Orleans showed their (**diffident, indomitable**) spirit by rebuilding.

5. Caring nothing about negative repercussions, Katy had the (**temerity, discrepancy**) to ask not only for a raise but also for a more flexible schedule.

6. I enjoy reading stories about King Arthur and his (**chivalrous, virulent**) knights.

7. We soon learned that behind his retiring and (**remiss, diffident**) manner, there is a keen mind and a strong will.

8. After boasting to me of your family's great wealth, how could you have the (**clemency, temerity**) to ask me for a loan?

9. As a state legislator, you should not give your (**assent, chivalry**) to any measure unless you truly believe in it.

10. I had no inkling of your deep-seated aversion to pop music until I overheard your (**diffident, virulent**) comments about it.

11. It would be (**remiss, indomitable**) of me, as editor-in-chief of the school newspaper, not to express appreciation for the help of our faculty advisor.

12. The lawyer (**plodded, assented**) through hundreds of pages of the trial record, hoping to find some basis for an appeal.

Completing the Sentence

Choose the word from the word bank that best completes each of the following sentences. Write the correct word or form of the word in the space provided.

assent	clemency	discrepancy	plod	temerity
chivalrous	diffident	indomitable	remiss	virulent

1. Refusing to admit defeat even when things looked completely hopeless, our _____ football team drove eighty-five yards in the last few minutes to score the winning touchdown.

2. Doctors attributed the epidemic to the rampant spread of a particularly _____ strain of influenza virus.

3. Emphasizing the youth of the convict, the defense attorney pleaded for _____.

4. It was quite _____ of you to give up your seat so that the man with the cane did not have to stand during the bus trip.

5. As a school cafeteria guard, I would be _____ in my duties if I failed to report a serious disturbance.

6. The exhausted refugees _____ along the dusty road, hoping to reach the Red Cross camp before nightfall.

7. The rash young lieutenant had the _____ to disregard the express orders of the commanding officer.

8. My parents will not _____ to my going to the dance unless I promise faithfully to be home no later than 1:00 A.M.

9. I rarely join in the discussions because I am _____.

10. The principal claimed that there were major _____ between what actually happened in the school and the way the incident was reported on television.

Synonyms

*Choose the word or form of the word from this Unit that is the same or most nearly the same in meaning as the **boldface** word or expression in the phrase. Write that word on the line. Use a dictionary if necessary.*

1. the spreading of **venomous** rumors   _____
2. would be **negligent** if I did not pay my bills   _____
3. **humanitarian** dedication to finding a cure   _____
4. generous **sponsors** of the foundation   _____
5. called for **leniency** for a minor offense   _____
6. refused to **accede** to the will of the majority   _____
7. found **serenity** in the shade of a tree   _____
8. found a(n) **inconsistency** in the story   _____
9. **start** on a new endeavor in his life   _____
10. has an **unerring** memory   _____
11. a **brutal** band of hardened criminals   _____
12. a **caustic** response to a hostile question   _____
13. made allowances for the **audacity** of youth   _____
14. **gallant** actions that showed respect   _____
15. had an **unyielding** spirit   _____

Antonyms

*Choose the word or form of the word from this Unit that is most nearly opposite in meaning to the **boldface** word or expression in the phrase. Write that word on the line. Use a dictionary if necessary.*

1. **scamper** across the field   _____
2. the teenager's **confident** manner   _____
3. gave a **labored** explanation   _____
4. screamed in **pretended** horror   _____
5. the **abundance** of supplies   _____

Writing: Words in Action

In a brief essay, identify the main tenets, or principles, of democracy. Explain how these principles continue to influence life in the United States today. Use at least two details from the passage (pages 68–69) and three or more Unit words to support your analysis.

Vocabulary in Context

*Some of the words you have studied in this Unit appear in **boldface** type. Read the passage below, and then circle the letter of the correct answer for each word as it is used in context.*

Ancient Athens under the leadership of Pericles (c.495–429 BCE) is often called one of the few golden ages in the history of Western civilization. Statesman, orator, and general, Pericles was also a distinguished **benefactor** of the arts. His circle of friends included Sophocles, the tragic playwright, and Phidias, the city's leading sculptor, as well as Anaxagoras, a pioneering philosopher. When Anaxagoras's controversial ideas and spirit of scientific inquiry got him into trouble with the Athenians, Pericles was scarcely **remiss** in the support of his friend. In a **chivalrous** gesture, he spoke out for the philosopher's cause at the trial of Anaxagoras and subsequently arranged for his friend's safety in exile.

Perhaps Pericles's most brilliant campaign was architectural, rather than military. Beginning soon after the year 450, he led the building campaign on the Athenian Acropolis. Within two decades, this effort resulted in the Parthenon, the temple to the city's patron, the goddess Athena, with its perfect proportions, matchless reliefs, and commanding style. More than any other public building of the age, the Parthenon gave substantiation to Pericles's proud boast that Athens was "the education of all Greece."

Pericles's final years were laden with conflict. In 431, the increasingly **truculent** accusations and **pungent** countercharges between Athens and her main rival, Sparta, erupted into open hostilities. The Peloponnesian War, in whose opening stages Pericles served as the leading Athenian strategist, was to last 27 years. It ended with Athenian defeat and the collapse of the democracy that the city had done so much to foster. A year after the outbreak of war, in 430, a ghastly plague broke out in Athens—perhaps similar to the Black Plague of fourteenth-century Europe and Asia. This **virulent** epidemic claimed the life of Pericles.

1. The word **benefactor** most nearly means
   a. scholar
   b. analyst
   c. patron
   d. advocate

2. A person who is **remiss** may be described as
   a. conscientious
   b. tardy
   c. cowardly
   d. lax

3. A **chivalrous** gesture is
   a. pliant
   b. honorable
   c. tactful
   d. impartial

4. **Truculent** accusations are
   a. ambiguous
   b. protracted
   c. harsh
   d. mild

5. The word **pungent** most nearly means
   a. sharp
   b. cozy
   c. competitive
   d. soothing

6. A **virulent** epidemic is
   a. boundless
   b. poisonous
   c. devious
   d. enigmatic

Read the following passage, taking note of the **boldface** words and their contexts. These words are among those you will be studying in Unit 6. It may help you to complete the exercises in this Unit if you refer to the way the words are used below.

When the Wall Came Tumbling Down
<Oral History>

The Brandenburg Gate behind the Berlin Wall

My grandparents' generation came of age in a divided country. In 1961, East Germany's Communist government built the Berlin Wall, which divided the city in two. The construction of this wall was a **premeditated** act, planned by a vengeful regime determined to **brandish** its power in the decades following the Allied victory over Hitler's Germany. My grandmother said isolating West Berlin from the rest of Soviet-controlled East Germany was a way for the regime to thumb its nose at Western democracies. In a **deft** statement of double-speak, East Germany's leaders claimed that the wall would shelter its people from "the ravages of capitalism." Even if the wall's real purpose had not been made **explicit** already, the truth was soon obvious to all: It prevented East Germans like my grandparents from fleeing to West Germany in search of freedom and a better life.

By the time I was born, that ugly concrete wall, with its **ominous** watchtowers, was a daily reminder of East German control and repression. Rather than protect us, the Berlin Wall was a cruel blockade that cost nearly 300 people their lives. Some tried to climb or fly over it, and others tried to dig under or around it, but most failed in their attempts to breach that barrier. They were all trying to escape a country in which everyday life was marked by our political leaders' **officious** rules. Every law was rigidly enforced by the **venal** secret police. We both despised and feared them.

Despite our fears, despite the guards, it was regular people like me who finally brought down the wall simply by walking through its checkpoints. **Ironic**, isn't it? What happened was this. During the late 1980s, the East German government gradually became less rigid. Bit by bit, it began offering its people more freedoms. Then in 1989, its leaders declared that on November 9, anyone who had a proper visa could visit West Germany. I did not have a visa, but I went to the wall anyway with some friends. Within hours, the crowd had become huge, and it was clear that the guards were overwhelmed. They could no longer keep back the thousands and thousands of people who wanted to pass through the checkpoints.

I'm not sure if it was that the guards were outnumbered and scared, or that they, too, wanted freedom. But suddenly, the barricades were open, and when people began to walk through, the guards let them. That's really when the wall came down. We did not physically tear it apart, brick by brick. But it was clear the wall no longer served as a threat or a barricade. In our minds, it was already gone.

Above: The scene as the wall fell in November 1989

I will never forget what it was like to be in Berlin that November. Everywhere in the streets people were dancing and laughing. You could hear horns and music from one end of the city to the other. I saw people spray-painting democratic slogans on the wall and even hammering off chunks to keep as souvenirs. Everyone was smiling and laughing—it was an amazing contrast to the gloom I used to feel when walking past the wall as a kid.

On November 10, my friend Anja and I went to the **stately** Brandenburg Gate, the centuries-old symbol of Berlin that had been cut in two by the wall. People were still gathering in the streets, still dancing, still laughing. We were all celebrating freedom, something most of us probably never thought we would experience. Suddenly, as Anja and I were dancing, an armed soldier left his post by the wall and walked toward us. That made Anja and me nervous. He reached out to shake our hands. Then he and I swapped caps. We each had a huge smile on our face—I swear, it was the **pinnacle** of our lives, the happiest day ever! Imagine the **solace** that comes from realizing that in just 24 hours, we had gone from being enemies to being friends.

Although joy was **rampant** and evident in everyone's eyes, within days, our delight was muted by concerns about what was ahead for our country. We were no longer trapped behind the wall, but we had lived for generations under a harsh regime. To get by, East Germans had learned to **suppress** their hopes and dreams. Citizens had to **accede** to the rules of the communist system, or face prison—or worse. Now that the wall was down and our government was weakened, how would we **extirpate** the fears and anxieties that had plagued our lives? These were the questions people asked in the days and weeks after the Berlin Wall fell. But during those glorious first days, all we knew was that we were making history—and that soon, the two Germanys would be reunited as a single nation.

Audio

For iWords and audio passages, go to SadlierConnect.com.

Definitions

Note the spelling, pronunciation, part(s) of speech, and definition(s) of each of the following words. Then write the appropriate form of the word in the blank space in the illustrative sentence(s) following.

1. accede
(ak sēd')

(*v.*) to yield to; to assume an office or dignity

Management was not willing to _____ to labor's initial demands, thus increasing the likelihood of a long and bitter strike.

2. comprise
(kəm prīz')

(*v.*) to include or contain; to be made up of

Classical symphonies usually_____ three or four movements of varying musical form, tempo, and character.

3. deft
(deft)

(*adj.*) skillful, nimble

The _____ fingers of Spanish seamstresses produced some of the finest, most delicate lace ever seen.

4. inopportune
(in äp ər tün')

(*adj.*) coming at a bad time; not appropriate

Why do my relatives always seem to turn up at the most _____ time imaginable?

5. musty
(məs' tē)

(*adj.*) stale, moldy; out-of-date

Houses that have been closed up for a very long time often have an unpleasantly _____ smell about them.

6. officious
(ə fish' əs)

(*adj.*) meddling; excessively forward in offering services or assuming authority

The manager of the store warned the entire sales force not to be too _____ when helping customers.

7. pinnacle
(pin' ə kəl)

(*n.*) a high peak or point

Some pop musicians reach the _____ of their careers comparatively early in life.

8. solace
(säl' əs)

(*n.*) comfort, relief; (*v.*) to comfort, console

Many world leaders seek _____ from the cares of state in the pages of great literature.

I could find no way to _____ my deeply troubled conscience.

9. stately
(stāt′ lē)

(*adj.*) dignified, majestic

The _____ procession slowly wound its way from the palace to the cathedral.

10. supple
(səp′ əl)

(*adj.*) bending easily; bending with agility; readily adaptable; servile

Have you ever read Robert Frost's famous poem about swinging on the _____ branches of a birch tree?

Using Context

*For each item, determine whether the **boldface** word from pages 82–83 makes sense in the context of the sentence. Circle the item numbers next to the six sentences in which the words are used correctly.*

1. Tonight's snowstorm comes at a very **inopportune** time, since I have an important job interview tomorrow morning.

2. The test will **comprise** three parts: a short answer section focusing on math and logic, a reading comprehension section, and an essay.

3. The fort's **supple** walls were built to withstand even the most powerful of assaults.

4. The books and toys that had been stored in the basement all had a **musty** smell and needed to be aired out.

5. The board of trustees was willing to **accede** to the residents' requests and began a study to determine how much the construction of a town swimming pool would cost.

6. Lawyers for both sides are awaiting the judge's **officious** ruling, and each side is confident the decision will be in its own favor.

7. The woman faced a **pinnacle**: whether to remain at an unexciting but well-paid job or accept a scholarship and attend graduate school for the next several years.

8. The Romantic poets found both inspiration and **solace** in nature at a time when the western world was becoming increasingly industrialized and polluted.

9. The **stately** waters of that shallow pond are nothing but a breeding ground for all sorts of foul-smelling algae.

10. A boxer must be both powerful and **deft** during a match in the ring.

Choosing the Right Word

*Select the **boldface** word that better completes each sentence. You might refer to the passage on pages 80–81 to see how most of these words are used in context. Note that the choices might be related forms of the Unit words.*

1. Eliza Doolittle was a poor flower seller, but she learned to conduct herself with the (**supple, stately**) bearing of a princess.

2. He is in for a rude awakening if he thinks that as the son of a rich family, he will simply (**comprise, accede**) to a position of wealth and power.

3. During the darkest hours of defeat, their only (**solace, pinnacle**) was the knowledge that they had fought hard to the very end.

4. She has the kind of (**supple, musty**) personality that can easily adapt itself to a wide variety of needs and conditions.

5. No matter how ticklish the situation, the hero of the cartoon always devised some (**deft, officious**) maneuver to avoid capture.

6. The senator finally (**solaced, acceded**) to the controversial legislation, handing his opponents a victory.

7. There's a world of difference between a helpful research assistant and a(n) (**supple, officious**) one!

8. Traveling in the dead of night, the weary travelers found (**solace, pinnacle**) knowing that their journey would lead them to freedom.

9. I have no patience with (**musty, stately**) old ideas about family roles based on gender.

10. Coming at a time when I was flat broke, your suggestion that we have a bite to eat and go to the movies was highly (**officious, inopportune**).

11. The actress felt that she had reached the (**solace, pinnacle**) of fame when the principal of her former school asked for her autograph.

12. Let's prepare a joint statement that will (**accede, comprise**) the various objections of all civic groups to the freeway plan.

Completing the Sentence

Choose the word from the word bank that best completes each of the following sentences. Write the correct word or form of the word in the space provided.

accede	deft	musty	pinnacle	stately
comprise	inopportune	officious	solace	supple

1. A great dancer, like a great athlete, must have a sharp sense of timing and a highly trained, responsive, and _____ body.

2. How can I ever forget that _____ inspector in the customs office who insisted that I empty every piece of luggage before him!

3. Who would have dreamed that the cluttered old attic, with all its darkness, dust, and _____ odor, contained such a treasure!

4. Accomplished portrait painters can usually reveal a person's character with a few _____ strokes of a brush.

5. It was touching to watch the girl help her little brother off the ground and _____ him about his scraped knee.

6. It is a sobering thought to realize that when one has reached the _____ of a mountain, there is nowhere to go but down.

7. We will never _____ to those selfish and unfair terms.

8. Unfortunately, the so-called recreational facilities _____ nothing more than a card table and a small-screen television.

9. "We could not have chosen a more _____ spot for our picnic," she observed as she swept ants off the blanket.

10. Who can forget the stirring sight of those _____ tall ships with their lofty masts and graceful lines as they sailed past the Statue of Liberty on the Fourth of July?

Definitions

Note the spelling, pronunciation, part(s) of speech, and definition(s) of each of the following words. Then write the appropriate form of the word in the blank space in the illustrative sentence(s) following.

1. brandish
(bran′ dish)

(*v.*) to wave or flourish in a menacing or vigorous fashion

I _____ my umbrella repeatedly in a vain effort to hail a cab.

2. destitute
(des′ tə tüt)

(*adj.*) deprived of the necessities of life; lacking in

Some people fled their homes so suddenly that they arrived at the refugee camp absolutely _____.

3. explicit
(ek splis′ it)

(*adj.*) definite, clearly stated

The more _____ your directions are, the easier it will be for all of us to find our way to the campsite.

4. extirpate
(ek′ stər pāt)

(*v.*) to tear up by the roots; to destroy totally

We must do everything we can to _____ racism from American society.

5. ironic
(ī rän′ ik)

(*adj.*) suggesting an incongruity between what might be expected and what actually happens; given to irony, sarcastic

The short stories of O. Henry are famous for their _____ endings.

6. ominous
(äm′ ən əs)

(*adj.*) unfavorable, threatening, of bad omen

The _____ sound of distant thunder warned us of the storm's approach.

7. premeditated
(prē med′ ə tāt id)

(*adj., part.*) considered beforehand, deliberately planned

Some crimes are spontaneous acts of passion; others are quite _____.

8. rampant
(ram′ pənt)

(*adj.*) growing without check, running wild

All kinds of odd rumors run _____ during a political campaign.

9. **suppress**
(sə pres')

(v.) to stop by force, put down
Totalitarian governments usually take strong measures
to _____ free speech.

10. **venal**
(vēn' əl)

(adj.) open to or marked by bribery or corruption
The presence of even one _____ official
may jeopardize the integrity of an entire organization.

Using Context

*For each item, determine whether the **boldface** word from pages 86–87 makes sense in the context of the sentence. Circle the item numbers next to the six sentences in which the words are used correctly.*

1. Most suspects will try to prove that their crimes were not **premeditated**, because a planned offense will warrant a more severe punishment.

2. When traveling abroad, I always make sure to **brandish** my wallet immediately after paying for something to avoid pickpockets.

3. Many parents try to **extirpate** good manners in their children by demonstrating how to be polite to others.

4. I prefer books and movies written with an **ironic** sense of humor, the incongruity of which can sometimes go over people's heads.

5. You might think the error in your calculations was **venal**, but, in fact, it had grave consequences for the company's financial projections.

6. I tried for as long as I could to **suppress** my cough, but I eventually had to leave the room to clear my throat sufficiently.

7. I left **explicit** instructions, as well as a diagram, for how to turn the sprinkler system on, but my neighbor still could not figure it out.

8. It's not uncommon for those who win the lottery to spend the money so quickly and irresponsibly that they end up **destitute**.

9. Now that so many people focus on what's trendy, reading classic literature is a pastime that has become **rampant**.

10. Just before the scariest part of the movie, the score slowly turned **ominous**, making everyone in the audience tense up in their seats.

Choosing the Right Word

Select the **boldface** word that better completes each sentence. You might refer to the passage on pages 80–81 to see how most of these words are used in context. Note that the choices might be related forms of the Unit words.

1. Was Oscar Wilde being (**ironic, explicit**) when he said that he could resist everything except temptation?

2. The way he (**brandishes, suppresses**) his facts and figures reminds me of a butcher swinging a meat cleaver.

3. Someone who believes that everyone has a price must think that human beings are (**premeditated, venal**) by nature.

4. Even in the prisoner-of-war camps, some basic feelings of decency and humanity were not completely (**brandished, extirpated**).

5. Her speech at first seemed highly dramatic and impressive, but we soon realized that she was quite (**destitute, rampant**) of new ideas.

6. How unfortunate that those in power are often presumed to have a(n) (**venal, explicit**) nature.

7. The only sure way to (**brandish, suppress**) social unrest is to make possible a decent, secure life for all the people.

8. You can try to explain away your insult as a slip of the tongue, but in my opinion it was deliberate and (**premeditated, ominous**).

9. No doubt there are some dishonest officials, but it is a gross exaggeration to say that graft and corruption are (**rampant, explicit**) in our government.

10. We were prepared for a sharp scolding but not for the (**ironic, ominous**) silence with which the principal greeted us.

11. (**Extirpating, Brandishing**) everything in its path, the deadly tornado left nothing but a desolate landscape.

12. If the law is intended to limit nonessential use of gasoline and heating oil, it should state this (**ironically, explicitly**).

Completing the Sentence

Choose the word from the word bank that best completes each of the following sentences. Write the correct word or form of the word in the space provided.

| brandish | explicit | ironic | premeditated | suppress |
| destitute | extirpate | ominous | rampant | venal |

1. In the mid-1800s, "Boss" Tweed controlled New York City through a(n) _____ political machine that fed on graft and extortion.

2. How _____ that they finally inherited all that money at a time when it could no longer help to solve their problems!

3. I vowed that I would _____ every weed that dared to show itself in our newly seeded lawn.

4. Even when the economy is strong, there are always a large number of _____ families in urgent need of assistance.

5. Attacking the present administration, the candidate said that crime has been _____ in the streets of our city.

6. The unruly mob retreated as the line of deputies moved forward slowly, _____ their riot sticks.

7. The referee gave a(n) _____ warning that if either team protested her decisions, she would be forced to call a technical foul.

8. Whether your act was _____ or the result of carelessness, the fact remains that you have caused great pain to someone who has always been very good to you.

9. The sudden drop in temperature and the unnatural stillness in the air were _____ signs of an unfavorable change in the weather.

10. The students couldn't _____ their groans of dismay when the teacher announced a surprise quiz.

Synonyms

*Choose the word or form of the word from this Unit that is the same or most nearly the same in meaning as the **boldface** word or expression in the phrase. Write that word on the line. Use a dictionary if necessary.*

1. annoyingly **intrusive** coworkers _____

2. **soothe** me during my grief _____

3. the **distinguished** language of the Gettysburg Address _____

4. warned not to **swing** the stick near the window _____

5. a **stuffy** old office building _____

6. left the orphans totally **impoverished** _____

7. refused to **surrender** to his demands _____

8. the **contradictory** conclusion to her promising career _____

9. at the very **height** of the social scene _____

10. **foreboding** clouds overhead _____

11. actions that were obviously **calculated** _____

12. an **unseemly** occasion for a feast _____

13. **consists of** bits and pieces of longer works _____

14. followed the **unambiguous** orders _____

15. a rule that is **adjustable** if circumstances require _____

Antonyms

*Choose the word or form of the word from this Unit that is most nearly opposite in meaning to the **boldface** word or expression in the phrase. Write that word on the line. Use a dictionary if necessary.*

1. sections of the garden where weeds are **restrained** _____

2. **foster** hateful language and attitudes _____

3. **honest** politicians in office _____

4. tried to **encourage** the women's vote _____

5. **clumsy** dance moves _____

Writing: Words in Action

Describe another wall (either real or symbolic) that continues to limit people's freedoms, and explore how to make that wall "come tumbling down." Use examples from the passage (pages 80–81), as well as your own studies or personal knowledge. Write at least three paragraphs, and use three or more words from this Unit.

Vocabulary in Context

*Some of the words you have studied in this Unit appear in **boldface** type. Read the passage below, and then circle the letter of the correct answer for each word as it is used in context.*

Shortly after the end of World War II, Romania's Communist Party took control of the government, and the country would remain behind the Iron Curtain for the next four decades. Although the Romanian government pursued an independent foreign policy—often clashing with the Soviet Union—at home it implemented strict communist policies. Free speech was not tolerated, the media were tightly controlled, economic decisions were made by state bureaucrats, and the secret police kept a vigilant eye on citizens.

The Romanian economy suffered under communism. A series of **inopportune** industrial decisions in the 1970s forced the government to export much of the country's agricultural and industrial output. Ordinary Romanian people soon found themselves **destitute** of basic necessities, from food to fuel and medicine. Houses and apartments became **musty** and decrepit because residents could not afford to maintain them. Hoping to **suppress** public knowledge of better living conditions outside of Romania, the government cut television programming to two hours of daily propaganda and heavily censored movies.

But a small group of courageous and enterprising citizens figured out a way to subvert the government's control measures. Working secretly, a translator with a unique and **supple** voice dubbed thousands of western films into the Romanian language. An underground entrepreneur then made copies of the movies, distributing them across the country through a network of "lieutenants." Citizens who got hold of these copies would organize secret screenings in their homes. Friends and neighbors—young and old—gathered at night to watch double and triple-bills **comprised** of Hollywood action, western, horror, and romance movies. Through ingenuity and daring, the Romanian people were thus able to get a glimpse of the life their government would not allow.

1. To be **inopportune** is to be
   a. unfortunate
   b. difficult
   c. inappropriate
   d. ill-planned

2. If you are **destitute** of something, you
   a. crave it
   b. lack it
   c. are poor
   d. are hungry

3. The word **musty** most nearly means
   a. dirty
   b. cramped
   c. unpleasant
   d. antiquated

4. To **suppress** public knowledge, a government
   a. supports it
   b. stops it by force
   c. issues decrees
   d. undermines it

5. A **supple** voice is
   a. adaptable
   b. educated
   c. devious
   d. thoughtful

6. The word **comprised** most nearly means
   a. excluded from
   b. selected from
   c. made up of
   d. presented to

Vocabulary for Comprehension
Part 1

*Read this passage, which contains words in **boldface** that appear in Units 4–6. Then choose the best answer to each question based on what is stated or implied in the passage. You may refer to the passage as often as necessary.*

Questions 1–10 are based on the following passage.

Education has long been a tool to make society more equitable: it is the only way to ensure that all students have the access to knowledge that will make them
(5) successful in life. But what is success? Is it simply the **attainment** of the highest personal goals? Is success ensuring that all people reach the **pinnacle** of their careers? Or is success achieved when
(10) an educated member is a good citizen, **altruistic** in all encounters? It is a complicated question, but educational sociologists and philosophers provide a way to consider the role of education
(15) in individual and societal success.
      Émile Durkheim, a French educational sociologist, was **affiliated** with the functionalist view of education. Functionalism asserts that the role of
(20) education is to guarantee that students grow to become citizens and workers who help society thrive. The modern model of public school education is based on this functionalist view. A competing view to the
(25) functionalist view is the conflict theory. The conflict theory argues that education promotes social inequality through tracking and standardized testing. The conflict theory stresses that because
(30) some schools suffer from a **dearth** of funding and have vast **discrepancies** in their learning conditions, education only serves to reinforce social inequality and **suppress** lower socioeconomic groups.
(35)   Even though they differ, both functionalism and conflict theory operate under the belief that education prepares

students for a workforce, regardless of the skill level that each student achieves.
(40) Within these frameworks, how can teachers educate students to participate in a democratic society? Educational philosophers have debated this conundrum for decades, and they have
(45) created a theory called democratic education. Democratic education is founded on educational philosophy from pioneering educators like John Dewey, Paulo Friere, and Margaret Mead. These
(50) educators asserted the importance of educating students in the values, practices, and beliefs of democratic societies and human rights. Democratic education takes a variety of forms, but
(55) many programs empower students to choose from a **finite** set of experiences designed to enhance their learning. These democratic education programs are often **comprised** of classroom time, individual
(60) projects, and out-of-school activities that go beyond the traditional curriculum. (One sample of a democratic education project would be a student leading an effort to reduce water usage in the community. In
(65) and out of school, this student would work on this project individually and with local agencies that share the same mission.) Thus, the goal of democratic education is to help students move beyond the
(70) standard idea of education and become active in their learning. Proponents of democratic education argue that it shapes students beyond the textbook curriculum, transforming them into engaged, informed
(75) citizens of the world.
      Just as there is no clear-cut definition of success, there is no straightforward answer for what the role of education

should be for all students. Unfortunately,
(80) there is no **panacea** that will make all
students come alive in the classroom,
ready to engage with the world beyond
them. Many democratic education
teachers would **assent** that democratic
(85) education should play a role in educating
any student for success in life, regardless
of what the definition of success may be.

1. What is the purpose of the first paragraph?
   A) To define success
   B) To interrogate ideas about success
   C) To describe how educational
   philosophers viewed success.
   D) To explain the difference between
   individual and societal success

2. As it is used in line 11, "altruistic"
most nearly means
   A) unselfish.
   B) friendly.
   C) intelligent.
   D) wise.

3. According to functionalists, the purpose
of education is to prepare children to
   A) become workers.
   B) become citizens
   C) help society thrive.
   D) take standardized tests.

4. As it is used in line 56, "finite"
most nearly means
   A) unexpected.
   B) determined.
   C) hurried.
   D) limited.

5. The main purpose of the third paragraph is
   A) to compare democratic education to
   functionalism and conflict theory.
   B) to introduce democratic education
   as a way to educate good citizens.
   C) to describe ways that democratic
   education can function in school.
   D) to explore one specific model of
   democratic education in detail.

6. What do democratic education and
functionalism have in common?
   A) Both philosophies seek to empower
   students to engage as citizens.
   B) Both philosophies emphasize projects.
   C) Both philosophies have informed the
   modern model of public education.
   D) Both philosophies emphasize testing.

7. As it is used in line 59, "comprise"
most nearly means
   A) to be compared with.
   B) to be confused by.
   C) to be made up of.
   D) to be connected to.

8. It can reasonably be inferred that the
author includes lines 61–67 in order to
   A) show how democratic education
   works in all schools.
   B) provide a successful example of
   democratic education in action.
   C) describe a project that would be
   unacceptable in democratic
   education curricula.
   D) suggest that all students in democratic
   education programs should work
   with local agencies.

9. According to the passage, the mission of
democratic education is to help students
   A) explore out-of-school activities.
   B) choose from a finite set of experiences.
   C) rethink education and be active
   citizens.
   D) investigate the work of John Dewey,
   Paulo Friere, and Margaret Mead.

10. Which choice provides the best evidence
for the answer to the previous question?
   A) Lines 46–49 ("Democratic. . . Mead")
   B) Lines 53–57 ("Democratic . . . learning")
   C) Lines 57–61 ("These . . . curriculum")
   D) Lines 68–71 ("Thus . . . learning")

Vocabulary for Comprehension

Part 2

*Read these passages, which contain words in **boldface** that appear in Units 4–6. Then choose the best answer to each question based on what is stated or implied in the passage(s). You may refer to the passages as often as necessary.*

Questions 1–10 are based on the following passages.

Passage 1

From behind the controls of a plane's cockpit to behind a car's steering wheel, the Global Positioning System, better known as GPS, has improved our lives.
(5) Businesses use GPS to track drivers and shipments—thus increasing profitability. From a safety perspective, many people who are not **facile** with maps or directions rely on GPS for navigation and would get
(10) lost without it. With a **deft** swipe of a finger before **embarking** on a drive, locations appear on the screen of the device and a tracker directs the car turn by turn until it reaches its destination. Consequently,
(15) GPS tracking has made driving safer by reducing distractions—drivers no longer need to look at maps.

GPS can be used to locate missing phones and missing pets. Phone number
(20) tracking and reverse tracking services can allow people to locate cell phones that have been lost or stolen; this same technology allows parents to find pets wearing a special GPS collar. GPS is also
(25) advantageous in an emergency; before GPS, emergency responders triangulated cell phone towers to estimate someone's location. Since the advent of GPS technology, GPS-enabled devices can
(30) provide an accurate location within several meters. When rescue personnel are dispatched, they can **converge** on the location and handle the emergency.

As GPS technology has evolved, it has
(35) benefited users by increasing efficiency for businesses, making transportation safer, and helping in search and rescue. GPS will continue to be integral to modern life.

Passage 2

Although GPS provides many benefits,
(40) there are drawbacks that come along with the convenience of this technology. Because GPS uses satellite technology to pinpoint the exact location of cellular devices, many argue that it is an invasion
(45) of privacy. This issue has even gone to the U.S. Supreme Court. In *United States vs. Jones*, the U.S. Supreme Court heard a case about whether law enforcement agencies can legally use GPS tracking
(50) devices to monitor suspects' families. Though the Supreme Court ruled in this case that using GPS was unconstitutional, this may not be the ruling in future cases.

Cell phone service providers have access
(55) to consumers' locations at all times, even at **inopportune** times; thus, service providers are becoming increasingly **omniscient** in the modern era. Although consumers may not **accede** to this information being
(60) collected, purchasing GPS-enabled cell phones and automobiles is equivalent to granting permission for this information to be made public. Information about where people live and shop is attractive to
(65) businesses and marketers, and cell phone service providers can sell this information to help companies decide who is in their target demographic and how to advertise to them.

No one is immune from this invasion
(70) of privacy: Even consumers who are
scrupulous about disabling GPS on their
phones can still be located by emergency
service providers and cell phone service
providers. Consumers would be **remiss** to
(75) ignore the drawbacks of GPS technology,
despite its many conveniences.

1. As it is used in line 10, "deft" most
nearly means
A) skillful.
B) awkward.
C) elaborate.
D) unnecessary.

2. As it is used in line 32, "converge"
most nearly means
A) to take separate routes.
B) to dispatch several vehicles.
C) to move toward one point.
D) to take an indirect path.

3. The main purpose of Passage 1 is to
A) describe how GPS is generally
useful for navigation purposes.
B) prove that GPS helps rescue
personnel in case of emergencies.
C) argue that GPS is a useful tool for
pilots and businesses.
D) explain how GPS technology makes
life safer and more efficient.

4. As it is used in line 57, "omniscient"
most nearly means
A) aware.
B) all-knowing.
C) efficient.
D) hazardous.

5. The author of Passage 2 includes the case
of *United States vs. Jones* in order to
A) illustrate the fact that the U.S. Supreme
Court is not hearing current GPS issues.
B) show that GPS privacy invasion is
becoming an increasingly serious issue.
C) demonstrate that people overreact to
GPS privacy invasion issues.
D) prove that the U.S. Supreme Court
has ruled in favor of using GPS.

6. As it is used in line 74, "remiss" most
nearly means
A) careless.
B) economical.
C) clever.
D) traditional.

7. The authors of Passage 1 and Passage 2
would most likely agree that
A) people rely too heavily on GPS.
B) people are careless with their GPS-
enabled devices.
C) GPS technology has been beneficial
in several ways.
D) more people need to use GPS devices.

8. Which statement best describes the
relationship between the passages?
A) Passage 1 has facts about GPS, and
Passage 2 has opinions about GPS.
B) Passage 1 presents problems with
GPS, and Passage 2 offers solutions.
C) Passage 1 compares GPS devices,
and Passage 2 contrasts them.
D) Passage 1 describes GPS's benefits,
and Passage 2 shows GPS's negatives.

9. In Passage 1, the author explores several
different ways that GPS can be used. In
Passage 2, the author mainly focuses on
A) U.S. Supreme Court cases involving
GPS technology.
B) GPS technology infringing on privacy.
C) cell phone service providers accessing
consumers' locations.
D) companies using GPS to target their
advertising.

10. Which choice provides the best evidence
for the answer to the previous question?
A) Lines 42–45 ("Because . . . privacy")
B) Lines 45–50 ("This issue . . . families")
C) Lines 54–58 ("Cell phone . . . era")
D) Lines 63–68 ("Information . . . them)"

Synonyms

*From the word bank below, choose the word that has the same or nearly the same meaning as the **boldface** word in each sentence and write it on the line. You will not use all of the words.*

brandish	expunge	plod	supple
chivalrous	extirpate	premeditated	truculent
disperse	facile	skulk	uncanny
embark	inopportune	stately	unfeigned

1. I was so awestruck by the **grand** manor in which we were to have dinner that I completely lost my appetite. _____

2. Running out of gas is never a good thing, but it happened to us at an **inconvenient** time when we were out in the rural countryside. _____

3. I **trudge** down the hallway toward the door, reluctant to step outside into the freezing cold rain. _____

4. It is often said that you never forget how to ride a bike, but it has not been such an **effortless** feat for me after years without practice. _____

5. Many Europeans left their homelands to **begin** on a journey to the United States in order to live better lives. _____

6. My dog's ability to sense when someone is not trustworthy is **inexplicable**, but her instincts always turn out to be right. _____

7. When I won first place in the state writing contest, I was both surprised and touched by the **genuine** joy all the runners-up showed for me. _____

8. I decided to have a relaxing weekend at the beach to try and **efface** the stress that had built up over the previous week. _____

9. The revelations about the politician's corrupt history the day before the election seemed coincidental but were in fact **prearranged** by his opponent. _____

10. I thought our cat had gotten lost until I finally saw him **prowl** around behind those bushes. _____

11. Your **belligerent** attitude will get you nowhere when speaking with any person of authority. _____

12. Taking some time to stretch before exercising will make your muscles more **limber** during your workout and, therefore, less prone to injury. _____

Two-Word Completions

Select the pair of words that best completes the meaning of each of the following sentences.

1. Nineteenth-century hucksters touted their elixirs as _____ for every ailment imaginable. Unfortunately, these concoctions often proved more _____ than the maladies they were supposed to cure.
   a. panaceas . . . virulent
   b. attainments . . . pungent
   c. benefactors . . . musty
   d. pinnacles . . . ominous

2. Pundits were quick to note the _____ when the councilman, who had campaigned on a reform platform, was discovered to be every bit as _____ as the corrupt bosses he had railed against.
   a. discrepancy . . . venial
   b. clemency . . . rampant
   c. irony . . . venal
   d. attainment . . . altruistic

3. While it is true that human beings are neither _____ nor _____, they can certainly use what they do know to avoid making foolish or unnecessary mistakes.
   a. omniscient . . . infallible
   b. altruistic . . . malevolent
   c. diffident . . . supercilious
   d. indomitable . . . invulnerable

4. During the long years that the painter struggled to _____ fame, her talents never failed her. However, once she had actually achieved the public _____ that she sought, her skills began to desert her.
   a. suppress . . . clemency
   b. comprise . . . nonchalance
   c. ascertain … pinnacle
   d. attain . . . esteem

5. The salesman pressed me to sign the contract, but I refused to give my _____ to the agreement until all the terms and provisions he mentioned so vaguely were spelled out _____.
   a. temerity . . . scrupulously
   b. assent . . . explicitly
   c. discrepancy . . . cogently
   d. esteem . . . officiously

6. The school trustees agreed to cease their attempts to _____ the identity of the donor when an intermediary explained that the mysterious _____ wished to remain anonymous.
   a. esteem . . . bequest
   b. comprise . . . affiliation
   c. accede . . . attainment
   d. ascertain . . . benefactor

7. The senator found some _____ after her electoral defeat in the comforting knowledge that she would now be able to enjoy a life of _____, far from the strife of the political arena.
   a. esteem . . . temerity
   b. clemency . . . destitution
   c. solace . . . repose
   d. panacea . . . dearth

Denotation and Connotation

When you look up a word in a dictionary, you will find the word's **denotation**—its formal, literal meaning. A denotation is a straightforward, *neutral* definition of a word.

Many words have synonyms—words that share similar denotations. These synonyms often differ from one another in their shades of meaning, or **connotations**—the positive or negative emotional associations that people make to particular words.

Consider these synonyms for the neutral word *casual.*

> *relaxed   nonchalant   indifferent   apathetic*

Relaxed and *nonchalant* have positive connotations, suggesting ease, effortlessness, and a lack of formality. *Indifferent* and *apathetic*, however, suggest ease or casualness taken too far, to the point where there is carelessness and a lack of concern.

Look at these examples of words that are similar in denotation but have different connotations.

NEUTRAL	POSITIVE	NEGATIVE
agree	consent	acquiesce
strong	indomitable	implacable
thorough	scrupulous	fussy

Expressing the Connotation

Read each sentence. Select the word in parentheses that expresses the connotation (positive, negative, or neutral) given at the beginning of the sentence.

neutral   **1.** Some people like spicy foods, but the (**strong, pungent**) aroma of certain peppers and herbs does not appeal to me.

neutral   **2.** I greatly (**esteem, respect**) those who do good deeds anonymously, without any expectation of reward.

positive   **3.** My grandfather loves to recite Shakespeare, and his performances of passages from the Bard's plays are (**infallible, skillful**).

positive   **4.** You must be (**clever, omniscient**) if you can understand the motivations of all your team's players.

neutral   **5.** We saw a young man (**skulking, roaming**) around the park this afternoon.

negative   **6.** After she had time to think about it, she realized that her sister's (**casual, truculent**) criticism of her was born of jealousy.

positive   **7.** I think it was a(n) (**kind, altruistic**) impulse that prompted her to donate her annual bonus to the homeless shelter.

negative   **8.** The situation seemed (**ominous, fateful**) to the queen, and she was convinced that nothing good could come of it.

Classical Roots

fac, fact—to make or do

This root appears in **facile** (page 70). The literal meaning is "easily accomplished or done." Some other words based on the same root are listed below.

artifact	**faction**	**factor**	**faculty**
facility	**factitious**	**factual**	**malefactor**

From the list of words above, choose the one that corresponds to each of the brief definitions below. Write the word in the blank space in the illustrative sentence below the definition. Use an online or print dictionary if necessary.

1. one of the elements that help to bring about a result; an agent

The ability to work together was a major _____ in the group's success.

2. based on fact; real

Our assignment is to write a detailed _____ report on the presidential election.

3. ease, skill; that which serves or acts as a convenience or for a specific function

By the time he was five years old, Mozart could play the piano with great _____.

4. artificial, not natural; sham

The enthusiasm of those cheering infomercial audiences seems to me to be _____.

5. a teaching staff; the ability to act or to do something

A school may be known for its outstanding science _____.

6. an object of historical or archaeological interest produced by human workmanship (*"something made with skill"*)

The museum has an outstanding collection of _____ from the pre-Columbian period.

7. a small group of people within a larger group

The Senate _____ that opposed the President's budget was soundly defeated.

8. one who commits a crime, evildoer (*"one who does evil"*)

The _____ will stand trial for their terrible deeds.

*Read the following passage, taking note of the **boldface** words and their contexts. These words are among those you will be studying in Unit 7. It may help you to complete the exercises in this Unit if you refer to the way the words are used below.*

Emmeline Pankhurst
<Biographical Sketch>

TIME magazine declared Emmeline Pankhurst to be "One of the 100 Most Important People of the 20th Century." Many people, though, have never heard of this influential woman and of how she transformed the lives of women in England at the beginning of that century.

Emmeline Goulden Pankhurst was born in 1858 to a wealthy family in Victorian England, where she proved a dutiful daughter, wife, and mother of five. She was also a **renegade**—an outspoken suffragist and a leader in the struggle to gain British women the right to vote. Mrs. Pankhurst (as she preferred to be called) was struck by an incongruous fact: Women could own property and pay taxes if they held a job, but they had no legal right to vote. By 1903, the traditional

Emmeline Pankhurst

women's suffrage organizations had met with little success. Disillusioned and angry over the government's backpedaling and broken promises, Pankhurst formed a more militant group, the Women's Social and Political Union (WSPU). The WSPU engaged in political activism: Members introduced **chaos** into a society that was used to order. They broke windows and started fires, shaking things up to draw attention to their cause. WSPU's battle cry was "Votes for Women!" Its motto was "Deeds, Not Words."

These were **turbulent** times. Most politicians (at this time, all men) were **vociferous** in their opposition to women's suffrage: They jeered and taunted and spoke as if they **abhorred** women. Newspapers published scathing, **corrosive** editorials that criticized the WSPU and its tactics. (One of London's daily papers originated the term *suffragette* to ridicule the protesters. The name stuck. In fact, WSPU members embraced it and used it themselves.)

Some of the activities of the suffragettes—such as breaking windows and starting fires—were viewed as **reprehensible**, but the actions of the government, police, and prison wardens were worse. Women were battered and

Pankhurst (right) and fellow suffragettes were arrested in a 1910 protest and escorted to jail by police officers.

buffeted in demonstrations, and some were **implicated** in plots to destabilize straitlaced British society. Arrested protesters were jailed in **squalid** conditions, and many who **waived** their right to food to protest their incarceration were brutally force-fed. Pankhurst was imprisoned 12 times in one year alone in an attempt to **obviate** her continued participation in WSPU activities. During one court hearing, she said, "We are here, not because we are lawbreakers. We are here in our efforts to become law*makers*."

Pankhurst influenced American suffragist Alice Paul, who led a celebrated march of 5,000 people—women and men—in Washington, D.C., in 1913. Paul had protested in London, been jailed, and forcibly fed, and this experience galvanized her into action when she returned home. The march she led was a turning point for U.S. women's suffrage, although it was to take seven more years before the 19th Amendment to the Constitution, giving women full voting rights, was ratified. Back in Britain,

women over 30 were awarded the right to vote in 1918. Ten years later, the year Pankhurst died, the law was **amended**, and women were accorded the same voting rights as men.

Pankhurst's historical legacy is controversial. Some people view her as a forward- and clear-thinking heroine who had **discerned** the only effective way to get the vote for women. Critics say she was a self-serving **martinet** who demanded complete loyalty from her followers. One thing most can agree on: The determination and courage of one genteel, soft-spoken woman inspired a revolution, the effects of which persist to this day.

Audio

For iWords and audio passages, go to SadlierConnect.com.

Posters like this captured the imagination of women on both sides of the Atlantic.

Definitions

Note the spelling, pronunciation, part(s) of speech, and definition(s) of each of the following words. Then write the appropriate form of the word in the blank space in the illustrative sentence(s) following.

1. **amend**
   (ə mend')

   (v.) to change in a formal way; to change for the better
   If you are not doing well in a particular subject, you may want to _____ your way of studying it.

2. **buffet**
   (bəf' ət)

   (v.) to slap or cuff; to strike repeatedly; to drive or force with blows; to force one's way with difficulty; (n.) a slap, blow
   Blinding snowstorms _____ the barren landmass of Antarctica for months on end.
   Few figures in history or literature are as severely tested by fortune's _____ as Job in the Old Testament.

3. **commodious**
   (kə mō' dē əs)

   (adj.) roomy, spacious
   No one would expect a tiny studio apartment to have particularly _____ closets.

4. **extant**
   (ek' stənt)

   (adj.) still existing; not exterminated, destroyed, or lost
   The paintings of animals and human hands in Spain's Altamira caves are among the oldest _____ specimens of Stone Age art.

5. **implicate**
   (im' plə kāt)

   (v.) to involve in; to connect with or be related to
   The suspects never stood trial because there was no solid evidence to _____ them in the daring series of robberies.

6. **martinet**
   (mär tə net')

   (n.) a strict disciplinarian; a stickler for the rules
   When it came to drilling troops, the Revolutionary War general Baron Friedrich von Steuben was something of a _____.

7. **obviate**
   (äb' vē āt)

   (v.) to anticipate and prevent; to remove, dispose of
   Vaccinations can do much to _____ the dangers of childhood illnesses.

8. **reprehensible**
   (rep rē hen' sə bəl)

   (adj.) deserving blame or punishment
   Stalin eliminated many potential rivals by accusing them of all sorts of _____ acts that they did not commit.

9. **squalid**
(skwäl' id)

(*adj.*) filthy, wretched, debased
Many laws prohibit the types of _____
working conditions found in sweatshops.

10. **turbulent**
(tər' byə lənt)

(*adj.*) disorderly, riotous, violent; stormy
Letters and diary entries may reveal a person's lifelong struggle
to gain some control over _____ emotions.

Using Context

*For each item, determine whether the **boldface** word from pages 102–103 makes sense in the context of the sentence. Circle the item numbers next to the six sentences in which the words are used correctly.*

1. The employees wondered how they would get along with the new manager, since he had a reputation for being a real **martinet**.

2. Those socks, which were made in Egypt and date from the eleventh century, are the earliest **extant** knitted items.

3. It's very **commodious** to live in a location where you can walk to town and the commuter train station instead of having to drive.

4. Once the principal presented the evidence, the student made the decision to **implicate** the others who were involved in the prank as well.

5. To **obviate** the need for frequent trips to the supermarket, my mother will sometimes order groceries online and have them delivered.

6. If a student does not **amend** school on at least 150 of the 180 days in the school year, he or she will not be promoted to the next grade level.

7. Organizing a food drive and volunteering in a hospital are both examples of **reprehensible** acts.

8. Although powerful gusts of wind **buffet** the campsite, all the tents remain secure and anchored to the ground.

9. The workhouses of Victorian England were **squalid** places where poor people spent many hours at various jobs, such as washing clothes and peeling potatoes, in order to earn their keep.

10. The passengers on the cruise ship are looking forward to two **turbulent** weeks of sailing the sea and visiting colorful ports of call.

Choosing the Right Word

*Select the **boldface** word that better completes each sentence. You might refer to the passage on pages 100–101 to see how most of these words are used in context. Note that the choices might be related forms of the Unit words.*

1. According to cryptozoologists—people who search for proof that legendary creatures exist—Bigfoot might be a large prehistoric humanoid that is still (**reprehensible, extant**).

2. The Founding Fathers set up a method of (**amending, obviating**) the Constitution that is neither too easy nor too difficult to use.

3. Instead of trying to help the people who had elected her, she became involved in a(n) (**squalid, extant**) little quarrel about handing out jobs.

4. A compromise agreement reached in the judge's chambers would clearly (**buffet, obviate**) the need for a long, costly lawsuit.

5. Some people prefer the (**martinet, turbulence**) of life in a big city to the more placid atmosphere of a small town.

6. I'm not so sure that I want to rent a bungalow so (**squalid, commodious**) that I'll have room for guests every weekend.

7. Didn't it occur to them that by signing the letter "Sophomores of Central High," they would (**implicate, obviate**) the entire class in the protest?

8. The custom by which a young man buys his bride through a payment to her father is still (**commodious, extant**) in some parts of the world.

9. When she accused me of playing fast and loose with the rules, I lost my temper and called her an officious (**buffet, martinet**).

10. Hoping it was not too late to (**amend, implicate**) their relationship, the young man purchased a lovely bouquet of roses.

11. I don't know which was more (**reprehensible, squalid**)—making improper use of the money or lying about it later.

12. Which great poet said that his head was "bloody but unbowed" under the (**buffeting, implication**) of fate?

Completing the Sentence

Choose the word from the word bank that best completes each of the following sentences. Write the correct word or form of the word in the space provided.

amend	commodious	implicate	obviate	squalid
buffet	extant	martinet	reprehensible	turbulent

1. We are petitioning the council to _____ its procedures so that all citizens will have a chance to express their opinions.

2. Although our drill instructor was determined to follow the rules, he was by no means an overbearing _____.

3. In a natural history museum, we can see physical remains of many species of animals that are no longer _____.

4. A person who has been _____ about by many dreadful misfortunes will either become stronger or suffer a complete breakdown.

5. We Americans are proud that each change of the national administration, far from being _____, is carried out in a peaceful and friendly manner.

6. Getting a good education will do much to _____ the problem of finding a job that pays well.

7. It is particularly _____ for citizens to fail to vote in national elections and then complain about the government.

8. Are we justified in showing visitors only the most attractive and interesting sections of our cities, towns, or villages while keeping them away from the _____ neighborhoods where so many people live?

9. The trunk of the car was so _____ that it held all of our skiing equipment as well as our other luggage.

10. Those accused of crimes are sometimes willing to _____ their accomplices in return for immunity from prosecution.

Definitions

Note the spelling, pronunciation, part(s) of speech, and definition(s) of each of the following words. Then write the appropriate form of the word in the blank space in the illustrative sentence(s) following.

1. abhor
(ab hôr')

(*v.*) to regard with horror or loathing; to hate deeply

A pacifist is someone who _____ violence in all its forms.

2. chaos
(kā' äs)

(*n.*) great confusion, disorder

A great many people lost their fortunes and even their lives in the _____ brought on by the French Revolution.

3. corrosive
(kə rō' siv)

(*adj.*) eating away gradually, acidlike; bitterly sarcastic

Sulfuric acid is one of the most _____ substances known to chemistry.

4. discern
(di sərn')

(*v.*) to see clearly, recognize

It is a jury's job to _____ the truth by carefully evaluating all the evidence presented at trial.

5. inter
(in tər')

(*v.*) to bury, commit to the earth; to consign to oblivion

Jewels and other objects once _____ with Egypt's pharaohs can now be seen in numerous museums all over the world.

6. renegade
(ren' ə gād)

(*n.*) one who leaves a group; a deserter, outlaw; (*adj.*) traitorous; unconventional, unorthodox

Many a writer has been labeled a _____ for refusing to conform to society's conventions.

_____ senators from the President's own party joined the opposition to defeat the bill.

7. somber
(säm' bər)

(*adj.*) dark, gloomy; depressed or melancholy in spirit

The atmosphere in the locker room of the losing team could best be described as _____.

8. vociferous
(vō sif' ə rəs)

(*adj.*) loud and noisy; compelling attention

Relief agencies regularly make _____ appeals for aid for victims of war, terrorism, and natural disasters.

9. **voluminous** (və lü′ mə nəs)	(*adj.*) of great size; numerous; writing or speaking at great length The task of summarizing the _____ reports issued by government agencies may fall to members of a legislator's staff.
10. **waive** (wāv)	(*v.*) to do without, give up voluntarily; to put off temporarily, defer The senator agreed to _____ opposition to the proposed bill if some of its more controversial provisions were substantially modified.

Using Context

*For each item, determine whether the **boldface** word from pages 106–107 makes sense in the context of the sentence. Circle the item numbers next to the six sentences in which the words are used correctly.*

1. I ask that you **discern** the information given in my previous email, as I now have more accurate details.

2. I am happy to gather such **voluminous** research on my essay topic, but it will be difficult to condense all the information into only a few pages.

3. His **corrosive** sense of humor is off-putting to some, but I enjoy his witty sarcasm.

4. The newscaster's **somber** expression implied that we were in store for a distressing broadcast.

5. The author chooses to **abhor** her critics, knowing that giving them any attention will only encourage more comments.

6. Our assignment was to fill a time capsule with memorabilia and **inter** it in the ground, in hopes that one day in the future someone would unearth it and find relics of the past.

7. She is known in the community as a **renegade** lawyer who passionately fights for her clients.

8. I joined my gym on the day they offered a special deal to **waive** the sign-up fee for new members.

9. We have become so dependent on modern technology that **chaos** would ensue if the Internet stopped working.

10. We were wondering why the crowd we saw on our hike was so **vociferous**, until we learned they were part of a silent meditation group.

Choosing the Right Word

Select the **boldface** word that better completes each sentence. You might refer to the passage on pages 100–101 to see how most of these words are used in context. Note that the choices might be related forms of the Unit words.

1. In 1940, Winston Churchill conveyed to the British people the (**somber, voluminous**) truth that they were fighting for their national existence.

2. At lunchtime, the room rang with the sound of (**renegade, vociferous**) debates between the fans of rival teams.

3. We can expect (**chaos, discernment**) later if we do not develop a realistic conservation policy now.

4. The time has come for us to (**waive, inter**) our ancient disputes and go forward as a truly united people.

5. Did you know that many soft drinks, especially colas, are so (**corrosive, voluminous**) that they can erode tooth enamel over time?

6. If you examine the evidence carefully, you will soon (**discern, inter**) the contradictions in the witness's story.

7. The Tech team was offside on the play; but since we had thrown them for an eight-yard loss, we (**waived, abhorred**) the five-yard penalty.

8. History gives us many examples of how the (**vociferous, corrosive**) effects of religious hatred can weaken the entire social structure.

9. I wouldn't say that I (**inter, abhor**) housework, but I must admit that I avoid it whenever I can.

10. Even in his old age, Thomas Jefferson kept up a (**voluminous, renegade**) correspondence with important people in America and abroad.

11. If you (**discern, abhor**) blood, then you should probably not be a nurse.

12. We sometimes forget that the great men who led our revolution were considered (**renegades, chaos**) by the British king.

Completing the Sentence

Choose the word from the word bank that best completes each of the following sentences. Write the correct word or form of the word in the space provided.

abhor	corrosive	inter	somber	voluminous
chaos	discern	renegade	vociferous	waive

1. I didn't expect you to like my suggestion, but I was shocked by your bitter and _____ criticism of it.

2. Confident that she could present the case effectively to a judge, the lawyer advised her client to _____ his right to a jury trial.

3. The records of the school board meeting on the proposed bond issue are so _____ that it would take me a week to read them.

4. Let me say frankly that I _____ prejudice in anyone, even a member of my own family.

5. The American writer Dorothy Parker was celebrated for her sharp tongue and _____ wit.

6. Who would not feel depressed on entering that _____ old courtroom, with its dim lighting and dark, massive furnishings?

7. Shakespeare tells us that "the evil that men do lives after them; the good is oft _____ with their bones."

8. One of the signs of maturity is the ability to _____ the difference between things that are secondary and things that are truly important.

9. A person who changes from one political party to another on the basis of honest conviction should not be regarded as a(n) _____.

10. In our frantic search for the missing papers, we overturned everything in the room, leaving it in complete _____.

Synonyms

*Choose the word or form of the word from this Unit that is the same or most nearly the same in meaning as the **boldface** word or expression in the phrase. Write that word on the line. Use a dictionary if necessary.*

1. the **solemn** tolling of church bells   _____
2. willing to **alter** long-standing company policy   _____
3. a **tumultuous** period in history   _____
4. **noticed** a change in public opinion   _____
5. the cruel **taskmaster**   _____
6. a **vast** and elegant hotel lobby   _____
7. **incriminated** by the evidence   _____
8. a treasure **laid to rest**   _____
9. in a great deal of **turmoil**   _____
10. **avert** further debate   _____
11. **despises** insects and creepy crawlers   _____
12. condemned by all as a **defector**   _____
13. **battered** by fluctuations in the stock market   _____
14. **copious** pieces of evidence   _____
15. a formerly endangered, now **thriving** species   _____

Antonyms

*Choose the word or form of the word from this Unit that is most nearly opposite in meaning to the **boldface** word or expression in the phrase. Write that word on the line. Use a dictionary if necessary.*

1. the government's **commendable** actions   _____
2. the **benign** salt air   _____
3. live in **clean** conditions   _____
4. **accept** all claims to the throne   _____
5. a **soft-spoken** opponent   _____

Writing: Words in Action

Suppose that you are a citizen living during Emmeline Pankhurst's time. Write an editorial in which you express your views about women's suffrage. Support your view using at least two details from the passage (pages 100–101) and three or more Unit words.

Vocabulary in Context

*Some of the words you have studied in this Unit appear in **boldface** type. Read the passage below, and then circle the letter of the correct answer for each word as it is used in context.*

In July 1848, Elizabeth Cady Stanton and Lucretia Mott held the first women's rights convention at the Wesleyan Chapel in Seneca Falls, New York, where a **commodious** hall held more than 300 attendees. Stanton and Mott initially met at the World Anti-Slavery Convention in London in 1840, where, because of the **extant** laws of the time, they were prohibited from being on the convention floor. They **abhorred** this shared experience of indignity, and the idea for the Seneca Falls Convention was born.

On July 19, the first day of the convention, approximately 200 women were in attendance while Stanton presented the "Declaration of Sentiments and Grievances"—a document modeled after the Declaration of Independence. This document highlighted the injustices that women had suffered, and Stanton read each reprehensible action aloud. Though this action could have set a **somber** tone for the women, they wanted to **inter** these grievances and forge a path toward equality. In addition to listing grievances, this document also petitioned for a list of women's rights that seemed **voluminous** at the time, including the right to vote, the right to equal education, and the right to equal treatment under the law.

On July 20, the convention was open to the public. Forty men, including abolitionist Frederick Douglass, joined the women who were already in attendance at the convention. After much debate about women's suffrage, the Declaration of Sentiments and Grievances was signed by the assembly. The Declaration of Sentiments and Grievances marked an important step during a turbulent time in history when women were viewed as unequal; it began the women's rights and suffrage movement in the United States.

---

1. A **commodious** location, as Wesleyan Chapel is said to be, is
   a. isolated   c. distant
   b. spacious   d. urban

2. The word **extant** most nearly means
   a. overly confusing   c. still existing
   b. not straightforward d. too general

3. To **abhor** is to
   a. hate deeply   c. compare falsely
   b. live fully   d. disagree strongly

4. A tone that is **somber** is
   a. fearful   c. angry
   b. gloomy   d. reserved

5. To **inter** grievances means to
   a. bury them   c. ignore them
   b. trade them   d. save them

6. A **voluminous** list of rights is
   a. of great value   c. controversial
   b. memorable   d. of great length

*Read the following passage, taking note of the **boldface** words and their contexts. These words are among those you will be studying in Unit 8. It may help you to complete the exercises in this Unit if you refer to the way the words are used below.*

Anita Stockton Talks about Risk and Reward on the Stock Market
<Interview with an Expert>

By Jon X. Paek
Published April 19, 2012

Although *the stock market affects all Americans—both those who invest in the market and those who don't—many people have little or no understanding of how it works. This reporter sat down with Anita Stockton, a retired stockbroker, to find out more about this important financial institution.*

JXP: What does the stock market do?
AS: The stock market plays a crucial role in the global economy, enabling companies to raise money by selling shares of ownership to investors. The cash generated by sales of stock helps many companies grow, which increases competition and growth in the economy and provides consumers with more goods and services at cheaper prices.

JXP: Some people get rich from the stock market. How do they make money?
AS: Owners of shares, or shareholders, seek to profit from investments in stocks, but there are no guarantees. Occasionally, some

companies distribute dividends, a sum of money to shareholders for each share they own. Shareholders also sell their shares to other investors through a stock exchange, and they may **revel** in their profits when they sell for more than the original cost. Stock trading has become increasingly complex, with thousands of companies publicly traded and **multifarious** strategies available to traders. But "buy low, sell high" is a rule that will never become **obsolete** and that investors will always **commend**.

JXP: Sounds like easy money. Is there risk involved?
AS: Unfortunately, there is no sure way to predict fluctuations in stock prices. There can be **reprisals** for careless investing. The market can be an **omnivorous** beast that will pick clean the portfolios of the savviest investors. Even the wise lose more money than they gain, so putting one's money in the stock market is not for the **ingenuous**. Stock analysts measure the value of a company in terms of its assets, debts, and earnings. But such analysts cannot project future earnings with certainty. Nevertheless, when analysts determine that a company is likely to grow faster than its competitors, investors rush to purchase shares. Consequently, demand for the company's stock increases along with expectations for future performance, and the price of the shares rises. When the company's earnings are **compatible** with expectations, the share price may continue to rise. Investors keep their shares in anticipation of further gains or sell for a profit at the new price. Sometimes, a

investors regard the stock market with **animosity** and buy low-risk investments with **parsimonious** payoffs, like government bonds. Conversely, many a daring investor in the stock market has **derided** himself for his insatiable appetite for risk once he felt the sting of losses. The volatility of the market scares many investors away and punishes the imprudent.

JXP: With so much uncertainty, who invests in the stock market?

AS: For many investors, the possible gains of the stock market prove too great to ignore. Disciplined investors balance potential losses against potential rewards. They diversify their investments, maintaining reasonable expectations and a moderate appetite for risk. They research the companies whose stocks they buy. In short, **apathy** is not recommended for potential investors, but if you have no interest in studying the market yourself, mutual funds and money managers can fill this role, affording you the opportunity to benefit from the power of the stock market and from professional expertise. Overall, cautious, prudent, and well-informed investment in the stock market has proven to be one of the best ways for investors to increase their wealth.

company's profits may fall short of expectations, and such results, once reported, can have a **stultifying** effect on the demand for the firm's stock. **Apprehensive** investors watch the value of their investment shrink as the share price drops.

JXP: What a roller-coaster ride! Do many people lose money?

AS: The uncertainties of the stock market put many would-be investors in a **quandary**. Some

For iWords and audio passages, go to SadlierConnect.com

Wall Street on the Black Monday stock market crash of October 18, 1987

Definitions

Note the spelling, pronunciation, part(s) of speech, and definition(s) of each of the following words. Then write the appropriate form of the word in the blank space in the illustrative sentence(s) following.

1. animosity
(an ə mäs′ ə tē)

(*n.*) strong dislike; bitter hostility

The deep _____ between the Montagues and Capulets could not prevent Romeo and Juliet from falling in love.

2. apprehensive
(ap rē hen′ siv)

(*adj.*) fearful or anxious, especially about the future

As the hurricane approached, _____ residents all along the coast prepared for the worst.

3. commend
(kə mend′)

(*v.*) to praise, express approval; to present as worthy of attention; to commit to the care of

The mayor _____ the young people for their volunteer work at local hospitals and soup kitchens.

4. decrepit
(di krep′ it)

(*adj.*) old and feeble; worn-out, ruined

"I may be aging," the famous movie star replied, "but I am hardly _____."

5. deride
(de rīd′)

(*v.*) to ridicule, laugh at with contempt

Most people find jokes that _____ somebody's national origin or social background extremely offensive.

6. multifarious
(məl tə far′ ē əs)

(*adj.*) having great variety; numerous and diverse

Leonardo da Vinci's notebooks reveal that he was a man of _____ interests.

7. omnivorous
(äm niv′ ə rəs)

(*adj.*) eating every kind of food; eagerly taking in everything, having a wide variety of tastes

An _____ animal has a greater chance of survival than one that depends on a single food source.

8. quandary
(kwän′ drē)

(*n.*) a state of perplexity or doubt

Try as I might, I could see no way out of the ethical _____ in which I found myself.

9. **recalcitrant**
   (ri kal' sə trənt)

(*adj.*) stubbornly disobedient, resisting authority

A _____ individual may have great difficulty adjusting to a job that requires a good deal of teamwork.

10. **reprisal**
    (ri prī' zəl)

(*n.*) an injury done in return for injury

The Highland clans of Scotland engaged in cattle rustling in _____ for real or imagined injuries.

 **Using Context**

*For each item, determine whether the **boldface** word from pages 114–115 makes sense in the context of the sentence. Circle the item numbers next to the six sentences in which the words are used correctly.*

1. It's extremely surprising that those **decrepit** old cars still run.

2. If all you need is a routine cleaning, there's no need to be **apprehensive** about going to the dentist.

3. As a **reprisal** for the increase in residents in the next decade, the state is asking the federal government for additional funds in a number of areas.

4. To **commend** the students for a job well done, the teacher gave them a pizza party.

5. When the world's first plastics were developed, no one could have imagined the **multifarious** uses that would be found for the synthetic materials.

6. Upon the death of the king, emergency plans were executed to **deride** the successor.

7. The sense of rivalry between the two teams as well as between their fans is so intense that it borders on **animosity**.

8. The speaker's **omnivorous** remarks stirred the members of the audience and motivated them to seek new solutions to environmental problems.

9. The opposing political parties agreed to hold discussions to reach a **quandary** that would work for both sides.

10. One of the challenges that doctors and other medical professionals face comes from **recalcitrant** patients who miss appointments and do not follow a prescribed course of medication.

Choosing the Right Word

*Select the **boldface** word that better completes each sentence. You might refer to the passage on pages 112–113 to see how most of these words are used in context. Note that the choices might be related forms of the Unit words.*

1. Mary Shelley is often (**commended, derided**) for having written one of the earliest examples of science fiction: the classic novel *Frankenstein*.

2. Those students who have been doing their work all term need not feel (**apprehensive, recalcitrant**) about the final examination.

3. Yes, there is some (**quandary, animosity**) between different racial and ethnic groups, but it can be overcome by education and experience.

4. If you can't (**deride, commend**) me for my efforts to help you, at least don't criticize me for not doing everything you want.

5. Some people are (**omnivorous, apprehensive**) readers, with a lively appetite for all types of fiction and nonfiction.

6. Our Constitution is more than 200 years old; but far from being (**multifarious, decrepit**), it is still a vital, dynamic, and highly practical plan of government.

7. Although our society must punish criminals, I don't think we should do so simply as a(n) (**reprisal, animosity**) for the wrongs they have committed.

8. The woman looked (**omnivorous, apprehensive**) when her guide announced that the group was going whitewater rafting in the afternoon.

9. Two of the chief strengths of modern American society are the variety and vitality that arise from its (**multifarious, decrepit**) cultures.

10. The owner of the used car dealership showed poor judgment when he decided to publicly (**deride, commend**) his employees' suggestions for improved customer service.

11. The handful of (**apprehensive, recalcitrant**) students who refuse to obey study hall regulations are violating the rights of the majority.

12. So we are faced with that old (**quandary, reprisal**)—an income that simply can't be stretched to cover the things that we simply must have.

Completing the Sentence

Choose the word from the word bank that best completes each of the following sentences. Write the correct word or form of the word in the space provided.

animosity	commend	deride	omnivorous	recalcitrant
apprehensive	decrepit	multifarious	quandary	reprisal

1. In spite of all the elaborate safety precautions, I couldn't help feeling a little _____ as I set out for my first skydiving lesson.

2. From all his growling and snapping, you would think our beagle felt a personal _____ toward every other dog on the block.

3. If we increase our tariff rates on the goods of other countries, we can be sure that they will raise their own rates in _____.

4. If you think of all the different kinds of food that human beings are able to consume, you will realize that we are truly a(n) _____ species.

5. I think that the phrase "on its last legs" is an apt description of that _____ old house down the block.

6. Political candidates who do nothing but _____ their opponents' character and abilities may alienate voters.

7. The _____ problems that will face America's presidents in the twenty-first century will make their job one of the most demanding in the world.

8. I trust you will never have the experience of trying to cross the desert with a(n) _____ mule that wants to remain where it is.

9. So there I was, having accepted invitations to two different parties on the same evening. What a(n) _____ to be in!

10. The board of directors voted to _____ her for the skill and enthusiasm with which she had managed the charity drive.

Definitions

Note the spelling, pronunciation, part(s) of speech, and definition(s) of each of the following words. Then write the appropriate form of the word in the blank space in the illustrative sentence(s) following.

1. apathy
(ap′ ə thē)

(*n.*) a lack of feeling, emotion, or interest
I was horrified when the sales force greeted my great idea for an ad campaign with total _____.

2. compatible
(kəm pat′ ə bəl)

(*adj.*) able to get along or work well together; capable of use with some other model or system
Eyewitness accounts of an accident rarely are totally _____.

3. condolence
(kən dō′ ləns)

(*n.*) an expression of sympathy
A few well-chosen words of _____ can be a great comfort to someone who has lost a loved one.

4. consecrate
(kän′ sə krāt)

(*v.*) to make sacred, hallow; to set apart for a special purpose
Traditionally most religious denominations hold special ceremonies to _____ a new house of worship.

5. ingenuous
(in jen′ yü əs)

(*adj.*) innocent, simple; frank, sincere
In his novels, Dickens has harsh words for those who take cruel advantage of _____ young people.

6. obsolete
(äb sə lēt′)

(*adj.*) out-of-date, no longer in use
In order to remain competitive, manufacturing companies periodically replace _____ machinery.

7. parsimonious
(pär sə mō′ nē əs)

(*adj.*) stingy, miserly; meager, poor, small
Many people who lost money in the Great Depression later adhered to a _____ lifestyle, even during more prosperous times.

8. revel
(rev′ əl)

(*v.*) to take great pleasure in; (*n.*) a wild celebration
Some movie stars do not _____ in the attention that their fans and the media pay them.
All around the world, the new millennium was ushered in with positive thoughts and _____.

9. **stultify**
   (stəl′ tə fī)

   (*v.*) to make ineffective or useless, cripple; to have a dulling effect on

   Oppressive heat may _____ the mind and spirit as well as the body.

10. **suave**
    (swäv)

    (*adj.*) smoothly agreeable or polite; pleasing to the senses

    Nick Charles, the clever detective in the *Thin Man* movies, is a _____ man-about-town.

Using Context

*For each item, determine whether the **boldface** word from pages 118–119 makes sense in the context of the sentence. Circle the item numbers next to the six sentences in which the words are used correctly.*

1. Although he'd had a disadvantaged childhood, he developed such **suave** mannerisms over time that everyone believed he had a distinguished background.

2. The defendant's key witness turned out to be **parsimonious** during testimony and gave abundant information.

3. While some people dislike the cold weather, I find that the crisp air tends to **stultify** my senses and make me more alert.

4. When my phone died, I searched endlessly for a charger but could not find one that was **compatible** with my device.

5. Someone had clearly decided to **consecrate** the library books that were returned with ripped pages and grease stains.

6. We urged our **ingenuous** friend to not be so trusting of everyone, as she could easily be taken advantage of.

7. Some people now see stores as **obsolete** since you can buy almost anything online.

8. We delivered a week's worth of meals as an act of **condolence** to our grieving neighbor.

9. Most people were indifferent to the candidate for Congress, but some people felt such **apathy** for him that they showed up at every event to protest his campaign.

10. Although I enjoy the company of my friends and family, I do **revel** in the rare moments I get to spend by myself.

Choosing the Right Word

*Select the **boldface** word that better completes each sentence. You might refer to the passage on pages 112–113 to see how most of these words are used in context. Note that the choices might be related forms of the Unit words.*

1. Clark Gable was a(n) (**obsolete, suave**) leading man who attracted women with his charm and good looks and impressed men with his strength and confidence.

2. Your unwillingness to study foreign languages is in no way (**compatible, parsimonious**) with your ambition to get a job in the foreign service.

3. Her moods seem to go from one extreme to the other— from deepest (**apathy, condolence**) to unlimited enthusiasm.

4. Can you be so (**suave, ingenuous**) that you don't realize she is paying us all those phony compliments to get something out of us?

5. The address was so dull and long-winded that it seemed to (**consecrate, stultify**) rather than inspire the audience.

6. I think we should offer congratulations rather than (**revels, condolences**) for the disappearance of that battered old heap you called a car.

7. The headwaiter was so (**suave, ingenuous**) and self-assured in his manner that we took him for a diplomat.

8. I must give you the sad news that correct spelling and good grammar are not, and never will be, (**obsolete, compatible**).

9. In this new century of our nation's life, let us (**stultify, consecrate**) ourselves anew to the ideals of human freedom.

10. When my friends appeared with an MP3 player and a docking station with amazing sound, I realized that our crash study session might become an all-day (**apathy, revel**).

11. She is so absorbed in herself that she has become (**parsimonious, suave**) in the normal expression of human sympathy and affection.

12. I am looking for a printer that is (**compatible, ingenuous**) with my computer.

Completing the Sentence

Choose the word from the word bank that best completes each of the following sentences. Write the correct word or form of the word in the space provided.

apathy	condolence	ingenuous	parsimonious	stultify
compatible	consecrate	obsolete	revel	suave

1. Throughout the hot, dusty journey, we _____ in the thought that soon we would be swimming in the cool lake.

2. Struggling to overcome her _____ inclinations, she finally reached into her pocket and handed me one thin dime!

3. Although I was unable to visit my old friend's widow in person, I offered my _____ in a heartfelt letter.

4. Simple _____ seems to be the main reason that such a large percentage of those eligible to vote fail to cast ballots in any election.

5. It was difficult for us to believe that such a(n) _____ and cultured gentleman was a member of a gang of international jewel thieves.

6. Technology changes so rapidly that a particular computer may be state-of-the-art one day and _____ the next.

7. It is surprising how often people with very different personalities turn out to be _____ when they get to know one another.

8. Now that I am a senior, it is hard to believe that I was ever as innocent and _____ as the members of the new freshman class.

9. "Today," said the speaker, "we _____ this monument to the memory of all those who fought and died in defense of their country."

10. In totalitarian regimes, censorship and violence are often employed to suppress criticism and _____ dissent.

Synonyms

*Choose the word or form of the word from this Unit that is the same or most nearly the same in meaning as the **boldface** word or expression in the phrase. Write that word on the line. Use a dictionary if necessary.*

1. rejected the author's **antiquated** theories   _____
2. your **candid** admission of the truth   _____
3. **dedicated** themselves to healing the sick   _____
4. an old house with a **dilapidated** porch   _____
5. surrounded by **like-minded** friends   _____
6. sent a sincere message of **empathy**   _____
7. a **boring** routine   _____
8. courting the most **debonair** bachelor   _____
9. **delight** in the applause   _____
10. **delegated** to the care of friends   _____
11. babysitting a **cantankerous** child   _____
12. a moral **dilemma**   _____
13. cruel acts of **retribution**   _____
14. are **voracious** readers   _____
15. **jeered at** by the protestors   _____

Antonyms

*Choose the word or form of the word from this Unit that is most nearly opposite in meaning to the **boldface** word or expression in the phrase. Write that word on the line. Use a dictionary if necessary.*

1. expressed **goodwill** toward the enemy   _____
2. a result of voter **fervor**   _____
3. was **generous** with donations to charity   _____
4. a person of **unvaried** pursuits   _____
5. **confident** about the upcoming surgery   _____

Writing: Words in Action

Write your own financial advice column for teens in which you explain the pros and cons of investing in the stock market. Use at least two details from the passage (pages 112–113) as well as your own observations and personal knowledge. Use three or more words from this Unit.

Vocabulary in Context

*Some of the words you have studied in this Unit appear in **boldface** type. Read the passage below, and then circle the letter of the correct answer for each word as it is used in context.*

In 1919, Charles Ponzi, an Italian immigrant living in Boston, received an international postal reply coupon from a friend in Italy. Such coupons were meant to facilitate small international transactions—recipients exchanged them for stamps, which could be redeemed for cash. Ponzi noticed that his coupon had been purchased with pesetas in Spain. At the current exchange rate, its purchase price was far below the value of the U.S. stamps it could get in Boston. The discrepancy gave this **recalcitrant** businessman an idea.

Early in 1920, Ponzi established the Security and Exchange Company, which sold notes promising a 50 percent return in forty-five days. The **suave** "financial wizard" explained that his company would buy postal reply coupons overseas, transfer them among countries, and finally bring them back to the United States, where they would be redeemed at great profit. Investors, mainly from the immigrant community of Boston's North End, lined up. Before long, the company was taking in $200,000 a day. But Ponzi was not buying postal coupons. He was using cash from recent investors to pay off the notes of earlier investors.

Later that year, a *Boston Post* article exposed the dubious underpinnings of the scheme. Hundreds of **apprehensive** investors gathered to demand payment. By then, Ponzi controlled Hanover Trust Bank, which he **consecrated** as his personal checking account, and so was able to pay the initial wave of customers. But the banking commissioner shut down Hanover and called for an audit. Desperate, Ponzi took a million dollars to the local racetrack, where he hoped to cover his enormous debt by betting on long-shot, **decrepit** horses. He failed. Jailed for grand larceny, Ponzi gave no **condolence** to investors who had lost money in his scheme.

---

1. The word **recalcitrant** most nearly means
   a. resisting authority   c. criminal
   b. working hard   d. deceitful

2. A **suave** person is
   a. smart   c. highly educated
   b. convincing   d. sophisticated

3. **Apprehensive** investors are
   a. preoccupied   c. anxious
   b. angry   d. greedy

4. To **consecrate** is to
   a. consolidate   c. corrupt
   b. reserve   d. deposit

5. **Decrepit** horses are
   a. low-cost   c. unruly
   b. slow   d. worn-out

6. A **condolence** expresses
   a. sorrow   c. spite
   b. sympathy   d. repentance

*Read the following passage, taking note of the **boldface** words and their contexts. These words are among those you will be studying in Unit 9. It may help you to complete the exercises in this Unit if you refer to the way the words are used below.*

My Last Day in Pompeii
<Diary Entry>

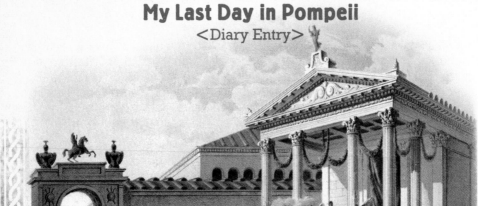

August 26, 79

I arrived in Pompeii the day before the volcano Vesuvius swallowed the city. Our ships were heavy with Syrian goods: leather works, dyes, and silk. I oversaw the men unloading the cargo, and when this job was done, I set out with two companions into the city. After our long journey, I **exulted** at the prospect of a decent meal and assumed my friends' desire to satisfy their appetites was as **ardent** as my own. One of them surprised me with a **spontaneous** plan: He insisted that we **deviate** from our goal to stop at the Temple of Fortuna Augusta.

If only we'd had an **inkling** of the city's fate, how many lives would have been spared! But who can predict the whims of the **capricious** gods? Having made our offering in haste, we descended the steps of the temple in a rush to fill our stomachs. We passed the market, winding through crowds of people carrying foodstuffs they had purchased: meat and fish, fruits, breads and cakes. Soon we found a restaurant and sat down to the business of eating grilled goat meat, **copious** servings of vegetables cooked in fish sauce, and a **palatable** wine. Satisfied, we made our way to the baths to wash off the grime of our voyage.

I parted ways with my companions and walked to the home of Marcus Durmius, a wealthy merchant who had invited me to be his guest. Along the way, I noticed an **emaciated** old nobleman

Amphorae were used to transport goods on ships.

People fled Pompeii as the volcano Vesuvius covered the town in ash.

dressed in purple silk. As our paths crossed, the ground trembled—one of those minor quakes with which the inhabitants of Pompeii were all too familiar. Afraid the nobleman might fall, I grabbed him by the arm to steady him. The tremor passed, but rather than thank me for my trouble, the old man looked at me with **rancor**, as if I had been impudent to assist him, and he walked off without a word.

I spent the rest of the day with Marcus Durmius in his garden. We exchanged news and discussed the price of wine, staring at the **limpid** water of his fountain, which was surroundedby the **gnarled** branches of his laurel trees. Excited by my report of prices in the East, the **assiduous** merchant outlined a plan for us to ship his wine immediately for sale in Palmyra. I awoke early in the morning and returned to the harbor to make the arrangements, and it was there, awaiting Marcus Durmius's porters, that I felt the shock of Vesuvius's eruption.

Looking over the city, I saw a plume of smoke climbing into the air. An uproar swept over the harbor, the shouts of men overwhelming the sounds of the bay. We watched in horror as the cloud approached, showering the temples in dust, setting rooftops ablaze. Our captain, recognizing the sign of an **omnipotent** god determined to **chastise** the city's inhabitants, commanded that we fill our vessel with as many souls as it could carry, and within two hours we were at sea. In the distance we now saw a second column of smoke rise from the mountain, much larger than the first, like a sinister tree sprouting in the sky. We watched the **poignant** scene as this new cloud spread over the city, and we were certain that Pompeii was doomed.

The city of Pompeii as it looks today

Audio

For iWords and audio passages, go to SadlierConnect.com.

Definitions

Note the spelling, pronunciation, part(s) of speech, and definition(s) of each of the following words. Then write the appropriate form of the word in the blank space in the illustrative sentence(s) following.

1. ardent
(är′ dənt)

(*adj.*) very enthusiastic, impassioned
The members of the winning team acknowledged the cheers of their _____ fans.

2. capricious
(kə prish′ əs)

(*adj.*) subject to whims or passing fancies
Our constitutional system of checks and balances is designed to prevent the _____ use of power by any branch of the federal government.

3. chastise
(chas tīz′)

(*v.*) to inflict physical punishment as a means of correction; to scold severely
State and federal laws now forbid the use of corporal punishment to _____ prisoners.

4. deviate
(*v.*, dē′ vē āt; *n.*, *adj.*, dē′ vē ət)

(*v.*) to turn aside; to stray from a norm; (*n.*) one who departs from a norm; (*adj.*) differing from a norm, heterodox, unconventional
Try not to _____ from the directions given in the owner's manual.
Those who disagreed with the Soviet form of government were often branded as _____ and imprisoned.
Under our system of justice, the mentally ill cannot be held responsible for their _____ behavior.

5. gnarled
(närld)

(*adj.*) knotted, twisted, lumpy
The _____ limbs of cypresses dominate many of the landscapes painted by the Dutch artist Vincent van Gogh.

6. indemnity
(in dem′ nə tē)

(*n.*) a payment for damage or loss
A certain type of life insurance contract provides double _____ for the accidental death of the policyholder.

7. omnipotent
(äm nip′ ə tənt)

(*adj.*) almighty, having unlimited power or authority
Many of the heroes of ancient myths and legends appear to be all but _____.

8. **palatable**
(pal′ ə tə bəl)

(*adj.*) agreeable to the taste or one's sensibilities; suitable for consumption

The addition of some seasonings will usually make even the blandest of dishes _____.

9. **poignant**
(poin′ yənt)

(*adj.*) deeply affecting, touching; keen or sharp in taste or smell

There is something truly _____ about the sight of falling leaves in autumn.

10. **sophomoric**
(säf ə môr′ ik)

(*adj.*) immature and overconfident; conceited

Adolescents aren't the only people whose behavior might at times be considered a bit _____.

Using Context

*For each item, determine whether the **boldface** word from pages 126–127 makes sense in the context of the sentence. Circle the item numbers next to the six sentences in which the words are used correctly.*

1. It was my grandparents' **ardent** wish that all three of their children attend college, even though they themselves did not have the opportunity to do so.

2. Before you can collect all or part of this **indemnity**, you must file the correct forms with the insurance company.

3. She is a **capricious** singer and dancer and has played the lead role in many musicals.

4. It is hard to imagine a situation where you would **chastise** someone for telling the truth.

5. The practice test was not at all useful because all the questions were ridiculously **palatable**.

6. The trunk of the huge tree was now almost completely covered by **gnarled**, woody vines.

7. Because her injuries from the bike accident are **omnipotent**, they will not take a long time to heal.

8. The works of the French Impressionist are now beloved and highly prized, so it is hard to believe that his style of painting was once thought to have come from a **deviate**.

9. Listening to old, familiar songs can often bring back **poignant** memories.

10. I thanked him for his **sophomoric** advice and assured him I would do my best to follow it.

Choosing the Right Word

*Select the **boldface** word that better completes each sentence. You might refer to the passage on pages 124–125 to see how most of these words are used in context. Note that the choices might be related forms of the Unit words.*

1. Lord Tennyson, the poet, speaks of "sorrow's crown of sorrow," by which he means the (**sophomoric, poignant**) experience of remembering happier times.

2. I spent the better part of an hour trying to untangle a badly (**gnarled, ardent**) heap of cables and electrical cords.

3. The lecturer explained that the UN is not (**palatable, omnipotent**) and that it can do only what the member states allow it to do.

4. We must show understanding and acceptance of those who (**chastise, deviate**) somewhat from our own standards of what is appropriate.

5. Most of the poetry written by the students was (**omnipotent, poignant**), filled with powerful imagery that conveyed a surprising depth of emotion.

6. The destruction wrought by a nuclear war would be so vast that any form of (**chastisement, indemnity**) to the injured would be impossible.

7. Your (**ardent, capricious**) interest in ecology shows that you care deeply about the welfare of this planet.

8. She seems to feel that it is her mission in life to (**chastise, deviate**) all those who fail to live up to her standards.

9. Since their loud talk and crude manners were anything but (**palatable, sophomoric**) to me, I politely declined their invitation to dine with them.

10. The tastes of the television audience are so (**capricious, gnarled**) that no one can predict in advance which programs will be successful.

11. He tries hard to sound well-informed, but his superficial answers only betray his (**poignant, sophomoric**) knowledge of world affairs.

12. My sister views my interest in horror films as (**deviate, omnipotent**) behavior.

Completing the Sentence

Choose the word from the word bank that best completes each of the following sentences. Write the correct word or form of the word in the space provided.

ardent	chastise	gnarled	omnipotent	poignant
capricious	deviate	indemnity	palatable	sophomoric

1. It is of no use to _____ my little brother for not keeping his room clean—he simply refuses to be tidy no matter how much he is scolded.

2. Under the American system of separation of powers, no government official or agency can ever become _____.

3. If you wish to recover quickly, you must not _____ in the slightest from the doctor's instructions.

4. When she told me that she was reading *Huckleberry Finn* for the ninth time, I realized that she was indeed a(n) _____ admirer of the novel.

5. We were fascinated to see the consummate grace and skill with which the _____ hands of the old carpenter manipulated his tools.

6. There can be no _____ for the pain and suffering that your carelessness has caused me!

7. Nothing can arouse _____ memories of long ago and far away like an old, well-loved song!

8. Some of my friends are mentally rather mature for their age; others are of a decidedly _____ turn of mind.

9. Far from being _____, the director's casting choices were based on a solid appreciation of each actor's abilities and limitations.

10. My travels have shown me that many exotic foods I once considered disgusting are really quite _____.

Definitions

Note the spelling, pronunciation, part(s) of speech, and definition(s) of each of the following words. Then write the appropriate form of the word in the blank space in the illustrative sentence(s) following.

1. allocate
(al′ ə kāt)

(*v.*) to set apart or designate for a special purpose; to distribute

In their wills many people _____ a portion of their wealth to favorite charities or educational institutions.

2. assiduous
(ə sij′ ü əs)

(*adj.*) persistent, attentive, diligent

Workers who are conscientious in the performance of their duties are, by definition, _____.

3. brash
(brash)

(*adj.*) prone to act in a hasty manner; impudent

Successful political candidates soon learn how to handle tough questions fired at them by _____ newspaper and TV reporters.

4. copious
(kō′ pē əs)

(*adj.*) abundant; plentiful; wordy, verbose

The _____ and detailed footnotes found in most scholarly books are designed to document the authors' sources.

5. emaciated
(i mā′ shē ā tid)

(*adj.*, *part.*) unnaturally thin

People who suffer from serious eating disorders may soon become woefully _____.

6. exult
(eg zəlt′)

(*v.*) to rejoice greatly

The campaign workers _____ in the unexpected victory of their candidate.

7. inkling
(iŋk′ liŋ)

(*n.*) a hint; a vague notion

I had absolutely no _____ of what to expect as I entered the room.

8. limpid
(lim′ pid)

(*adj.*) clear, transparent; readily understood

Snorkelers flock to the _____ waters of the Caribbean to view schools of brightly colored fish.

9. **rancor**
(raŋ′ kər)

(*n.*) bitter resentment or ill-will

An unusual degree of _____ may creep into the tone of the political debate in an election year.

10. **spontaneous**
(spän tā′ nē əs)

(*adj.*) arising naturally; not planned or engineered in advance

Actors try to make their performances seem as _____ as possible.

Using Context

*For each item, determine whether the **boldface** word from pages 130–131 makes sense in the context of the sentence. Circle the item numbers next to the six sentences in which the words are used correctly.*

1. It broke my heart to see the **emaciated** figures of the dogs that had been abandoned at the shelter.

2. I thought it was quite **brash** of my friend to correct our teacher's grammar, but he seemed to appreciate my friend's attention to detail.

3. Her **assiduous** reaction to winning a trip to Europe seemed snobbish, but in reality, she was blasé because she has already traveled to so many places.

4. The **copious** amount of food left in the house will hardly get us through the snowstorm this weekend.

5. Although I usually like to make plans ahead of time, there's nothing quite like going on a **spontaneous** trip and just seeing what happens.

6. The book had received many great reviews, but I found the writing far too **limpid** and incoherent for my tastes.

7. I try to **allocate** at least an hour of my day to reading for pleasure, since so many other duties often get in the way.

8. The soccer team had every right to **exult** in the locker room after experiencing the crushing defeat.

9. Because it was my birthday, I had an **inkling** that a surprise party was in store for me, but I did my best to act shocked when I entered the room.

10. The **rancor** between the two presidential candidates intensified as they each hurled insults at each other during the debate.

Choosing the Right Word

Select the **boldface** word that better completes each sentence. You might refer to the passage on pages 124–125 to see how most of these words are used in context. Note that the choices might be related forms of the Unit words.

1. George Gershwin's early songs gave only a dim (**inkling, allocation**) of the genius that was to express itself in *Porgy and Bess.*

2. Your simple, (**spontaneous, emaciated**) expression of appreciation meant more to me than all the elaborate, carefully phrased tributes I received.

3. Far from being effortless, her direct, (**limpid, copious**) writing style is the result of the most painstaking effort.

4. Our meeting last week was marred by a heated debate over how to (**allocate, exult**) the funds in this year's budget.

5. During the depression of the 1930s, the nation seemed to take strength from President Roosevelt's (**spontaneous, copious**) energy and enthusiasm.

6. Perhaps you have been treated unfairly, but what good will it do to allow your sense of (**inkling, rancor**) to control your mood and behavior?

7. The entire student body (**allocated, exulted**) when our team finally won the citywide basketball championship after years of losing to our bitter rivals.

8. In the concentration camps, the liberating troops found thousands of victims horribly (**limpid, emaciated**) as the result of starvation.

9. What she lacks in skill, she makes up for in (**assiduous, spontaneous**) attention to every last detail and requirement of the job.

10. During the scene in which the deer returns to the forest, leaving the young boy behind, our eyes filled with (**brash, copious**) tears.

11. To make an impression on his fiancée, the young man saved his money to purchase a large faceted diamond that was sparkling and (**limpid, emaciated**).

12. She was (**assiduous, brash**) enough to tell her mother she was going to the dance in spite of the doctor's orders.

Completing the Sentence

Choose the word from the word bank that best completes each of the following sentences. Write the correct word or form of the word in the space provided.

allocate	brash	emaciated	inkling	rancor
assiduous	copious	exult	limpid	spontaneous

1. General Grant accepted Lee's surrender with quiet dignity, refusing to _____ over the defeat of a worthy foe.

2. If you were as _____ in studying foreign affairs as you are in memorizing batting averages, you would have known how to reply to her comments on the situation in the Middle East.

3. How can you say that the audience's reaction was _____ when the director held up a sign reading "Applause"?

4. Wasn't it rather _____ of you to offer the soccer coach advice on your very first day as a candidate for the team?

5. Somewhere in a(n) _____ pool in the Canadian Rockies is the large trout that will someday grace the wall of my den.

6. Remembering my old friend as a robust 200-pounder, I was shocked to see how _____ he had become during his long illness.

7. As the speaker's voice droned on endlessly in the hot, crowded room, I suddenly realized that I hadn't the slightest _____ of what she was saying.

8. The teacher decided to _____ a corner of the classroom for an exhibition of student science projects.

9. Friends and relatives can be counted on to give _____ amounts of advice on child rearing to the parents of a new baby.

10. _____ is never so bitter as when it arises among people who were once close friends.

Synonyms

*Choose the word or form of the word from this Unit that is the same or most nearly the same in meaning as the **boldface** word or expression in the phrase. Write that word on the line. Use a dictionary if necessary.*

1. **celebrated** the news from the front _____

2. the survivors' **gaunt** faces _____

3. could find nothing **delectable** on the menu _____

4. **restitution** equal to our loss _____

5. **zealous** supporters of liberty _____

6. your **impromptu** display of affection _____

7. required **unremitting** attention _____

8. had no **clue** about the surprise party _____

9. **crooked** and weather-beaten fingers _____

10. asked **impertinent** questions _____

11. an **all-powerful** ruler _____

12. **apportioned** supplies to each member of the group _____

13. **juvenile** literary style _____

14. a **bittersweet** tale of love and loss _____

15. **diverge** from the path _____

Antonyms

*Choose the word or form of the word from this Unit that is most nearly opposite in meaning to the **boldface** word or expression in the phrase. Write that word on the line. Use a dictionary if necessary.*

1. a master of **dense** prose _____

2. noted the **goodwill** in her tone _____

3. were **rewarded** for their actions _____

4. a **meager** harvest _____

5. **consistent** with one's affections _____

Writing: Words in Action

Write a brief encyclopedia entry about the eruption of Vesuvius. Base your account on information from the diary entry (pages 124–125), but present the information from the third-person point of view. Include just the facts, without personal opinions. Use three or more words from this Unit to support your account.

Vocabulary in Context

*Some of the words you have studied in this Unit appear in **boldface** type. Read the passage below, and then circle the letter of the correct answer for each word as it is used in context.*

When Gaius Plinius Caecilius Secundus (c.62–c.115) lost his father in early childhood, he was adopted by his illustrious uncle, Gaius Plinius Secundus (23–79), cavalry commander and admiral of the fleet based in Misenum, at the northwestern tip of the Bay of Naples. His greatest achievement, however, was his *Natural History*, a 37-volume encyclopedia that aimed to describe in precise and **copious** detail the nature of the physical world. Gaius Plinius Secundus saw to it that his nephew had the finest teachers, was protected from the **brash** and the bothersome, and got to know the most powerful people in Rome. In time, nephew and uncle came to be known as Pliny the Younger and Pliny the Elder.

Pliny the Younger spent the summer of 79 in the port of Misenum. He studied assiduously and wrote **sophomoric** poetry, while his uncle oversaw repairs to the ships. In the early afternoon of August 24, an unusual cloud appeared across the bay. Many years later Pliny the Younger recalled that cloud in a letter to his friend Tacitus, the historian: It was, he wrote, "like an umbrella pine, for it rose to a great height on a sort of trunk and then split off into branches, I imagine because it was thrust upwards by the first blast and then left unsupported as the pressure subsided." The cloud was volcanic ash from Mount Vesuvius as it buried the city of Pompeii.

This letter is one of a series that forms an intensely personal and often **poignant** narrative of the eruption—and perhaps creates a sort of **indemnity** for Pliny the Younger's loss. The letter describes his uncle's initial scholarly interest in the eruption and how he **allocated** boats to evacuate those in danger. It also pays tribute to his uncle's courage as he sailed into the firestorm to save lives, but lost his own.

---

1. If details are **copious**, they are
   a. sufficient
   b. abundant
   c. superfluous
   d. accurate

2. To be **brash** is to be
   a. intermittent
   b. overrated
   c. ridiculous
   d. impetuous

3. The word **sophomoric** most nearly means
   a. precocious
   b. superficial
   c. incomplete
   d. creative

4. To find something **poignant** is to be
   a. moved by it
   b. depressed by it
   c. soothed by it
   d. amused by it

5. An **indemnity** is a
   a. compensation
   b. repayment
   c. punishment
   d. pardon

6. To **allocate** is to
   a. assign
   b. ignore
   c. sail
   d. board

Vocabulary for Comprehension
Part 1

*Read this passage, which contains words in **boldface** that appear in Units 7–9. Then choose the best answer to each question based on what is stated or implied in the passage. You may refer to the passage as often as necessary.*

Questions 1–10 are based on the following passage.

The passage is adapted from the novel *Shirley*, by Charlotte Brontë. Originally published in 1849. The novel is set during the period 1811–1815, when craftsmen and laborers known as Luddites mounted attacks on mills and factories that used machinery for tasks formerly assigned to their workers.

The highroad was now to be quitted, as the remaining distance to Hollow's Mill might be considerably reduced by a shortcut across fields. These fields

(5) were level and monotonous, and so, determined not to **deviate** from his goal, Malone took a direct course through them, jumping hedge and wall. He passed but one building here, and that seemed large

(10) and hall-like, though irregular. You could see a high gable, then a long front, then a low gable, then a thick, lofty stack of chimneys. It was dark, and not a candle shone from any window. It was absolutely

(15) still, and the rain ran from the eaves, and the rather **turbulent** but very low whistle of the wind round the chimneys and through the boughs were the sole sounds in its neighborhood.

(20) This building passed and the fields, hitherto flat, declined in a rapid descent. Evidently a vale lay below, through which you could hear the water run. One light could be **discerned** in the **somber** depth,

(25) and for that beacon Malone steered.

He came to a little white house—you could see it was white even through this dense darkness—and knocked at the door. A fresh-faced, **assiduous** servant

(30) opened it, and by the candle she held was revealed a narrow passage, terminating in a narrow stair. Two doors covered with crimson fabric, a strip of crimson carpet down the steps,

(35) contrasted with light-colored walls and white floor, made the little interior look clean and fresh.

"Mr. Moore is at home, I suppose?"

"Yes, sir, but he is not in."

(40) "Not in! Where is he then?"

"At the mill—in the counting-house."

Here one of the crimson doors opened.

"Are the wagons come, Sarah?" asked a female voice, and a female head at the

(45) same time was apparent. It might not be the head of a goddess, indeed a screw of curl-paper on each side the temples quite forbade that supposition, but neither was it the head of a Gorgon, though

(50) **apprehensive** Malone seemed to take it in the latter light. Big as he was, he shrank bashfully back into the rain at the view thereof, and saying, "I'll go to him," hurried in seeming trepidation down a

(55) short lane, across an obscure yard, towards a **commodious** black mill.

The work-hours were over, the "hands" were gone, the machinery was at rest, the mill shut up. Malone walked round it and

(60) somewhere in its great sooty flank he found another **parsimonious** chink of light, and he knocked at another door, using for the purpose the thick end of his shillelagh, with which he beat a rousing

(65) tattoo. A key turned, and the door unclosed.

"Is it Joe Scott? What news of the wagons, Joe?"

"No; it's myself. Mr. Helstone would

(70) send me."

"Oh! Mr. Malone." The voice in uttering this name had the slightest possible **inkling** of disappointment, but after a moment's pause it continued—

(75)   "I beg you will come in, Mr. Malone, and I regret extremely Mr. Helstone should have thought it necessary to trouble you so far. There was no necessity—I told him so—and on

(80)   such a night, but walk forwards."

1. The primary purpose of the passage is to
A) describe the obstacles encountered by Malone on his visit to Mr. Moore.
B) explain why the workers at Hollow's Mill disliked Mr. Moore.
C) lead up to a nighttime meeting between Malone and Mr. Moore.
D) show Malone as courageous and Mr. Moore as cowardly.

2. As it is used in line 6, "deviate" most nearly means
A) stray.
B) abide.
C) propel.
D) align.

3. Overall, the description of the setting in lines 13–19 inspire a mood of
A) trepidation.
B) suspense.
C) melancholy.
D) hilarity.

4. Malone's state of mind in lines 38–56 can best be described as changing from
A) proud to embarrassed.
B) patient to impatient.
C) calm to angry.
D) confident to shy.

5. Which choice provides the best evidence for the answer to the previous question?
A) Lines 26–32 ("He came . . . stair")
B) Lines 38–40 ("Mr. Moore . . . then")
C) Lines 42–45 ("Here one . . . apparent")
D) Lines 51–56 ("Big as . . . mill")

6. As it used in line 50, "apprehensive" most nearly means
A) confident.
B) jittery.
C) insightful.
D) fanciful.

7. The "hands" in line 57, refer to
A) the hands of the mill clock.
B) textile machinery.
C) the mill workers.
D) Moore's relatives.

8. Which of the following statements is supported by the passage?
A) Malone is in love with the woman with curl papers in her hair.
B) Mr. Moore is suspicious of Malone and his intentions.
C) Mr. Moore is expecting wagons at the mill late at night.
D) Mr. Helstone sent Malone to interfere with Mr. Moore's plans.

9. As it is used in line 61, "parsimonious" most nearly means
A) meager.
B) opulent.
C) sumptuous.
D) satisfactory.

10. It can reasonably be inferred from the dialogue in lines 67–80 that
A) Mr. Moore told Mr. Helstone not to send Malone to the mill no matter what.
B) Mr. Moore warmly welcomed Malone.
C) Both Mr. Moore and Sarah were expecting the wagons to arrive at the mill.
D) Malone's errand at the mill seemed puzzling and worrisome to Mr. Moore.

Vocabulary for Comprehension
Part 2

*Read this passage, which contains words in **boldface** that appear in Units 7–9. Then choose the best answer to each question based on what is stated or implied in the passage. You may refer to the passage as often as necessary.*

Questions 1–10 are based on the following passage.

This passage is adapted from the novel *Evelina*, by Frances Burney. Published in 1778. Mrs. Mirvan is the daughter of the letter-writer, Lady Howard. Maria is Mrs. Mirvan's daughter. Rev. Mr. Villars is Evelina's guardian. Madame Duval is Evelina's grandmother.

LADY HOWARD TO THE REV. MR. VILLARS Howard Grove, March 26.

Be not alarmed, my worthy friend, at my troubling you again; I seldom wait for
(5) answers, or write with any regularity, and I have at present immediate occasion for begging your patience.

Mrs. Mirvan, my daughter, has just received a letter from her long absent
(10) husband, containing the welcome news of his reaching London by the beginning of next week. My daughter and the Captain have been separated almost seven years, and it would therefore be needless to
(15) say what joy, surprise, and consequently confusion, his at present unexpected return has caused at our house. Mrs. Mirvan, you may infer, will go instantly to town to meet him; her daughter, Maria,
(20) is under a thousand obligations to attend her; I grieve that I cannot.

And now, my good Sir, I am **brash** to ask, and almost blush to proceed; but, tell me, may I ask—will you permit—that your child
(25) may accompany Mrs. Mirvan and Maria? Our life here is **ingenuous**, so consider the many inducements which conspire to make London the happiest place at present that your child can **exult** in. The joyful occasion
(30) of the journey; the **revels** of the whole party, opposed to the dull life she must

lead, if left here with me, a **decrepit** old woman, for her sole companion, while she so well knows the cheerfulness and felicity
(35) enjoyed by the rest of the family—are circumstances that seem to merit your consideration. Mrs. Mirvan desires me to assure you that one week is all she **allocates** for the trip, as she is certain
(40) that the Captain, her husband, who hates London, will be eager to revisit our home at Howard Grove; and Maria is so very earnest in wishing to have the company of her friend, that, if you are **recalcitrant**, she
(45) will be deprived of the **copious** pleasures she otherwise hopes to receive.

However, I will not deceive you into an opinion that they intend to live in a retired manner, as that cannot be fairly expected.
(50) But allow me to **obviate** any uneasiness you may have concerning Evelina's grandmother, Madame Duval; she has not any correspondent in England, and obtains no intelligence but by common
(55) report. She must be a stranger to the name your child bears; and, even should she hear of this excursion, so short a time in town upon so particular an occasion, though previous to their meeting, cannot
(60) be construed into disrespect to herself.

Mrs. Mirvan desires me to assure you, that if you will oblige her, the two children shall equally share her time and her attention. She has sent a commission to a
(65) friend in town to take a house for her; and while she waits for an answer concerning it, I shall wait for one from you to our petition. However, your child is writing herself; and that, I doubt not, will more
(70) avail than all we can possibly urge.

My daughter desires her best compliments to you if, she says, you will

grant her request but not else. Adieu, my dear Sir, we all hope everything from
(75) your **ardent** goodness.

M. HOWARD.

1. Which choice best summarizes the letter?
   A) Lady Howard asks Mr. Villars to allow his child to accompany her daughter and granddaughter on a short trip to London.
   B) Lady Howard tells Mr. Villars about her daughter's husband's return to London after an absence of seven years.
   C) Lady Howard asks Mrs. Mirvan to accompany Mr. Villars's child on a brief but joyful journey to Howard Grove.
   D) Lady Howard desires the Captain to allow Mrs. Mirvan, Maria, and her friend to enjoy a week in London.

2. It can reasonably be inferred from the first paragraph of the letter (lines 3–7) that Lady Howard is
   A) reclusive and inactive.
   B) domineering and overbearing.
   C) impulsive and unpredictable.
   D) indecisive and forgetful.

3. As it is used in line 26, "ingenuous" most nearly means
   A) dangerous.
   B) simple.
   C) dull.
   D) hectic.

4. As it is used in line 29, "exult" most nearly means
   A) lament.
   B) rejoice.
   C) yearn.
   D) regret.

5. The letter indicates that Lady Howard wishes she could
   A) accompany the Mirvans to London.
   B) meet Mr. Villars and Mrs. Mirvan in London.
   C) prevent Maria from going to London.
   D) persuade Mr. Villars to meet his child in London.

6. As it is used in line 45, "copious" most nearly means
   A) benign.
   B) apparent.
   C) abundant.
   D) worrisome.

7. Which strategy does Lady Howard use in order to persuade Mr. Villars?
   A) Contrasting the excitement and gaiety of London with the dull routine of Evelina's everyday life at Howard Grove
   B) Emphasizing the Mirvans' influential connections in high society
   C) Stressing that Captain Mirvan will be greatly disappointed if Mr. Villars withholds his permission
   D) Showing that Madame Duval has been less than generous to Evelina

8. Which choice provides the best evidence for the answer to the previous question?
   A) Lines 3–7 ("Be not . . . patience.)
   B) Lines 12–21 ("My daughter . . . cannot")
   C) Lines 29–37 ("The joyful . . . consideration")
   D) Lines 47–49 ("However . . . expected")

9. In the fourth paragraph of the letter (lines 47–60), Mrs. Howard anticipates
   A) that Mr. Villars will willingly give his assent to the plan.
   B) Mr. Villar's objections based on the possibility of his child meeting Madame Duval.
   C) that the family may extend their stay in London to as long as two weeks.
   D) bad weather that may force the cancellation of the London expedition.

10. The tone of Lady Howard's letter to Mr. Villars is predominantly
    A) persuasive.
    B) ironic.
    C) enigmatic.
    D) jocular.

Synonyms

*From the word bank below, choose the word that has the same or nearly the same meaning as the **boldface** word in each sentence and write it on the line. You will not use all of the words.*

allocate	decrepit	limpid	quandary
commodious	emaciated	obsolete	rancor
condolence	gnarled	omnipotent	reprisal
corrosive	inkling	poignant	somber

1. The new commuter bus line is hoping to attract passengers by offering **comfortable** seating along with a movie and snacks. _____

2. That **rickety** old mansion is rumored to be haunted. _____

3. Novelists can write in all sorts of styles, but journalists should aim for straightforward, **lucid** prose. _____

4. The river's color changes with the changing sky; sometimes the water is a crisp steely-blue and sometimes it is a **drab** grayish-brown. _____

5. A good debate should focus on facts and substance while totally avoiding any form of personal attack or **bitterness**. _____

6. We have only one week to complete every part of the project, so we will have to manage it well and **allot** our time wisely. _____

7. The girl's family got their first **intimation** of her musical talent when she composed an impressive original song at age nine. _____

8. It can be frustrating when equipment that still works perfectly well becomes **outmoded** because the latest software cannot support it. _____

9. Because the pharaoh was **all-powerful**, no one dared to question his actions or decisions. _____

10. By tradition, poppies are a **heartrending** reminder of the soldiers who died in World War I. _____

11. Many people fear that the **spiteful** accusations that are being exchanged by the two governments will lead to a breakdown in the peace talks. _____

12. It can be difficult to write a note of **sympathy** to someone who has lost a parent, but the best approach is just to be caring and sincere. _____

Two-Word Completions

Select the pair of words that best completes the meaning of each of the following sentences.

1. Though I am perfectly willing to give praise where I feel praise is due, I refuse to _____ an action that I consider underhanded and _____.
   a. commend . . . reprehensible
   b. abhor . . . extant
   c. amend . . . apprehensive
   d. deride . . . sophomoric

2. "My years of foreign service have taught me to be as _____ as possible," the veteran diplomat observed, his tongue firmly in his cheek. "These days, turning up one's nose at another country's national dish, no matter how _____, might just trigger a very unpleasant international incident."
   a. omnivorous . . . unpalatable
   b. suave . . . chaotic
   c. compatible . . . squalid
   d. recalcitrant . . . disingenuous

3. As the storm's intensity increased, the calm waters of the lake became more and more _____. Strong gusts of wind slapped at our sails, and our tiny craft was _____ about like a golf ball in an electric blender.
   a. capricious . . . derided
   b. vociferous . . . waived
   c. turbulent . . . buffeted
   d. voluminous . . . deviated

4. It would be impossible for a career to _____ a person as dynamic and unstoppable as Claire. She has such _____ talents that, if she felt bored or unchallenged by one job, she could readily turn to another occupation.
   a. implicate . . . parsimonious
   b. stultify . . . multifarious
   c. chastise . . . capricious
   d. obviate . . . spontaneous

5. The soldiers who fell in the engagement were _____ in a portion of the battlefield on which they had fought. The spot where they were laid to rest was not technically "hallowed ground." Still, it was considered appropriate because they had, in effect, _____ it with their blood.
   a. chastised . . . waived
   b. discerned . . . commended
   c. implicated . . . buffeted
   d. interred . . . consecrated

6. Infuriated by their treacherous behavior, the enraged party leader severely _____ the _____ who had unexpectedly bolted to the opposition during the crucial vote.
   a. derided . . . revelers
   b. implicated . . . martinets
   c. consecrated . . . deviates
   d. chastised . . . renegades

7. I hoped that my project proposal would be hailed by my classmates with _____ enthusiasm. Instead, it was greeted with "deafening" _____.
   a. compatible . . . animosity
   b. vociferous . . . apathy
   c. sophomoric . . . indemnity
   d. copious . . . chaos

WORD STUDY

Idioms

In the passage about Emmeline Pankhurst (see pages 100–101), the author writes that Pankhurst liked to "shake things up"—an idiom that means "to create changes" or "to challenge the status quo." The idiom tells us that Pankhurst actively worked to bring about change.

An **idiom** is an expression, often a figure of speech, that conveys an action or idea in a colorful, clever way. Idiomatic expressions are important to everyday language, creating memorable images and serving as a kind of "shorthand" for getting meanings across. Idioms cannot be taken literally and may be hard to interpret if you try to simply analyze the meaning of each individual word. That is why it can be useful to memorize the meanings of common idioms.

Choosing the Right Idiom

*Read each sentence. Use context clues to figure out the meaning of each idiom in **boldface**. Then write the letter of the definition for the idiom in the sentence.*

1. Of course I know what Marisa scored on the test; I just heard it **straight from the horse's mouth**. _____

2. After Abe dropped the football five times, the coach really **chewed him out**. _____

3. Andrea always starts working on her reports **at the eleventh hour**; then she wonders why she gets so stressed. _____

4. I heard you were **in hot water** when your father found out you borrowed the car without asking. _____

5. Why don't you just **cut to the chase** and tell me why you won't come to my party? _____

6. I've been on **pins and needles** waiting to find out how I did on the SAT. _____

7. It's your first day at work, so I am assigning Jade to **show you the ropes**. _____

8. The doctor reported that the hit-and-run victim is recovering, but she is still not **out of the woods**. _____

9. When you move, you have to **get your ducks in a row**: pack, hire a mover, close your bank account, cancel your utilities, and fill out change of address forms. _____

10. My four-year-old sister talks all the time and just **drives me up a wall**. _____

a. become well organized

b. get to the point quickly

c. free from danger

d. provide basic instruction

e. feeling very nervous

f. yelled at and criticized

g. at the last possible minute

h. irritates or annoys

i. from the most reliable authority; from a firsthand source

j. in serious trouble

Classical Roots

voc, vok—to call

This root appears in **vociferous,** "loud or noisy" (page 106). Some other words based on the same root are listed below.

advocate	convocation	evoke	revoke
avocation	equivocal	invoke	vocalize

From the list of words above, choose the one that corresponds to each of the brief definitions below. Write the word in the blank space in the illustrative sentence below the definition. Use an online or print dictionary if necessary.

1. a meeting, especially of members of a college or clergy (*"a calling together"*)
   The President will attend the _____ of world leaders.

2. to call forth; bring to mind (*"to call out"*)
   The tone of the poem *La Mer* _____ the sounds of the sea.

3. to plead in favor of; one who defends a cause; one who pleads the cause of another
   Our senators _____ reform of the tax code.

4. to bring or call back; to annul by recalling
   A judge can _____ the license of a driver who has a record of repeated violations.

5. an occupation or activity pursued for enjoyment, in addition to one's regular work; a hobby
   Bird-watching can be a lifelong _____.

6. open to two or more interpretations, ambiguous; uncertain or doubtful in nature
   The reporter's pointed question drew an _____ response from the candidate.

7. to call in for help or support; to appeal to as an authority; to put into effect; to make an earnest request for (*"to call on"*)
   The lawyer tried to _____ the sympathy of the jurors.

8. to give voice to; to sing without words
   Therapists encourage their patients to _____ their hopes and fears.

*Read the following passage, taking note of the **boldface** words and their contexts. These words are among those you will be studying in Unit 10. It may help you to complete the exercises in this Unit if you refer to the way the words are used below.*

Hakoah Athletes: From Strength to Victory
<Historical Nonfiction>

By the mid-1930s, while swimmer Judith Deutsch was still an Austrian teenager, the **sinuous** freestyle form that she brought to competition had enabled her to claim every women's middle- and long-distance record in her country. She was awarded Austria's prestigious Golden Badge of Honor in 1936. It was not a surprise, then, when Deutsch was chosen to represent her nation in that year's Summer Olympics in Berlin; the surprise was that Deutsch refused to compete at those games. The **allure** of Olympic gold had a less powerful hold on her than the Jewish athlete's moral convictions. "I refuse to enter a contest in a land which so shamefully persecutes my people," she stated, publicly protesting the German Nazis' politics of hatred.

The pressure on the 17-year-old swimmer was enormous, but Deutsch refused to **acquiesce**. Calm and displaying a **sonorous**

dignity when she spoke, she stood firm in her protest against the treatment of Jews by Germany's new führer, Adolph Hitler, thus infuriating the Nazis allied with Germany. In **retribution**, the Austrian government banished Deutsch from all competition. Soon, the Austrian authorities expunged her many victories from their record books as well. In an abhorrent time, hers was a righteous human act.

To those who believe there's no education like adversity, it would seem fitting that Deutsch got her athletic training from an organization founded as a bulwark against prejudice. Hakoah was a Jewish sports club started in Vienna in 1909, a time of **contentious** Aryan Laws that barred organizations from including Jewish participants. The founders of Hakoah were **exponents** of political views **professed** by the Hungarian social critic Max Nordau. He believed that "muscular Judaism" was a way to challenge the widely

Judith Deutsch as a 17-year-old swimmer

The Hakoah swim team with their coach

held image of the intellectual but physically weak Jew. The name chosen for the sports organization, *Hakoah*, was thus no **misnomer**. The word means "strength." Hakoah encouraged its members to train vigorously in order to demolish this damaging stereotype. Respect, as much as winning, is what its athletes **coveted**.

Hakoah Vienna grew rapidly, and by the 1920s, it had become one of Austria's largest sports clubs. Members found there not only a stage upon which to exhibit their athletic prowess, but also a **respite** from the growing anti-Semitism of their time. As a result, Hakoah was in the **vanguard** of community and civil rights groups, serving as a model for the many that followed.

Judith Deutsch is only one of Hakoah Vienna's success stories. Many other club athletes ranked among the finest in early 20th century Europe. Consider the 1923 men's soccer team. Its players traveled to England and defeated the fierce West Ham United players. If the humbled West Ham athletes and their fans were **crestfallen**, the victorious Jewish players were jubilant; they became the first visiting team to defeat a British squad on its own soil. Two years later, the same team won Austria's national championship. And at the 1932 Olympics in Los Angeles, Hakoah wrestler Micky Hirschl earned two medals.

After the Nazi takeover of Austria in 1938, life for Jews in Vienna became untenable as the Nazis intensified their anti-Semitic campaign. Hakoah Vienna was forced to disband. Friendships and connections forged during the club's heyday enabled many of its members to flee what was first seen as **lamentable**, then became deadly, persecution. A tip from Hakoah's swim-team president, for example, saved the life of a young swimmer named Fred Marcus. After escaping the Nazis, Marcus was placed aboard a ship, alone, to Uruguay. There he became a celebrated swimming and diving champion before emigrating to the United States.

Watermarks, a documentary film from 2004, examines the rise and fall of Hakoah Vienna and its athletes. The poignant return to the pool, where Deutsch and other members of the women's swim team had once **blithely** spent many youthful hours, shows the emotional reunion, after 65 years apart, of many of these extraordinary athletes. In celebrating both the athletes and the organization that brought them together at a dangerous time in history, the film is a powerful tribute, one that is more lasting than any medal or trophy.

Audio

For iWords and audio passages, go to SadlierConnect.com.

The Hakoah men's soccer team, 1928

Definitions

Note the spelling, pronunciation, part(s) of speech, and definition(s) of each of the following words. Then write the appropriate form of the word in the blank space in the illustrative sentence(s) following.

1. acquiesce
(ak wē es')

(*v.*) to accept without protest; to agree or submit

Management is not likely to _____ to union demands for raises because the company's profits have recently been on the decline.

2. blithe
(blīth)

(*adj.*) cheerful, lighthearted; casual, unconcerned

It is difficult to deflate the _____ optimism of the young.

3. crestfallen
(krest' fô lən)

(*adj.*) discouraged, dejected, downcast

Despite the loss of an important labor endorsement, the candidate appeared in no way _____.

4. disheveled
(di shev' əld)

(*adj.*) rumpled, mussed; hanging in disorder

Most people look a little bit _____ when they get up in the morning.

5. garrulous
(gar' ə ləs)

(*adj.*) given to much talking, tediously chatty

If you are conversing with a _____ individual, you may find it hard to get a word in edgewise.

6. misnomer
(mis nō' mər)

(*n.*) an unsuitable or misleading name

The term *World Series* is a _____ because only North American teams participate in this annual event.

7. profess
(prə fes')

(*v.*) to affirm openly; to state belief in; to claim, pretend

My music teacher _____ herself satisfied with my technical progress so far this year.

8. retribution
(re trə byü' shən)

(*n.*) a repayment; a deserved punishment

In most ancient societies _____ was swiftly visited on those who broke their promises.

9. **sonorous**
(sə nôr′ əs)

(*adj.*) full, deep, or rich in sound; impressive in style
The _____ tolling of church bells announced the passing of the monarch.

10. **wastrel**
(wās′ trəl)

(*n.*) a wasteful person, spendthrift; a good-for-nothing
Many a novel has told the sorry tale of a charming but self-destructive _____.

Using Context

*For each item, determine whether the **boldface** word from pages 146–147 makes sense in the context of the sentence. Circle the item numbers next to the six sentences in which the words are used correctly.*

1. In the painting, a knight kneels before a king and queen to **profess** his loyalty.

2. Because the word *starfish* is something of a **misnomer**, most people now refer to these invertebrate marine creatures as *sea stars*.

3. Frankly, your **blithe** attitude seems inappropriate during this serious time.

4. The weary travelers were **crestfallen** at the news that their connecting flight was indefinitely delayed.

5. The traveler said she preferred not to take the ferry because any kind of boat ride left her feeling queasy and **disheveled**.

6. The invitation to the **garrulous** annual event indicated that guests were expected to be in formal attire.

7. The long, **sonorous** essay was badly in need of editing.

8. In Greek mythology, a figure named Nemesis is the goddess of revenge and **retribution**.

9. Before we rescued our dog Buddy, he was a skinny, homeless **wastrel** who wandered the streets and would often try to follow people home.

10. The mayor's office is expected to **acquiesce** to the reporter's request for an interview.

Choosing the Right Word

Select the **boldface** word that better completes each sentence. You might refer to the passage on pages 144–145 to see how most of these words are used in context. Note that the choices might be related forms of the Unit words.

1. The poet Shelley, entranced by the joyous song of the skylark, addressed the bird as "(**garrulous, blithe**) spirit."

2. The wicked may seem to prosper, but I am convinced that sometime, somehow, in this life or the next, there will be (**misnomer, retribution**).

3. Although we really don't agree with Mother's musical taste, we decided to (**profess, acquiesce**) to her appeal and get tickets to the concert.

4. Since Ben was confident he could play varsity ball, he was extremely (**blithe, crestfallen**) when the coach cut him from the squad.

5. It would be a (**misnomer, retribution**) to label as biography a book that is clearly a work of fiction, even though its main character is historical.

6. Because it was the duty of town criers to deliver public proclamations, they were often chosen for their (**sonorous, crestfallen**) voices.

7. She should have known that Andre was a (**wastrel, retribution**), unworthy of her attentions, when he announced that he had no interest in holding a job.

8. When we ended up in the lake, we realized that the skipper was not the expert boatman he (**acquiesced, professed**) to be.

9. With hair styles what they are these days, many men now seem to look somewhat (**disheveled, garrulous**) when they come home fresh from the barber.

10. The church bells could be heard (**sonorously, blithely**) ringing through the valley, announcing the end of the war.

11. Anyone who spends hours, days, and weeks just hanging around is a (**wastrel, misnomer**) with the most precious thing we have—*time*.

12. The taxi driver was so (**disheveled, garrulous**) during the long trip that it was a relief to return to my silent hotel room.

Completing the Sentence

Choose the word from the word bank that best completes each of the following sentences. Write the correct word or form of the word in the space provided.

acquiesce	crestfallen	garrulous	profess	sonorous
blithe	disheveled	misnomer	retribution	wastrel

1. Excessively _____ people usually don't have the imagination to realize that their endless chatter is boring everyone else.

2. The _____ personality that had made her so charming and popular was unaffected by the passage of the years.

3. The body of the slain hero was accompanied to its final resting place by the _____ strains of a funeral march.

4. After I heard my new parrot's harsh call, I decided that "Melody," the name I had planned for it, was something of a(n) _____.

5. I do not _____ to be heroic, but I hope I have the nerve to stand up for unpopular ideas that I believe are right.

6. It isn't likely that the school administration will _____ to your recommendation to do away with all examinations and grades.

7. In spite of her rain-soaked clothing and _____ appearance, it seemed to me that she had never looked lovelier.

8. For the innumerable crimes and cruelties he had committed, the tyrant had good reason to fear _____.

9. He says that he is spending the family fortune "to promote the art of good living " but I consider him no more than a(n) _____.

10. After all my high hopes, I was utterly _____ when the notice arrived that I had failed my driver's test.

Definitions

Note the spelling, pronunciation, part(s) of speech, and definition(s) of each of the following words. Then write the appropriate form of the word in the blank space in the illustrative sentence(s) following.

1. allure
(a lür′)

(*v.*) to entice, tempt; to be attractive to; (*n.*) a strong attraction; the power to attract, charm

Dreams of stardom _____ many gifted young performers from all over the country to the bright lights of Broadway.

The _____ of get-rich-quick schemes may lead people down the road to financial ruin.

2. askew
(ə skyü′)

(*adj., adv.*) twisted to one side, crooked; disapprovingly

Some people cannot refrain from straightening lampshades that are a little _____.

All our plans for a picnic on the beach went suddenly _____ when it began to rain very heavily.

3. contentious
(kən ten′ shəs)

(*adj.*) quarrelsome, inclined to argue

The members of the on-line discussion group were annoyed by the newcomer's _____ and rude remarks.

4. covet
(kəv′ ət)

(*v.*) to desire something belonging to another

Those who _____ the good fortune of others are likely to be unhappy with their own lot in life.

5. exponent
(ek spō′ nənt)

(*n.*) one who advocates, speaks for, explains, or interprets; (*math*) the power to which a number, symbol, or expression is to be raised

President Theodore Roosevelt was one of the first _____ of conservation.

In the equation $x^2 + y^2 = z^2$, the small raised 2s are all _____.

6. insuperable
(in sü′ pər ə bəl)

(*adj.*) incapable of being overcome

To the composer Ludwig van Beethoven, increasing deafness was not an _____ handicap.

7. lamentable
(lam′ ən tə bəl)

(*adj.*) to be regretted or pitied

After a long, hard winter, city streets may be in a truly _____ state of disrepair.

8. **respite**
(res′ pit)

(*n.*) a period of relief or rest

A vacation provides a _____ from the worries and responsibilities of everyday life.

9. **sinuous**
(sin′ yü əs)

(*adj.*) winding, having many curves; lithe and flexible

The trunk of the tree was almost completely encased by _____ wisteria vines.

10. **vanguard**
(van′ gärd)

(*n.*) the foremost part of an army; the leading position in any field

If a high-tech company is to survive in today's marketplace, it must remain in the _____ of innovation.

Using Context

*For each item, determine whether the **boldface** word from pages 150–151 makes sense in the context of the sentence. Circle the item numbers next to the six sentences in which the words are used correctly.*

1. To see bright, young people give up on their dreams is truly **lamentable**.

2. While most people were done with the race within the hour, the officials had to wait for the last few **vanguards** to cross the finish line before declaring the race over.

3. My father glanced at me **askew** when I suggested my homework could wait until after I watched TV.

4. Those who **covet** the lives of others so intensely can't even appreciate their own achievements.

5. After hearing him complain for hours, I was grateful for the **respite** from his chatter when he had to take a phone call.

6. The smell of breakfast cooking is usually all it takes to **allure** me to the kitchen table.

7. The **exponents** of the new bill staged a protest outside the statehouse.

8. While listening to the **insuperable** lecture, which was full of information I already knew, I nearly fell asleep.

9. I try to avoid her when she's in a **contentious** mood and will attack everything I say.

10. Her **sinuous** build hinted at the strict running routine that she kept.

Choosing the Right Word

Select the **boldface** word that better completes each sentence. You might refer to the passage on pages 144–145 to see how most of these words are used in context. Note that the choices might be related forms of the Unit words.

1. The (**vanguard, allure**) of "gold in them thar hills" brought many immigrants to California in 1849.

2. The (**sinuous, insuperable**) road to Hana is both unnerving and breathtaking.

3. With her lipstick smeared, her hair disarranged, and her hat (**askew, lamentable**), she certainly was a strange sight.

4. His willingness to experiment with interesting new ideas clearly put him in the (**vanguard, exponent**) of social reform in his time.

5. Walking out on the empty stage and speaking the opening lines of the play seemed a(n) (**covetous, insuperable**) difficulty to the young actors.

6. After we had been playing our favorite music at top volume for several hours, Mother entered the room and begged for some (**respite, allure**).

7. As I watched the gymnastic meet on TV, nothing impressed me more than the incredibly graceful and (**askew, sinuous**) movements of the athletes.

8. Marshall McLuhan, a leading (**allure, exponent**) of TV's importance in modern life, coined the phrase "the medium is the message."

9. Seeking (**vanguard, respite**) from the cold weather, the hikers entered the cave and immediately built a small fire.

10. Wasteful use of energy at a time when there is a critical shortage of such resources is indeed (**lamentable, insuperable**).

11. He is so (**contentious, sinuous**) that if someone says "Nice day," he'll start a full-scale debate on the weather.

12. The intently longing gaze that he fixed upon my plate told me that Rover (**allured, coveted**) my lunch.

Completing the Sentence

Choose the word from the word bank that best completes each of the following sentences. Write the correct word or form of the word in the space provided.

allure	**contentious**	**exponent**	**lamentable**	**sinuous**
askew	**covet**	**insuperable**	**respite**	**vanguard**

1. With the publication of her famous book *Silent Spring*, Rachel Carson moved into the _____ of those seeking to protect our natural environment.

2. A staunch believer in the equality of the sexes, Susan B. Anthony was one of the most effective _____ of women's rights.

3. Retailers who seek to _____ unwary consumers with false claims should feel the full penalties of the law.

4. You certainly have a right to your opinions, but you have become so _____ that you immediately challenge opinions expressed by anyone else.

5. We can all agree that the crime situation in this community is truly _____, but what are we going to do about it?

6. "The blinds are hanging _____ because the pull cord is all knotted and tangled," I said.

7. The pioneers succeeded in settling the West because they refused to admit that any obstacle, however formidable, was _____.

8. Driving a car along those _____ mountain roads at a height of ten thousand feet calls for stronger nerves than I have.

9. Now that the football season has ended, don't you think our school's athletes deserve a brief _____ before beginning basketball practice?

10. I confess I suffered a twinge of envy when I learned that my rival had won the prize I had _____ so dearly.

Synonyms

*Choose the word or form of the word from this Unit that is the same or most nearly the same in meaning as the **boldface** word or expression in the phrase. Write that word on the line. Use a dictionary if necessary.*

1. a **serpentine** river flowing to sea _____

2. a well-known **defender** of human rights _____

3. proved to be something of a **squanderer** _____

4. **a breather** from the hectic city _____

5. **payback** for a life of crime _____

6. had a **combative** disposition _____

7. the **front line** of medical science _____

8. awoken by his **resounding** voice _____

9. **desire** the leading role _____

10. a **long-winded** talk show host _____

11. advised to **yield** and retreat _____

12. looking **unkempt** and confused _____

13. a commonly used **inappropriate name** _____

14. a still-life arrangement that seemed **off-kilter** _____

15. faced **unbeatable** odds _____

Antonyms

*Choose the word or form of the word from this Unit that is most nearly opposite in meaning to the **boldface** word or expression in the phrase. Write that word on the line. Use a dictionary if necessary.*

1. **disavowed** her allegiance _____

2. was **elated** when the results were tallied _____

3. **commendable** test scores _____

4. had a **glum** attitude about his job prospects _____

5. **repelled** by the prospect of anonymity _____

Writing: Words in Action

Think about Judith Deutsch's hopes and ambitions as an athlete. Do you think she made the right decision by refusing to participate in the Summer Olympics in Berlin? Write a brief essay explaining why or why not. Support your position using at least two details from the passage (pages 144–145) and three or more Unit words.

Vocabulary in Context

*Some of the words you have studied in this Unit appear in **boldface** type. Read the passage below, and then circle the letter of the correct answer for each word as it is used in context.*

By 1936, anti-Semitism was the official policy of the Nazi Party. Under the Nuremberg Laws of 1935, Jewish Germans had been stripped of their citizenship and reduced to the status of "state subjects." In Hitler's **garrulous** autobiography and political manifesto, the dictator's grasp of history was characteristically **askew**, but his dislike of people of African heritage was quite clear. Even so, by 1936 the Nazis had formulated no coherent policy with regard to Afro-Germans—probably because there were so few of them. Senior advisors in the party recommended a total ban on black athletes in the Berlin Olympics, but the number of athletes boycotting the Games had already compromised their legitimacy and Hitler was afraid a total ban would cause more countries to withdraw. Besides, he sincerely believed that German athletes were **insuperable**, and expected them to trounce every non-Aryan "**wastrel**" who dared to challenge them.

Meanwhile, there were 10 African American athletes on the United States team who could not wait to disprove Hitler's notions of Aryan supremacy. The issue of American involvement in the Games had been **contentious**. Many people felt that participation would legitimize the Nazi regime. Others, like Avery Brundage of the U. S. Olympic Committee (who had once won American hearts as a **disheveled** teenage track star), insisted that politics had no place in sports. Brundage prevailed.

The 10 African American athletes left Berlin with seven gold medals, three silver, and three bronze. Four gold medals were won by one man: Jesse Owens—an achievement that Hitler acknowledged by leaving the stadium. And in November 1936, the Nuremberg Laws expanded their discriminatory policies to include Afro-Germans.

---

1. A **garrulous** person
   a. is too loud
   b. makes friends easily
   c. talks too much
   d. knows a lot

2. The word **askew** most nearly means
   a. honest
   b. twisted
   c. ignorant
   d. wishful

3. An **insuperable** opponent is
   a. unbeatable
   b. overbearing
   c. arrogant
   d. vulnerable

4. A **wastrel** is a
   a. thief
   b. man-about-town
   c. good-for-nothing
   d. liar

5. If an issue is **contentious**, it is
   a. not open to debate
   b. undecided
   c. indisputable
   d. controversial

6. The word **disheveled** most nearly means
   a. carefree
   b. mussed
   c. long
   d. unstylish

*Read the following passage, taking note of the **boldface** words and their contexts. These words are among those you will be studying in Unit 11. It may help you to complete the exercises in this Unit if you refer to the way the words are used below.*

Should Government Sponsor the Arts?
<Debate>

Members of Alvin Ailey
American Dance Theater

Moderator: Today's topic for the debate teams of Central High School and Western High School is this one: *Be it resolved, that government should provide sponsorship of the arts.* Central High is taking the Affirmative, which has first response, and Western High will take the Negative. This debate is being broadcast over local public radio by Central High's student DJs.

Affirmative: Without government subsidies, arts such as regional dance companies, local playhouses, and art institutes face **stark** and unpleasant futures. Museums will be unable to maintain their artistic **integrity** if they have to **placate** wealthy donors who possess a merely **superficial** knowledge of art—or no knowledge at all. Artists could not afford to take the risks that come with new and innovative art forms, and cultural and societal decline will be the inevitable result. Art is the daughter of freedom, and a country should be proud to support it.

Negative: There are many **potent** arguments against government sponsorship of the arts. Our national test scores are far lower than those of other countries with **exemplary** education systems. Government cannot ignore the fact that schools need more funds for math and science

programs. It is wrong to take tax money from where it is desperately needed—to fund extra classes and school lunches—and fritter it away on elitist pastimes.

Affirmative: It is difficult to **fathom** what would happen if government withdrew its support. One would have to be **clairvoyant** to foresee all of the consequences. No doubt, museums would have to charge admissions. The opposing side **alluded** to children on school lunches, and those same children might never go to a museum because of the cost. Our shared wealth of culture and beauty would be shut off to the average person—a clear disadvantage to the very people the opposing side wishes to support.

Negative: There are dangers inherent in government subsidies for the arts—and not just the fact that the money might support projects some citizens find **disreputable** and **obnoxious**. History proves that government patronage can backfire if it is just a **pretext** for making artists promote a regime's goals and values. In the past, artists worked to please the monarchs who paid them and, more recently, subsidized artists disseminated the ideologies of tyrants and dictators.

Furthermore, a responsible government should use its limited funds where the needs and **endemic** problems are greatest. The best arts organizations will sustain themselves through the powers of the free market and, if they cannot, they **misconstrue** their importance to society. One example of such a policy is the case of the local public radio station. When government support for this station was withdrawn, listeners contributed money to the station, and it is still on the airways.

Affirmative: It is easy to recognize the connection between defunding the arts and the disintegration of social structure. Consider the example of one county that cut funding for its after-school choral society. Low-income students who took part in this activity at no cost had higher GPAs than the county's average. When the county defunded

The Stuyvesant High School Chamber Choir

the program, 75 percent of the choral members saw their GPAs drop, and some former members were turned down for scholarships they had been on track to receive. This is **conclusive** evidence that supporting the arts is money well spent.

Moderator: Thank you. Our judge will now consider your arguments and determine the winner of today's debate.

Audio

For ¡Words and audio passages, go to SadlierConnect.com.

Students work as radio DJs.

Definitions

Note the spelling, pronunciation, part(s) of speech, and definition(s) of each of the following words. Then write the appropriate form of the word in the blank space in the illustrative sentence(s) following.

1. conclusive
(kən klü′ siv)

(*adj.*) serving to settle an issue; final
When they weighed all the evidence in the case, the members of the jury found the testimony of the expert witness to be _____.

2. disreputable
(dis rep′ yə tə bəl)

(*adj.*) not respectable, not esteemed
Supermarket tabloids frequently publish stories about the _____ behavior of celebrities.

3. exemplary
(eg zem′ plə rē)

(*adj.*) worthy of imitation, commendable; serving as a model
The Medal of Freedom is awarded to U.S. civilians for _____ achievements in various fields.

4. fathom
(fath′ əm)

(*v.*) to understand, get to the bottom of; to determine the depth of; (*n.*) a measure of depth in water
It is sometimes difficult to _____ the motives behind another person's actions.
The great passenger liner *Titanic* still lies buried several thousand _____ beneath the ocean's surface.

5. integrity
(in teg′ rə tē)

(*n.*) honesty, high moral standards; an unimpaired condition, completeness, soundness
Scholars debated the _____ of the text of a newly discovered poem attributed to Shakespeare.

6. misconstrue
(mis kən strü′)

(*v.*) to interpret wrongly, mistake the meaning of
Young children sometimes _____ their parents' motives.

7. placid
(plas′ id)

(*adj.*) calm, peaceful
There was no wind to disturb the _____ surface of the lake.

8. protrude
(prō trüd′)

(*v.*) to stick out, thrust forth
Dentists commonly use various kinds of braces to correct the alignment of teeth that _____ or are crooked.

9. reparation
(rep ə rā′ shən)

(*n.*) a payment made for a wrong or an injury

Both Germany and Japan paid _____ to Britain, France, and the United States after WWII.

10. stark
(stärk)

(*adj.*) harsh, unrelieved, desolate; (*adv.*) utterly

Many a young idealist has found it difficult to accept the _____ realities of life.

By the end of his brief reign, the Roman emperor Caligula was clearly _____ raving mad.

Using Context

*For each item, determine whether the **boldface** word from pages 158–159 makes sense in the context of the sentence. Circle the item numbers next to the six sentences in which the words are used correctly.*

1. If you read a poem quickly and inattentively you may well **misconstrue** its meaning.

2. How can a company that is so **disreputable** and has so many lawsuits pending manage to remain in business?

3. We cannot afford to waste time and must take **exemplary** action to repair the damaged equipment.

4. The building's clean, modern exterior and sleek, uncluttered interior may appeal to some people, but the whole design is too **stark** for my taste.

5. Venus is the closest planet to Earth, and yet it is more than one hundred million **fathoms** away.

6. Louis Armstrong's music displays a marvelous **integrity** of musical styles that was influenced not only by jazz and blues but also by folk and popular music.

7. According to the panel of scientists, the evidence of the new drug's effectiveness is **conclusive**, and so the medication should be made available to the public.

8. The painting depicted a **placid** scene of storm clouds gathering over a harbor.

9. My cat's tail would **protrude** from underneath the sofa whenever she ran there to hide from thunder and other loud noises.

10. The two sides agreed to negotiate the amount of a fair **reparation** for the damage the faulty equipment had caused.

Choosing the Right Word

Select the **boldface** word that better completes each sentence. You might refer to the passage on pages 156–157 to see how most of these words are used in context. Note that the choices might be related forms of the Unit words.

1. It is all very well for science fiction writers to speculate, but is there any (**exemplary, conclusive**) evidence that UFOs exist?

2. Mother was as upset as any of us, but she managed to conceal her fears so that she looked positively (**stark, placid**).

3. The agency was created for the sole purpose of providing (**integrity, reparation**) to victims of human rights violations.

4. Although most of us cannot hope to match Mother Teresa's pure idealism, we may regard her noble life as inspiring and (**exemplary, conclusive**).

5. Modern scientists use all kinds of high-tech gadgetry to (**fathom, misconstrue**) the depths of the ocean.

6. A candidate for the highest office in the land should be, above all, a person of unshakable (**reparation, integrity**).

7. In that neighborhood of small homes, a few massive apartment buildings (**fathom, protrude**) like giants set down in a community of dwarfs.

8. Is it any wonder that your parents are worried, knowing that you are associating with such a (**placid, disreputable**) group of people?

9. The spectacular remains of that brilliant period stand in (**stark, conclusive**) contrast to the poverty of archaeological finds from previous eras.

10. In times of crisis, the utmost care must be taken to prevent ordinary military maneuvers from being (**fathomed, misconstrued**) as hostile acts.

11. The children cut holes in their paper bag masks to allow for their (**exemplary, protruding**) noses.

12. Most of his paintings portray (**stark, disreputable**) and barren desert landscapes.

Completing the Sentence

Choose the word from the word bank that best completes each of the following sentences. Write the correct word or form of the word in the space provided.

conclusive	exemplary	integrity	placid	reparation
disreputable	fathom	misconstrue	protrude	stark

1. The tapes of the conversations were regarded as _____ proof that the official had been aware of the crime.

2. In 1722, Daniel Defoe published his famous account of the _____ history of Moll Flanders.

3. The man has filed a lawsuit seeking _____ payments on behalf of all families who were forced to live in internment camps.

4. When we consider the _____ misery of the last years of his life, we must conclude that he paid in full for all his offenses.

5. If you allow your foot to _____ into the aisle, someone may trip over it.

6. I selected them as my business partners not only because I respect their ability but also because I have unlimited confidence in their character and _____.

7. Their idea of a(n) _____ student is someone so perfect in so many ways that he or she would be too good to exist.

8. By disregarding the flood of excuses, explanations, and justifications, we were able to _____ the true reasons for her actions.

9. Neither misfortunes nor happy events seem to have the slightest effect on my friend's _____ disposition.

10. Legally a defendant is innocent until proven guilty, so do not _____ a refusal to testify as an admission of guilt.

Definitions

Note the spelling, pronunciation, part(s) of speech, and definition(s) of each of the following words. Then write the appropriate form of the word in the blank space in the illustrative sentence(s) following.

1. allude
(ə lüd′)

(*v.*) to refer to casually or indirectly

In his speech, the candidate _____ to his opponent's lack of military experience.

2. clairvoyant
(klâr voi′ ənt)

(*adj.*) supernaturally perceptive; (*n.*) one who possesses extrasensory powers, seer

Few people are taken in by the _____ pronouncements of fortune-tellers and mediums.

The police sometimes use _____ to help them solve difficult missing-person cases.

3. endemic
(en dem′ ik)

(*adj.*) native or confined to a particular region or people; characteristic of or prevalent in a field

Scientists have yet to identify many plant and animal species _____ to the rain forests.

4. guile
(gīl)

(*n.*) treacherous cunning, deceit

Folklore has it that a serpent's most outstanding trait is _____, just as a fox's is craftiness.

5. itinerary
(ī tin′ ə rer ē)

(*n.*) a route of travel; a record of travel; a guidebook

Tour companies regularly provide potential customers with detailed _____ of the trips they offer.

6. obnoxious
(äb näk′ shəs)

(*adj.*) highly offensive, arousing strong dislike

The speeches Hitler delivered at the Nuremberg rallies were full of racial slurs and other _____ language.

7. placate
(plā′ kāt)

(*v.*) to appease, soothe, pacify

Sponsors of the controversial bill modified some of its original provisions in order to _____ the opposition.

8. potent
(pōt′ ənt)

(*adj.*) powerful; highly effective

Music has been called the most _____ agent for inducing people to forget their differences and live in harmony.

9. **pretext**
(prē' tekst)

(*n.*) a false reason, deceptive excuse

I sought some _____ for excusing myself from the weekly staff meeting I did not want to attend.

10. **superficial**
(sü pər fish' əl)

(*adj.*) on or near the surface; concerned with or understanding only what is on the surface, shallow

A _____ analysis of a complex problem is not likely to produce a viable or long-lasting solution.

Using Context

*For each item, determine whether the **boldface** word from pages 162–163 makes sense in the context of the sentence. Circle the item numbers next to the six sentences in which the words are used correctly.*

1. Most of the produce we buy during the winter months is **endemic** to the United States and imported from another country.

2. The **potent** waves lapping onto the shore provided a relaxing background noise as I read on the beach.

3. I'm not sure that the artist appreciated your **guile** when you said that her painting reminded you of something a toddler would make.

4. She tried to hide her **superficial** understanding of the subject in her essay by using unnecessarily big words and complicated sentence structure.

5. I headed into the kitchen on the **pretext** of grabbing a snack, but really I wanted to eavesdrop on my parents discussing what to get for my birthday.

6. I believe you **allude** to my lack of skill in the kitchen when you suggest that I should not bring an appetizer to your party.

7. Most citizens lost respect for their mayor when he made **obnoxious** statements about how the city would go to ruin without him.

8. Before each game, the coach tries to **placate** the team members with a rousing pep talk.

9. I was reluctant to stray from our **itinerary**, but the unexpected side trip to the Grand Canyon was worth shuffling some things around.

10. Unless you have **clairvoyant** senses, it is impossible to know for sure whether or not a financial investment is sound.

Choosing the Right Word

*Select the **boldface** word that better completes each sentence. You might refer to the passage on pages 156–157 to see how most of these words are used in context. Note that the choices might be related forms of the Unit words.*

1. Tom Sawyer used (**guile, pretext**) to get the other boys to do his work by convincing them that whitewashing a fence was fun.

2. I find no one more (**obnoxious, clairvoyant**) than a person who insists on talking instead of listening to the brilliant and important things I have to say.

3. Why not include Mount Vernon in the (**guile, itinerary**) of our spring vacation?

4. Do not be taken in by any (**superficial, potent**) resemblances between their half-baked ideas and the sensible program we proposed.

5. If the British government had made a sincere effort to (**placate, allude**) the colonists, would the American Revolution have occurred?

6. Marge produced a convenient headache as her (**pretext, itinerary**) for having to leave early.

7. Some people maintain that intelligent life must exist elsewhere in the universe, but I firmly believe that it is (**endemic, obnoxious**) to Earth.

8. When I said you were flying too close to the sun, I was (**placating, alluding**) to the myth about Daedalus and Icarus.

9. With some psychics it is difficult to tell where the (**clairvoyant, itinerary**) leaves off and the con artist begins.

10. The prospect of extremely high starting salaries is a(n) (**endemic, potent**) argument for pursuing a career in computer science.

11. Though all the lights were on, the restaurant refused to serve us, using the (**pretext, guile**) that it was closed for the evening.

12. Instead of (**alluding, placating**) so often to your own achievements and successes, why not wait for other people to mention them?

Completing the Sentence

Choose the word from the word bank that best completes each of the following sentences. Write the correct word or form of the word in the space provided.

allude	endemic	itinerary	placate	pretext
clairvoyant	guile	obnoxious	potent	superficial

1. His skillful use of flattery and double-talk to persuade us to agree to his scheme was a typical example of his _____.

2. Although the cut on my arm was bleeding quite heavily, it proved to be quite _____ and required only a tight bandage.

3. Phyllis was too polite to mention John's crude behavior at the party, but she certainly _____ to it when she spoke of "unnecessary unpleasantness."

4. It is quite useless to try to _____ dissatisfied customers who actually enjoy being angry and making complaints.

5. His conceit and his cold disregard of other people's feelings make him utterly _____!

6. America's most _____ weapon in the struggle for world influence is its great tradition of democracy and freedom.

7. Sherlock Holmes assured Dr. Watson that it was simple deduction, not some _____ faculty, that led him to the document's hiding place.

8. Blue jeans, once _____ to the cowboys of the American West, are now a familiar part of the whole world's wardrobe.

9. We spent many pleasant hours poring over all kinds of maps and guidebooks, planning the _____ for our trip across the United States.

10. On the _____ of delivering a package, the burglar sought to gain entrance to the house.

Synonyms

*Choose the word or form of the word from this Unit that is the same or most nearly the same in meaning as the **boldface** word or expression in the phrase. Write that word on the line. Use a dictionary if necessary.*

1. an advantage gained by **duplicity**   _____
2. a hectic **agenda** with no time for relaxation   _____
3. failed to **comprehend** the severity of the situation _____
4. recognized for **meritorious** service   _____
5. deliberately **mistook** my words   _____
6. signs that **obtrude** from the front of the building   _____
7. gave his **repugnant** opinion   _____
8. **reimbursement** for the destruction of property   _____
9. a leader with **high moral standards**   _____
10. could find no plausible **justification** to stay   _____
11. **hinted at** the existence of embarrassing secrets   _____
12. her **unperturbed** and reassuring manner   _____
13. fish **indigenous** to New England   _____
14. a **bleak** and barren landscape   _____
15. made **insightful** observations   _____

Antonyms

*Choose the word or form of the word from this Unit that is most nearly opposite in meaning to the **boldface** word or expression in the phrase. Write that word on the line. Use a dictionary if necessary.*

1. **aboveboard** business practices   _____
2. **questionable** proof of innocence   _____
3. **provoke** the angry crowd   _____
4. conducted a **thorough** examination   _____
5. prescribe **ineffectual** medications   _____

Writing: Words in Action

In what ways can the arts be restricted in society? What might be the effects of such restriction? Write a brief essay supporting your viewpoint. Use examples from your studies, the passage (pages 156–157), or your personal experience. Use three or more words from this Unit.

Vocabulary in Context

*Some of the words you have studied in this Unit appear in **boldface** type. Read the passage below, and then circle the letter of the correct answer for each word as it is used in context.*

The Bureau of Educational and Cultural Affairs, part of the United States Department of State, sponsors many international exchange programs for U.S. citizens. One of the largest programs for international educational exchange is the Fulbright Program, which offers dozens of experiences abroad for the purposes of study, research, and cultural exchange. Fulbright operates in 155 different countries on six continents; students can create an **itinerary** that best serves what they want to learn. For example, students can complete research on a doctoral dissertation about the Swiss Revolution on the **placid** banks of Lake Zurich, where the Albis and Zimmerberg hills **protrude** on the north side of the lake. Other students can travel to Japan to learn more about the effect on that country of the **reparations** that it paid to the Allies after World War II. Projects and programs are as varied as the students who submit proposals to the program.

The Fulbright Program has long been an **exemplary** model for other government-sponsored international educational exchange programs. Some government-sponsored programs familiarize educators with other cultures so that they can bring that information back to their classrooms. Other programs promote English-language learning abroad and provide people with the opportunity to teach English around the globe. It may seem too good to be true that the U.S. government will pay for people to travel abroad, but there is no **guile** involved. Applicants do not need to concoct some elaborate pretext to receive these grants. The application process is rigorous, but hundreds of thousands of students have taken advantage of these government-sponsored travel programs.

---

1. The word **itinerary** most nearly means
   a. a route of travel
   b. a flexible plan
   c. a difficult path
   d. an uncertain destination

2. To be **placid** is to be
   a. vast
   b. artificial
   c. distant
   d. calm

3. The Albis and Zimmerberg hills **protrude** because they
   a. are jagged
   b. stick out
   c. surround water
   d. are steep

4. A **reparation** is
   a. an amount owed on a loan
   b. an apology for a mistake
   c. a payment made for a wrong
   d. a promise for future payments

5. Something that is **exemplary** is
   a. worthy of imitation
   b. unique in form
   c. easy to criticize
   d. prone to change

6. **Guile** is
   a. understanding
   b. purpose
   c. deceit
   d. mystery

*Read the following passage, taking note of the **boldface** words and their contexts. These words are among those you will be studying in Unit 12. It may help you to complete the exercises in this Unit if you refer to the way the words are used below.*

Do Not Forget Our Earliest Cultures
<Letter to the Editor>

To the Editor:

In an otherwise excellent article on early cultures of South America ("South America's Ancient Diversity," April 22), author Rigoberto Ruiz-Nunez ignores the lasting significance of the Aymara people. Although the Aymara Empire collapsed over 1,000 years ago, the Aymara are not an **irrelevant** footnote in the history books today. Their empire once spanned the south-central Andes Mountains, and today, an estimated two million of their descendents live in Bolivia and another 500,000 in Peru. The Aymara have made an **indelible** mark on this region.

Saying that the Aymara suffered during colonization is a **platitude** that explains nothing. Millions of Aymara were **callously** worked to death in Spanish silver mines. The Aymara were forced to **abjure** their traditional religion and culture, although some practices continued in a **clandestine** way. For almost 500 years, Bolivian leaders showed no **compunction** about the mistreatment of the Aymara. Not until 1952 did Bolivia adopt a more **indulgent** policy, granting the Aymara the same civil rights as other Bolivians.

How did the Aymara survive such adversity? For one thing, there has always been a **tacit** agreement among the Aymara to help members of their community. In times of crisis, the Aymara work together—an arrangement that strengthens the group. In addition, centuries of high-altitude living gave the Aymara extraordinary lung capacity. They could live at elevations that left the colonizers faint—a further challenge to any attempts to **quell** rebellions in Aymara communities.

High in the Andes today, many Aymara continue their **inveterate** traditions, including their reliance on potato farming—they were among the first to cultivate this food—and llama and alpaca herding. Others have settled into modern society with **tangible** results. An Aymara political party sends members to the Bolivian Congress, and Aymara TV shows and music groups are popular. The tourist trade provides a ready market for sought-after Aymara woolen goods and weavings. So more than a millennium after the fall of their **august** empire, the Aymara remain a vibrant people, carrying on age-old traditions while exploring modern possibilities.

The Aymara have their own language—Aymara. Many also speak Spanish.

The Moche civilization arose 2,000 years ago in the river valleys and coastal plain of northern Peru.

To the Editor:

Your recent article about the diverse peoples who populated early South America gave short shrift to an important ancient culture. The Moche people inhabited the river valleys and coastal plain of northern Peru between AD 100 and AD 800. You rightly note that archaeologists are **elated** by recent discoveries in the region: The sophisticated Moche built pyramids, temples, and irrigation canals and produced extraordinary ceramics and murals. Yet the article offers no **trenchant** explanation for why the Moche "disappeared."

Scholars have long **ruminated** on the causes of the Moche collapse. Evidence from glacial ice cores shows that the area experienced 30 years of flooding followed by 30 years of

Although they had no written language, the Moche people excelled at ceramics.

drought. This weather event, from AD 536–594, could have disrupted the Moche food supply.

Furthermore, Moche leaders were charged with ensuring stable weather through religious practices, and their failure to do so may have destabilized the people's faith in their leadership.

Although the Moche had no known enemies, a few of their later settlements did have fortifications. What was the purpose of these defenses? Perhaps food shortages led to bitter infighting among the Moche. Such **acrid** conflicts could have led to the death of thousands and hastened the civilization's decline. The full story of the Moche collapse may never be known. However, I hope articles such as yours will inspire some of your readers to study this and other ancient civilizations.

Audio

For iWords and audio passages, go to SadlierConnect.com.

Ruins of a Moche pyramid

Definitions

Note the spelling, pronunciation, part(s) of speech, and definition(s) of each of the following words. Then write the appropriate form of the word in the blank space in the illustrative sentence(s) following.

1. august
(ô gəst′)

(*adj.*) majestic, inspiring admiration and respect

The _____ visages of four of America's great presidents are carved on the face of Mount Rushmore.

2. callous
(ka′ ləs)

(*adj.*) emotionally hardened, unfeeling

Protesters accused the mayor of _____ indifference to the plight of the homeless.

3. compunction
(kəm pəŋk′ shən)

(*n.*) remorse, regret

In some religious writings _____ is used as a synonym for *contrition* to express profound regret for one's sins.

4. conflagration
(kän flə grā′ shən)

(*n.*) a large destructive fire

A large number of wooden structures quite literally added fuel to the _____ that swept through San Francisco in 1906.

5. indelible
(in del′ ə bəl)

(*adj.*) not able to be erased or removed; memorable

The brutal crimes against humanity committed by the Nazis left an _____ stain on the history of the twentieth century.

6. inveterate
(in vet′ ər ət)

(*adj.*) firmly established, long-standing; habitual

It has been claimed that many writers and artists have an _____ hostility to criticism.

7. nocturnal
(näk tər′ nəl)

(*adj.*) of or occurring in the night; under cover of darkness

Most _____ creatures have keen eyesight and acute hearing.

8. platitude
(plat′ ə tüd)

(*n.*) a commonplace, stale, or trite remark

The sentiments expressed in most greeting cards seldom rise above the level of timeworn _____.

9. quiescent
(kwī es′ ənt)

(*adj.*) inactive; at rest
Although some volcanoes are believed to be truly extinct, many are merely _____.

10. tacit
(tas′ it)

(*adj.*) unspoken, silent; implied, inferred
The neighbors had a _____ understanding that they would help each other in an emergency.

Using Context

*For each item, determine whether the **boldface** word from pages 170–171 makes sense in the context of the sentence. Circle the item numbers next to the six sentences in which the words are used correctly.*

1. Over a hundred firefighters had battled the **conflagration** by the time it was put under control.

2. It was both moving and humbling for us to think about all the teachers and students who had passed through the great university's **august** halls.

3. The opening of five new restaurants added to the general **compunction** that the neighborhood was becoming popular and trendy.

4. I regretted my **callous** remarks immediately after uttering them.

5. During their pupal stage, butterflies and other insects are **quiescent** and do not move or feed.

6. The opposing team's top player received a penalty for hurling a **platitude** at us in the middle of the point.

7. Because the microphones in the auditorium were not working, the principal's welcoming remarks were completely **indelible**.

8. **Nocturnal** animals, such as bats, owls, and coyotes, are often regarded as spooky.

9. The subtle, **inveterate** taste of the soup was due to a complex blend of herbs and spices.

10. For centuries, people have been fascinated by the Mona Lisa's mysterious and **tacit** smile.

Choosing the Right Word

Select the **boldface** word that better completes each sentence. You might refer to the passage on pages 168–169 to see how most of these words are used in context. Note that the choices might be related forms of the Unit words.

1. Alexander the Great's meteoric career of world conquest made a(n) (**indelible, quiescent**) impression on the thoughts and institutions of antiquity.

2. An insightful writer usually has no need to rely on hollow generalities or threadbare (**compunctions, platitudes**).

3. We may criticize Americans for many things, but they are never (**nocturnal, callous**) when appeals for help come from distressed people.

4. The major powers intervened to prevent the brushfire war from engulfing the entire region in a full-scale (**conflagration, platitude**).

5. Like so many (**callous, inveterate**) pack rats, she has found that great self-discipline is needed to break the cluttering habit.

6. Millions of Americans were thrilled as they witnessed on TV the simple but (**august, quiescent**) ceremony of the presidential inauguration.

7. We hoped that the strange noises outside the tent were merely the foraging sounds of small (**nocturnal, inveterate**) creatures like possums and raccoons.

8. Since my parents offered no objections, I felt that I had their (**indelible, tacit**) consent to go ahead with my plans for a summer trip to California.

9. The deep-seated resentment of the populace, which had long been (**august, quiescent**), suddenly blossomed into open rebellion.

10. Because their misconduct was clearly deliberate, we have no feelings of (**compunction, conflagration**) in sentencing them to ten days of detention.

11. Just before going to sleep, we set traps to discourage the (**tacit, nocturnal**) raids of the raccoons on our food supply.

12. The old (**compunction, platitude**) "You can't teach an old dog new tricks" is based on the principle that old dogs and people do not learn as well as the young.

Completing the Sentence

Choose the word from the word bank that best completes each of the following sentences. Write the correct word or form of the word in the space provided.

august	compunction	indelible	nocturnal	quiescent
callous	conflagration	inveterate	platitude	tacit

1. Some people are so completely wrapped up in their own concerns that they often seem to be _____ about the feelings of others.

2. The streets seemed safe and familiar during the day, but now we had to face unknown _____ dangers.

3. Though we were angry with each other, we had a(n) _____ agreement to act politely in front of our parents.

4. Their behavior was so rude and offensive that I had no _____ about telling them to leave the house.

5. In the presence of such a(n) _____ assemblage of spiritual leaders representing all the major beliefs, I felt very humble.

6. The years of close association with outstanding teachers had left a(n) _____ mark on the students' characters.

7. The audience seemed to be stirred by the speaker's remarks, but in my opinion they were no more than a series of _____.

8. How can we possibly accept the testimony of someone who is known to be a(n) _____ liar?

9. Although the disease had been _____ for several years, the doctors warned her that its symptoms could appear again at any time.

10. According to legend, Mrs. O'Leary's cow kicked over an oil lamp and started the _____ that consumed four square miles of Chicago in 1871.

Definitions

Note the spelling, pronunciation, part(s) of speech, and definition(s) of each of the following words. Then write the appropriate form of the word in the blank space in the illustrative sentence(s) following.

1. abjure
(ab jür′)

(*v.*) to renounce, repudiate under oath; to avoid, shun
Toward the end of Shakespeare's last play, *The Tempest*, the magician Prospero _____ his powers over nature.

2. acrid
(ak′ rid)

(*adj.*) harsh in taste or odor; sharp in manner or temper
The _____ stench of a fire lingers in the air long after the flames have been extinguished.

3. clandestine
(klan des′ tən)

(*adj.*) secret, concealed; underhanded
During the early stages of the American Revolution, _____ colonial printing presses churned out quantities of anti-British propaganda.

4. elated
(i lā′ tid)

(*adj., part.*) in high spirits, jubilant; extremely pleased
_____ fans lined the city's streets to cheer the World Series champions.

5. indulgent
(in dəl′ jənt)

(*adj.*) yielding to the wishes or demands of others
A heightened sense of compassion has induced the federal government to adopt a more _____ policy toward illegal aliens.

6. irrelevant
(i rel′ ə vənt)

(*adj.*) not to the point, not applicable or pertinent
When you take notes, it's best to record only the main ideas and eliminate all _____ details.

7. quell
(kwel)

(*v.*) to subdue, put down forcibly
The English poet John Dryden believed that music has the power either to arouse or to _____ strong emotions.

8. ruminate
(rü′ mə nāt)

(*v.*) to meditate, think about at length
In old age many people sadly _____ on mistakes made and opportunities missed.

9. tangible
(tan′ jə bəl)

(*adj.*) capable of being touched; real, concrete

After months of intensive negotiation, diplomats reported that they had made _____ progress toward reaching a settlement of the bitter dispute.

10. trenchant
(tren′ chənt)

(*adj.*) incisive, keen; forceful, effective; cutting, caustic; distinct, clear-cut

Scholars consider the _____ satires of Jonathan Swift to be the greatest works of their kind in the English language.

Using Context

*For each item, determine whether the **boldface** word from pages 174–175 makes sense in the context of the sentence. Circle the item numbers next to the six sentences in which the words are used correctly.*

1. I like staying at my aunt's house because she is more **indulgent** than my parents, letting me sleep in as late as I want.

2. I always need some time to myself before I go to sleep to **ruminate** on the day's events.

3. When the former friends who had not spoken in years both entered the room, a **tangible** air of hostility settled around us.

4. The principal expected some students to be displeased by the school's new lunch menu, but she could not have anticipated such a **clandestine** backlash.

5. Even though I only have a small role in the play, I'm **elated** just to be part of the cast.

6. Her **acrid** remarks about every site we saw on the trip made us wonder why she had even come.

7. Their **trenchant** conversation about which lane they prefer to drive in nearly put me to sleep.

8. He became so enraged that he started bringing up **irrelevant** topics that had nothing to do with our original conversation.

9. The professor attempted to **quell** the class's attention by singing at the top of his lungs.

10. Most romantic comedy movies end when the lead couple finally decides to **abjure** their love for each other.

Choosing the Right Word

*Select the **boldface** word that better completes each sentence. You might refer to the passage on pages 168–169 to see how most of these words are used in context. Note that the choices might be related forms of the Unit words.*

1. In a large city, it is difficult to avoid the (**acrid, indulgent**) smoke emitted from cars.

2. In these days of presidential primaries, candidates can no longer be chosen at (**elated, clandestine**) meetings of a few powerful politicians.

3. I've noticed that many professional football players become (**irrelevant, tangible**) only a few years after their retirement.

4. As part of the settlement, the company must henceforth (**abjure, ruminate**) unsubstantiated claims for its product.

5. Taking third place in the hundred-meter dash in the intramural track meet left me satisfied but scarcely (**irrelevant, elated**).

6. Although there was no (**tangible, clandestine**) reason for my alarm, I could not shake off the feeling that something terrible was about to happen.

7. We should seek not to (**quell, elate**) the idealism and enthusiasm of youth but, rather, to direct those impulses into useful channels.

8. The judge has a reputation for being generally (**indulgent, trenchant**), but not when confronting an individual convicted of reckless driving.

9. How will you write your novel if you spend most of your time (**abjuring, ruminating**) about the title?

10. After listening to the senator's (**trenchant, tangible**) analysis, I have a clearer idea of what is involved and where I should stand on the issue.

11. His invariably (**acrid, indulgent**) remarks on the state of the world soon earned him the nickname of "Old Sourpuss."

12. Though the anecdote was amusing, it was totally (**clandestine, irrelevant**) to the matter we were discussing at the moment.

Completing the Sentence

Choose the word from the word bank that best completes each of the following sentences. Write the correct word or form of the word in the spaces provided.

abjure	clandestine	indulgent	quell	tangible
acrid	elated	irrelevant	ruminate	trenchant

1. I tried to _____ my feeling of panic by assuring myself that there is simply no such thing as a ghost.

2. The documents showed that, years before, the companies had made a(n) _____ agreement to divide the market among them.

3. Who wouldn't be _____ at winning a huge prize on a television quiz show?

4. There was no _____ evidence of his sincerity, but somehow we were confident that he would do all he could to help us.

5. I have no patience with a(n) _____ parent who gives in to every whim and demand of an undisciplined child.

6. The debate was decided in our favor when Carole's _____ rebuttal tore the other side's arguments to pieces.

7. Abraham Lincoln's plan for reconstruction simply had the former rebels _____ allegiance to the Confederacy and vow to support the Union.

8. The fumes released by the volcano were so _____ that they caused great discomfort among people in the nearby villages.

9. Your statement may be correct, but since it has no bearing on the point now under discussion, I must reject it as _____.

10. I stretched out under the old maple tree in the backyard and began to _____ on the strange events of that remarkable day.

Synonyms

*Choose the word or form of the word from this Unit that is the same or most nearly the same in meaning as the **boldface** word or expression in the phrase. Write that word on the line. Use a dictionary if necessary.*

1. the **irritating** smoke from a burning log   _____

2. a terrifying **inferno** that destroyed thousands of acres   _____

3. **lenient** grandparents spoiling grandkids   _____

4. **reflect** on the validity of the statement   _____

5. observe nature in a **dormant** state   _____

6. **palpable** signs of long neglect   _____

7. a **covert** meeting with the President   _____

8. just one **tired expression** after another   _____

9. a known **chronic** liar who can't tell the truth   _____

10. tried to **suppress** their fears   _____

11. creatures that are **active during the night**   _____

12. broke the rules without **shame**   _____

13. saw the actor's **unforgettable** performance   _____

14. willingly **recanted** their old beliefs   _____

15. **delighted** by the day's events   _____

Antonyms

*Choose the word or form of the word from this Unit that is most nearly opposite in meaning to the **boldface** word or expression in the phrase. Write that word on the line. Use a dictionary if necessary.*

1. **material** to the topic at hand   _____

2. a descendant of **humble** lineage   _____

3. had **explicit** permission to borrow the car   _____

4. the critic's **imperceptive** remarks   _____

5. a reputation for being **kind**   _____

Writing: Words in Action

Write a brief essay explaining why it is important for scholars to continue researching and making discoveries about civilizations that no longer exist. Support your position with examples from your studies and the passage (pages 168–169). Write at least three paragraphs, and use three or more words from this Unit.

Vocabulary in Context

*Some of the words you have studied in this Unit appear in **boldface** type. Read the passage below, and then circle the letter of the correct answer for each word as it is used in context.*

For thousands of years the Modoc people lived on the rugged, high plateau of what is now the border between Oregon and California. A semi-nomadic tribe, the Modoc left their winter villages as soon as wildflowers began to bloom. During spring and summer, Modoc bands established temporary camps along the banks of rivers and lakes, where they hunted, fished, and gathered nuts and berries. Forest fires were a normal part of life, but since tree cover was sparse in the arid region, blazes rarely grew into **conflagrations**. Autumn camps were busy, as Modoc of all ages collected and prepared food—from acorns to dried salmon and smoked duck—for the coming winter. Once the heavy snows fell, hunting and gathering necessarily subsided; however, life in the winter villages was anything but **quiescent**. People used the coldest season to repair tools, weave baskets, and, of course, **ruminate** on the year's accomplishments.

To open land for settlers, the U.S. Army relocated the Modoc to a newly created reservation in 1864. A year later, a Modoc leader named Captain Jack (known as Kintpuash to his fellow Modoc) led his people back to their ancestral land, where they were **elated** to readopt their traditional way of life. After several more failed attempts to force the Modoc onto the reservation, fighting broke out in 1872. Captain Jack led 52 warriors and a band of about 150 Modoc to the lava beds south of Tule Lake. Taking advantage of their knowledge of the difficult terrain, Modoc warriors staged **nocturnal** raids and won several battles. Newspapers covered the Modoc War extensively, and journalists' accounts of the fierce adversary and brutal conditions created an **indelible** impression with the American public.

---

1. **Conflagrations** are
   a. deserts
   b. campfires
   c. large destructive fires
   d. natural disasters

2. A **quiescent** village is
   a. quiet
   b. asleep
   c. lazy
   d. inactive

3. The word **ruminate** most nearly means
   a. to think about at length
   b. to chant and sing
   c. to summarize
   d. to rhapsodize

4. **Elated** people are
   a. content
   b. eager
   c. jubilant
   d. excited

5. A **nocturnal** raid occurs
   a. at night
   b. by surprise
   c. on foot
   d. at dawn

6. An **indelible** impression is
   a. casual
   b. fantastic
   c. sobering
   d. memorable

Vocabulary for Comprehension
Part 1

*Read this passage, which contains words in **boldface** that appear in Units 10–12. Then choose the best answer to each question based on what is stated or implied in the passage. You may refer to the passage as often as necessary.*

Questions 1–10 are based on the following passage.

One problem with building an economic system that depends on a nonrenewable natural resource such as oil is that the natural resource will eventually run out.

(5) As the oil fields of Alaska's North Slope are slowly drained, less and less oil flows through the Trans-Alaska Pipeline. This fact is important because revenue from taxes levied on oil companies make up

(10) about 90 percent of Alaska's budget. In other words, oil industry money largely supports public schools, courts, hospitals, and infrastructure. Compounding Alaska's oil decline, hydraulic fracturing, or

(15) "fracking," in the lower 48 states has greatly increased the nation's overall oil supply, helping spur a dramatic drop in oil prices. So not only is less oil moving through Alaska's famous pipeline, but the

(20) price of oil is under pressure. When the price of oil drops, the state faces serious budget deficits.

One possible solution, of course, is to find new oil deposits. The most promising

(25) area lies offshore, beneath the Arctic Ocean, which geologists have long suspected of harboring substantial deposits of oil and natural gas. The challenges of drilling in Arctic waters are

(30) daunting, or, according to many critics, **insuperable**. Temperatures are extreme, pushing ships, drilling rigs, and people to the limits of their capabilities. Even during the short summer months, **placid** seas

(35) can quickly give way to fierce storms, massive waves, and grinding ice floes. Despite these challenges—and without

conclusive evidence of oil deposits—the federal government opened large tracts

(40) of the ocean to drilling.

The move divided the community of Barrow, the town nearest to any offshore drilling operation. More than three-quarters of Barrow's residents are Inupiat, people

(45) who still raise their families on a traditional diet of whale, caribou, and seal. Whaling, in particular, is crucial to the Inupiat, both as a source of food and as a touchstone of cultural identity. For thousands of years,

(50) Inupiat men have headed out to sea each spring in a flotilla of umiak, or seal-skin boats, to hunt bowhead whales. The bowhead is **endemic** to this **august** region, migrating among the Bering,

(55) Chukchi, and Beaufort Seas. Any oil spill in these waters would be **lamentable**, opponents argue, devastating the bowhead population—and the people who depend on it.

(60) Perhaps surprisingly, a leading **exponent** of offshore oil development is one of Barrow's whaling captains. The benefits of a strong oil industry, he argues, are **tangible**. The Inupiat of Barrow enjoy

(65) better schools, healthcare service, and infrastructure because of oil revenue, and many Inupiat are employed, directly or indirectly, by the oil industry. Others in the community, however, take a very different

(70) position. For them, the dangers posed by offshore drilling are not worth the risk. Promised oil revenue is a negligible blip in the timeline of the Inupiat, whose oral history goes back to woolly mammoth

(75) hunts. For now, the argument may be hypothetical. After years of mishaps and disappointing results—and a $7 billion

bill—the only company exploring for oil in Barrow's icy seas has **abjured** its
(80) drilling rights.

1. The main purpose of the passage is to
   A) inform the reader about Alaska's oil industry.
   B) summarize the key points of Alaskan history.
   C) describe benefits and risks of Alaska's oil industry.
   D) explain why some Inupiat support oil development.

2. According to the first paragraph, Alaska faces budget deficits when
   A) a nonrenewable natural resource runs out.
   B) oil production declines and oil prices fall.
   C) hydraulic fracturing increases oil prices.
   D) environmental regulations curtail production.

3. Lines 28–36 summarize
   A) the reasons for oil exploration in the Arctic Ocean.
   B) why geologists believe oil deposits lie beneath the Arctic Ocean.
   C) the difficulties of oil production in the Arctic Ocean.
   D) how the federal government controls oil exploration in the Arctic Ocean.

4. As it is used in line 38, "conclusive" most nearly means
   A) serving to settle an issue.
   B) more likely than not.
   C) final.
   D) scientific.

5. As it is used in line 53, "endemic" most nearly means
   A) native to a particular region.
   B) prevalent in a field.
   C) enormous.
   D) migratory.

6. According to the passage, why are some Inupiat opposed to offshore oil production?
   A) They still have a traditional diet.
   B) Few Inupiat would work on drilling rigs.
   C) They are a whaling community, not an oil community.
   D) An oil spill would endanger the whales on which they depend.

7. Which choice provides the best evidence for the answer to the previous question?
   A) Lines 43–46 ("More than ... and seal")
   B) Lines 46–49 ("Whaling ... identity")
   C) Lines 49–52 ("For ... bowhead whales")
   D) Lines 55–59 ("Any ... depend on it")

8. It can reasonably be inferred from information in the fourth paragraph (lines 60–80) that the whaling captain
   A) is not popular.
   B) is an environmentalist.
   C) is focused on the risks, not the benefits.
   D) will have his livelihood threatened by any oil spills.

9. As it is used in line 64, "tangible" most nearly means
   A) capable of being touched.
   B) taken for granted.
   C) obvious.
   D) real.

10. What point does the author make by mentioning the Inupiat's oral history in the last paragraph?
    A) The Inupiat used to hunt wooly mammoths.
    B) The Inupiat are master storytellers.
    C) The Inupiat have lived in the region a very long time.
    D) There is no written history of the Inupiat.

Vocabulary for Comprehension
Part 2

*Read these passages, which contain words in **boldface** that appear in Units 10–12. Then choose the best answer to each question based on what is stated or implied in the passage(s). You may refer to the passages as often as necessary.*

Questions 1–10 are based on the following passages.

Passage 1

The Klamath Basin Restoration Agreement signals a potential end to the **inveterate** animosity surrounding water rights in this arid region of southern

(5) Oregon and northern California. Since the early twentieth century, farmers, Native American tribes, commercial fishermen, and environmentalists have disputed the allocation of the river's water. The more

(10) water used to irrigate farms, the less water there is to support the river's salmon runs. Klamath, Yurok, and Karuk people have depended on the fish for millennia.

The roots of the Restoration Agreement

(15) can be traced to a severe drought that began in 2001. To protect endangered fish, federal officials reduced water flows to farms, but the next year the officials reversed course. Bowing to

(20) political pressure—and showing **callous** disregard for the effects of their actions— water managers diverted flows from the drought-stricken river to irrigation canals. More than 70,000 salmon perished.

(25) Recognizing that such an environmental catastrophe served no one's interest, the various factions began negotiating. Their final agreement focuses on the "decommissioning" of four obsolete dams.

(30) Once the dams are removed, salmon will be able to reach much more of their historic spawning grounds. The **integrity** of some riverside ecosystems will be

restored. In exchange, farmers will get a

(35) share of the Klamath's upstream water. A **respite** from this bitter conflict is at hand.

Passage 2

Proponents of the Klamath Basin Restoration Agreement **misconstrue** the position of farmers and ranchers who

(40) oppose the deal. These hardworking men and women are not **contentious**. They will not block reasonable measures to protect salmon stocks in the Klamath watershed. But they do insist that their long-

(45) established legal rights to Klamath River water be respected so that future droughts do not result in their economic ruin. Remember the aftermath of the 2001 drought. In a misguided attempt to protect

(50) a fishery that had been declining for decades, government officials curtailed water flow to farms and ranches. Families who had been working the land for more than a century watched as their crops

(55) withered and cattle died. According to some estimates, the region's agricultural losses totaled as much as $47 million.

The proposed agreement makes an array of **indulgent** promises to various

(60) "stakeholders." Many of these environmental groups have little history in the area and are simply trying to wring concessions for their constituencies. Long before any environmental organization

(65) had heard of the Klamath River, local ranchers and farmers were using its waters to turn arid scrubland into fertile farmland and ranchland. Instead of addressing the concerns of these

Two-Word Completions

Select the pair of words that best completes the meaning of each of the following sentences.

1. During the evening, Ned must have _____ to his close acquaintance with at least a dozen celebrities. Afterward, we all agreed that his nickname, "Name-dropper Ned," was no _____.
   a. alluded … misnomer
   b. misconstrued … pretext
   c. protruded … reparation
   d. protruded … platitude

2. I had hoped that the candidates would make a few _____ observations during the course of the debate. All I got, however, were the same tired old _____ that politicians have been mouthing for decades.
   a. superficial … ruminations
   b. trenchant … platitudes
   c. irrelevant … reparations
   d. exemplary … pretexts

3. The trail known as "Dead Man's Curves" is so steep and _____ that even the most proficient and experienced skiers often must stop for a brief _____ before completing the course.
   a. stark … itinerary
   b. clandestine … compunction
   c. sinuous … respite
   d. disreputable … pretext

4. After romping around with my six-year-old nephew all afternoon, I had become woefully _____. My trousers were rumpled, my shirttails were hanging out, and my tie was all _____.
   a. lamentable … sinuous
   b. garrulous … acrid
   c. disreputable … crestfallen
   d. disheveled … askew

5. Utterly _____ at their upset defeat, the Belleville squad looked on dismally as the trophy they had so much _____ was awarded to their archrivals from Henderson.
   a. crestfallen … coveted
   b. lamentable … abjured
   c. blithe … professed
   d. disheveled … ruminated

6. In view of the countless crimes the dictator had committed while in power, the revolutionary tribunal expressed no _____ in seeking the sternest _____ on behalf of the people.
   a. pretext … vanguard
   b. compunction … retribution
   c. integrity … respite
   d. guile … conflagration

7. High winds fanned the flames; and in no time at all, the _____ had spread to a nearby tire factory. Clouds of thick black smoke billowed up into the sky, and the _____ stench of burning rubber filled the air.
   a. compunction … potent
   b. contention … obnoxious
   c. conflagration … acrid
   d. retribution … indelible

Denotation and Connotation

The literal meaning of a word is its **denotation**. It is the formal meaning of the word found in a dictionary. A word's denotation conveys a *neutral* tone.

Conversely, a word's **connotation** is the informal, implied meaning a reader or listener associates with it. That connotation can be either *positive* or *negative*.

Consider these synonyms for the neutral word *agree*:

> *concur   consent   acquiesce   comply*

Concur and *consent* have positive connotations, suggesting that an accord has been reached through mutual agreement. *Acquiesce* and *comply*, however, have negative connotations, suggesting that one side has given in to the demands of the other and that whatever agreement has been reached benefits one side more than the other.

Look at these examples of words that are similar in denotation but have different connotations.

NEUTRAL	POSITIVE	NEGATIVE
grand	august	intimidating
direct	incisive	trenchant
quiet	pacify	quell

Expressing the Connotation

Read each sentence. Select the word in parentheses that expresses the connotation (positive, negative, or neutral) given at the beginning of the sentence.

positive   **1.** Michael was amazed by his young daughter's (**guile, cleverness**) as she explained how she had dealt with a problem at school.

positive   **2.** Don't you find that most grandparents are (**lenient, indulgent**) when it comes to their relationship with their grandchildren?

negative   **3.** Very few officials knew about the (**clandestine, devious**) operation.

neutral   **4.** On a dark, cloudy day, the desert can seem (**desolate, stark**) and harsh.

negative   **5.** For many people, the danger of talking on a cell phone while driving is a (**debatable, contentious**) matter.

neutral   **6.** The argument he gave was (**irrelevant, unrelated**) to the problem we had presented to him.

negative   **7.** When the trial was postponed for several months, the rancher decided to take action and seek his own (**retribution, revenge**) for the cattle theft.

positive   **8.** The dancer's (**twisting, sinuous**) movements suggested a swaying tree.

Classical Roots

dem—people; pan— all, every

The root *dem* appears in **endemic**, "native or confined to a particular region or people" (page 162). The root *pan* appears in **panacea**, "a remedy for all ills" (page 58). Some other words based on these roots are listed below.

demagogue	demotic	pandemonium	panorama
demographics	pandemic	panoply	pantheon

From the list of words above, choose the one that corresponds to each of the brief definitions below. Write the word in the blank space in the illustrative sentence below the definition. Use an online or print dictionary if necessary.

1. view of an area in every direction; a comprehensive presentation of a subject
   The _____ from the rim of the Grand Canyon is truly awe-inspiring.

2. a leader who gains or holds power by appealing to the emotions or prejudices of the populace and by making false claims
   _____ may cloak their true motives in the guise of patriotism.

3. a wild uproar, din, or commotion; literally, the dwelling place of all demons
   At midnight on New Year's Eve, _____ breaks out among the revelers in Times Square.

4. a temple or building dedicated to heroes or other famous persons; all the gods of a people
   In the Greek _____, Zeus is the father of the gods.

5. a full suit of armor; ceremonial attire; any splendid or impressive array
   Figures of knights and horses in full _____ make up one of the museum's most popular exhibits.

6. taking place over a wide area and affecting a very large number of people
   Twenty-one million people died in the influenza _____ of 1918.

7. statistics on human populations, such as number of people, location, migration, age, and income
   The U.S. Census, which is taken every ten years, is an important source of _____.

8. relating to the common people, especially the language of the people; connected with the colloquial form of Greek spoken in modern times
   Homer's epic poems *The Iliad* and *The Odyssey* are written in classical, rather than _____, Greek.

*Read the following passage, taking note of the **boldface** words and their contexts. These words are among those you will be studying in Unit 13. It may help you to complete the exercises in this Unit if you refer to the way the words are used below.*

Life on the High Seas
<Log>

This is an imaginary log of a sailor aboard the HM Bark *Endeavour* during Captain James Cook's epic 1768–1771 first voyage of discovery in the Pacific Ocean. Captain Cook visited Tahiti and charted New Zealand and the east coast of Australia. Botanists and artists on the *Endeavour* made important records of the people, flora, and fauna of each land.

5 September 1768
Nine days at sea and we are getting our sea legs. Tonight, we dined on salted beef and slabs of cheese, but I fear this is the last of our cheese ration. Ah, for an endless supply instead of what lies ahead: dried meats and—horrors!— cabbage preserved in vinegar. Still, Captain Cook has told us we must eat plenty of this dish to prevent scurvy and to set an example for the crew.

12 December 1768
Thomas, our ship's cat, is **sedate** after a busy day of ratting. His **exuberance** for his job is an inspiration. He is always cheerful and willing and never seasick. If only that could be said of his shipmates!

21 July 1769
Endless days with no sight of land: We are **infinitesimal** specs on a vast sea. The men are restless due to the relentless and **implacable** boredom. Casks of beer and rum were damaged in last night's storm, and I fear the crew will **imbibe** the contents before long.

10 November 1769
The crew is kept busy with sail and rope repair. I heard Sam Jones grumbling that the breakfast biscuits are full of weevils and not fit to be consumed. I told him the weevils added flavor, but my **innocuous** attempt at humor fell flat.

9 January 1770
Mr. Evans, the quartermaster, is not himself. He harbors **antipathy** to all who question his navigational skills. Perhaps he has eaten bad meat?

6 April 1770
The captain has shown time and again what an **asset** he is to our king and country. Some are fearful of his **stentorian** commands that boarder on **duress**, but I say he must be forceful to keep order. We want no mutiny here!

Captain James Cook rose through the ranks, from ordinary seaman to legendary commander and explorer.

12 June 1770
Disaster! We are **beset** with troubles. Our ship ran aground on a massive reef and sustained great damage to the hull. Midshipman Munkhouse may have saved us: His idea to plug the holes has worked well as a temporary fix, and we are proceeding north in search of a harbor in which to make more thorough repairs.

3 July 1770
Weeks on land and all signs of **decorum** and discipline in the crew have vanished. Some good news: We enjoyed tasty fish and greens for dinner—a welcome change from ship's rations. The men sang songs late into the night. As they say, better poor on land than rich at sea.

16 July 1770
Captain Cook has given us an **ultimatum**: We must complete all necessary repairs and set sail again by early August.

29 July 1770
Dined this evening with the captain; Mr. Green, the astronomer; and Mr. Banks, the botanist. Mr. Banks is excited about the many new plants he has encountered. He showed me great **compassion** when I spoke of missing my wife and children.

3 August 1770
We depart. Huzzah! Pilot whales accompanied us as we left the harbor, perhaps a good omen. We pray for good weather, calm seas, and the continued **prowess** of our brave and skilled captain to guide us to the end of our journey.

Audio

For iWords and audio passages, go to SadlierConnect.com.

The British Royal Naval vessel HM Bark Endeavour, *also known as* HMS Endeavour

Definitions

Note the spelling, pronunciation, part(s) of speech, and definition(s) of each of the following words. Then write the appropriate form of the word in the blank space in the illustrative sentence(s) following.

1. **antipathy**
   (an tip' ə thē)

   (*n.*) a strong dislike, hostile feeling

   Sensible people normally view any form of bigotry with the most profound _____.

2. **beset**
   (bē set')

   (*v.*) to attack from all sides; to surround, hem in; (*adj., part.*) harassed, troubled; studded (as with jewels)

   Every federal administration must grapple with the economic woes that _____ the nation.

   The crown worn by England's monarchs is a gorgeous object _____ with precious stones.

3. **compassion**
   (kəm pash' ən)

   (*n.*) sympathy for another's suffering; pity

   Without the _____ and generosity of donors and volunteers, many charitable organizations would close.

4. **duress**
   (dù res')

   (*n.*) compulsion by threat; forcible confinement

   Political prisoners are sometimes subjected to a mild form of _____ called *house arrest*.

5. **implacable**
   (im plak' ə bəl)

   (*adj.*) not to be satisfied or pacified; unyielding

   The peoples of the Arctic have shown that nature need not be an _____ foe.

6. **innocuous**
   (i näk' yü əs)

   (*adj.*) harmless, inoffensive; insignificant

   Conversation at a dinner party may sometimes be confined to pleasant and _____ generalities.

7. **militate**
   (mil' ə tāt)

   (*v.*) to have effect or force on or against someone or something, fight against

   Health experts _____ strongly against a diet that is high in calories, fat, and salt.

8. **patent**
   (pat' ənt)

   (*n.*) exclusive rights over an invention; copyright; (*v.*) to arrange or obtain such rights; (*adj.*) plain, open to view; copyrighted

   When the _____ on a drug expires, any manufacturer may produce it.

   Thomas Alva Edison had _____ over two thousand inventions before his death in 1931.

   A skilled lawyer may catch a key hostile witness in a _____ falsehood.

9. **prowess**
   (praú' əs)

(*n.*) distinguished bravery; superior skill or ability
The Greek hero Achilles won fame for his
_____ in the Trojan War.

10. **stentorian**
    (sten tôr' ē ən)

(*adj.*) extremely loud
Some public speakers favor a _____
delivery and emphatic gestures to drive home their
message to their listeners.

Using Context

*For each item, determine whether the **boldface** word from pages 190–191 makes sense in the context of the sentence. Circle the item numbers next to the six sentences in which the words are used correctly.*

1. An inventor should research if a **patent** has already been granted before investing time and money into an idea.

2. During the 1930s, when the country was **beset** by the Great Depression, many Americans found escape in movies that depicted glamorous settings and ways of life.

3. By any standard, a 100th birthday is truly a **stentorian** occasion.

4. Thousands of local animal rescue organizations have been founded by people who feel deep **compassion** for homeless and abused pets.

5. A confession made under **duress** is not generally considered to be legally valid.

6. There is a big difference between a boss who is tough but fair and one who is unreasonable and **implacable**.

7. When writing a persuasive essay, it is important to state your opinion clearly and **militate** it with reasons and evidence.

8. Some patients show remarkable **antipathy** and recover from illnesses much earlier than normal.

9. The art gallery's owners would prefer a groundbreaking and even controversial show to a dull and **innocuous** one.

10. The lawyer apologized to the judge for the **prowess** that she showed while cross-examining the witness.

Choosing the Right Word

Select the **boldface** word that better completes each sentence. You might refer to the passage on pages 188–189 to see how most of these words are used in context. Note that the choices might be related forms of the Unit words.

1. Unable to roar and intimidate those around him, the Cowardly Lion hoped the Great Wizard could help him exhibit his (**prowess, compassion**) as king of the beasts.

2. The tough leadership we need in this new century will not come from uncertain and (**patented, innocuous**) personalities.

3. You are in deep trouble if you combine a strong taste for high living with an equally strong (**antipathy, prowess**) for hard work.

4. The authorities suspected that the hostage's statement was made not voluntarily but under (**patent, duress**).

5. Mistaking the (**innocuous, stentorian**) backfire of the truck for a sudden burst of gunfire, we ducked behind a parked car for safety.

6. Although he was (**beset, militated**) by creditors, a tough employer, and medical problems, he never seemed to lose his zest for living.

7. As he watched his house go up in flames, he felt that he was the victim of an (**stentorian, implacable**) fate.

8. His (**prowess, duress**) as a speaker quickly made him a leading figure in the Senate.

9. It does little good to feel (**antipathy, compassion**) for those less fortunate than ourselves if we are not willing to make sacrifices to help them.

10. The mistake in identification was so (**patent, implacable**) that the suspect was released with the apologies of the arresting officer.

11. The politician's poor showing in the polls and the failure of her fund-raising efforts (**militated, beset**) against her entering the presidential race.

12. Her grandmother passed on her ancient gold bracelet (**duressed, beset**) with rubies.

Completing the Sentence

Choose the word from the word bank that best completes each of the following sentences. Write the correct word or form of the word in the space provided.

antipathy	compassion	implacable	militate	prowess
beset	duress	innocuous	patent	stentorian

1. American law prohibits police from arresting and holding suspects in any type of _____ without formally charging them.

2. We could hear the quarterback's _____ signals even above the roar of the crowd.

3. Her refusal to discuss even the possibility of a compromise convinced me that I was faced with a(n) _____ opponent.

4. How can you expect them to concern themselves with your problems when they are so _____ with troubles of their own?

5. The player's chronic shoulder injury _____ against his plan to extend his baseball career for another season.

6. Centuries-old ethnic _____ have more than once led to bloody conflict in the Balkans.

7. Dr. Albert Schweitzer had not only great scientific ability but also a deep sense of _____ for suffering humanity.

8. I am well on the road to becoming a millionaire because I have just been awarded the _____ for an automatic homework machine.

9. If only he could match his _____ on the playing field with a high level of excellence in the classroom!

10. The "monster" that frightened you so much during the hike last week was just a(n) _____ water snake.

End Set A

Definitions

Note the spelling, pronunciation, part(s) of speech, and definition(s) of each of the following words. Then write the appropriate form of the word in the blank space in the illustrative sentence(s) following.

1. applicable
(ap′ lə kə bəl)

(*adj.*) capable of being applied; relevant, suitable
The protection against being tried for the same crime twice is not _____ in some cases.

2. asset
(as′ et)

(*n.*) something of value; a resource; an advantage
By law, an annual report must include a detailed breakdown of a company's _____ and liabilities.

3. decorum
(di kôr′ əm)

(*n.*) proper behavior, good taste; orderliness
Legislative assemblies preserve _____ by operating under the rules of parliamentary procedure.

4. exuberant
(eg zü′ bər ənt)

(*adj.*) high-spirited, enthusiastic, unrestrained; excessive, abundant
Unable to control their _____ spirits, the fans of the popular singer cheered their idol loudly.

5. facsimile
(fak sim′ ə lē)

(*n.*) an exact copy
A _____ of the U.S. Constitution is displayed in many social studies classrooms.

6. imbibe
(im bīb′)

(*v.*) to drink; to take in, absorb
An inquisitive person can _____ knowledge from many sources.

7. infinitesimal
(in fin ə tes′ ə məl)

(*adj.*) so small as to be almost immeasurable; minute
To a fussy housekeeper, even an _____ amount of dust on a tabletop is unacceptable.

8. sedate
(sə dāt′)

(*adj.*) quiet, settled, sober; (*v.*) to administer a tranquilizer
At concerts of classical music, audiences generally behave in a _____ and attentive manner.
A doctor may decide to _____ a patient who has suffered a severe emotional shock or physical injury.

9. **stipulate**
(stip' yə lāt)

(v.) to arrange specifically; to require as a condition of agreement

A financial institution may _____ that all its employees be fingerprinted.

10. **ultimatum**
(əl tə mā' təm)

(n.) a final proposal or statement of conditions

As a strike deadline draws near, both labor and management can be expected to issue

_____.

Using Context

*For each item, determine whether the **boldface** word from pages 194–195 makes sense in the context of the sentence. Circle the item numbers next to the six sentences in which the words are used correctly.*

1. We all marveled at the **infinitesimal** view from the top floor of the skyscraper.

2. The teacher expected the class to be rowdy and excited on the first day of school, but her students were a surprisingly **sedate** group.

3. Not even the dark rain clouds could dampen her **exuberant** spirits that morning.

4. The **facsimile** of the newest smart phone comes with even more features than the previous version.

5. Jane Austen's novels make a great deal of commentary on society that is still **applicable** today.

6. The manager gave the worker an **ultimatum:** either start getting to work on time, or find a new job.

7. When he becomes interested in a subject, he will **imbibe** all the information he can find from books, the Internet, and documentaries until he feels he knows everything about it.

8. He may **stipulate** any wrongdoing on his part, but the statue did not simply fall on its own.

9. My ability to talk to anyone about anything is usually what people point out as my best **asset**.

10. The **decorum** he displayed at the dinner party guaranteed that he would not be invited to their home again.

Choosing the Right Word

*Select the **boldface** word that better completes each sentence. You might refer to the passage on pages 188–189 to see how most of these words are used in context. Note that the choices might be related forms of the Unit words.*

1. One of the many (**assets, facsimiles**) of the Globe Theater is its costumes—elaborate outfits that are made from luxuriant fabrics.

2. Did you (**stipulate, imbibe**) that you wanted the recliner, not the rocking chair?

3. "Here's the (**ultimatum, asset**)," said Father. "Pass all your courses or forget about attending the senior prom."

4. A person's modest and (**applicable, sedate**) appearance may mask an iron determination and a sharp temper.

5. They were so (**exuberant, infinitesimal**) in their praise that I soon began to suspect either their judgment or their sincerity.

6. At my niece's birthday party, I was concerned about the enormous amounts of punch, soda, and other sugary drinks the children were (**imbibing, sedating**).

7. Her sense of (**ultimatum, decorum**) is so strict that she often makes other people feel stiff and uncomfortable.

8. What good does it do to include all those (**stipulations, facsimiles**) in the agreement if there are no provisions for enforcing them?

9. My study of astronomy gave me a sense of the importance of (**infinitesimal, applicable**) human beings and our tiny planet in a boundless universe.

10. To show their (**decorum, exuberance**) during the play-offs, many football fans paint their faces and wear wild costumes.

11. In this synthetic world of ours, I sometimes wonder if my life is genuine or just a(n)(**ultimatum, facsimile**) of the real thing.

12. Some of the lessons that we learned during the Great Depression are (**exuberant, applicable**) to our economic problems today.

Completing the Sentence

Choose the word from the word bank that best completes each of the following sentences. Write the correct word or form of the word in the space provided.

applicable	decorum	facsimile	infinitesimal	stipulate
asset	exuberant	imbibe	sedate	ultimatum

1. How quickly their _____ holiday mood became quiet and sober when they had to return to work on Monday morning!

2. The landlord's _____ was simple and direct: Pay the rent increase or get out.

3. If the contract is framed by a good lawyer, it will _____ exactly when, where, and how payment is to be made.

4. During the long summer afternoons, we used to sit on the shaded veranda, _____ iced drinks and talking about life.

5. I was amazed to see how a few years had transformed an unruly and mischievous child into a well-bred, _____ young adult.

6. He has his shortcomings, but compared with his great services to his community and nation, they seem all but _____.

7. The reference material you have given me is interesting, but most of it is not _____ to my term paper.

8. I enjoy his jokes, but he ought to bear in mind that there are certain standards of _____ to be observed at the graduation ceremony.

9. Her chief _____, both in business and in social life, are her keen intelligence and pleasant manner.

10. Although the artist's latest work was acclaimed by the critics, it seemed to me to be no more than a(n) _____ of a cardboard cereal box.

Synonyms

*Choose the word or form of the word from this Unit that is the same or most nearly the same in meaning as the **boldface** word or expression in the phrase. Write that word on the line. Use a dictionary if necessary.*

1. spoke in a **booming** voice   _____
2. **hostility** between the opposing groups   _____
3. **defy** the adoption of the policy   _____
4. felt **empathy** for the grieving parents   _____
5. a **reproduction** of a famous painting   _____
6. an **unappeasable** enemy   _____
7. **assimilate** the wisdom of a lifetime   _____
8. **assailed** by the protestors   _____
9. forced to sell all their **possessions**   _____
10. providing the **pertinent** papers for admission _____
11. extorted evidence under **pressure**   _____
12. asked an **unobjectionable** question   _____
13. **spell out** the duties to be performed   _____
14. the **obvious** stupidity of the remark   _____
15. rejected the dictator's **threat**   _____

Antonyms

*Choose the word or form of the word from this Unit that is most nearly opposite in meaning to the **boldface** word or expression in the phrase. Write that word on the line. Use a dictionary if necessary.*

1. an **agitated** mood   _____
2. exhibited **bad taste** during the ceremony   _____
3. **incompetence** on the playing field   _____
4. an **immense** amount of rainfall   _____
5. her **sulky** personality   _____

Writing: Words in Action

Suppose you are Captain Cook, commander of the *Endeavor*. Write a letter to your family, describing your experiences on the voyage and assuring them that you are well. Use at least two details from the passage (pages 188–189) and three or more words from this Unit.

Vocabulary in Context

*Some of the words you have studied in this Unit appear in **boldface** type. Read the passage below, and then circle the letter of the correct answer for each word as it is used in context.*

Over 5000 years ago Phoenician traders used celestial navigation to create trade routes from the Eastern Mediterranean to what are now the British Isles. They steered by a "celestial calendar," created from their observations of the Little Bear constellation. The apparent height of each star above the horizon varied according to the time of year and the location of the observer. Every night they would measure the distance of each star from the horizon—their unit of measure was the width of an index finger, held horizontally at arm's length. As long as they followed the celestial calendar, the Phoenicians knew their way.

Until the eighteenth century navigation remained a matter of gazing at the horizon and measuring. Accuracy improved, but even the most sophisticated instruments could only measure latitude. Expanding trade and crowded sea-roads demanded longitude. In 1707 the British government offered a reward of 20,000 pound sterling (now $6 million) for an invention capable of measuring longitude, **stipulating** that it must be **applicable** to naval requirements.

Longitude fixes the location of any point on Earth in relation to the *prime meridian*—a north-south line that runs from pole to pole, passing through Greenwich, London. Any point on Earth must therefore be within 180° east or 180° west of the prime meridian. Since a complete rotation of Earth (360°) takes 24 hours, if you know the exact time wherever you are, and compare it to the time in London, you'll know your exact longitude.

The project was **beset** with problems. No timepiece could keep time *exactly*—and movement of the ocean would **militate** against accuracy. It was not until 1759 that John Harrison, an English clockmaker, was ready to **patent** and present his "Marine Chronometer." James Cook used a **facsimile** of Harrison's chronometer on his voyages of discovery. At last, navigators could make an X on the map and say, "We are here."

---

1. To **stipulate** is to

   a. ignore   **c.** precede

   b. require   **d.** record

2. If a method is **applicable**, it is

   a. suitable   **c.** insufficient

   b. desirable   **d.** in working order

3. To be **beset** is to be

   a. beaten   **c.** harassed

   b. belabored   **d.** intimidated

4. The word **militate** most nearly means

   a. oppose   **c.** disprove

   b. deplete   **d.** galvanize

5. If an invention has a **patent**, it has

   a. a copyright   **c.** a use

   b. approval   **d.** profits

6. A **facsimile** is

   a. a memento   **c.** a new gadget

   b. a diagram   **d.** an exact copy

Read the following passage, taking note of the **boldface** words and their contexts. These words are among those you will be studying in Unit 14. It may help you to complete the exercises in this Unit if you refer to the way the words are used below.

A Short History of Hygiene
<Informational Essay>

Hygeia, goddess of health and cleanliness

Cleanliness has deep roots in human civilization. The word *hygiene* is derived from the name of an ancient Greek goddess. Hygeia, the goddess of health and cleanliness, was said to prevent disease, and when an epidemic threatened, the Greeks went with **alacrity** to her temples. Ancient Romans worshipped Hygeia, too, and Rome was famous for its advanced hygienic standards. Historians **laud** the Romans for both building aqueducts that carried fresh water into Rome and public toilets that collected waste. Dotting the city were comfortable bathhouses, where people would gather to **loll** in the waters. Perhaps it was here that Romans first earned their reputation as a **loquacious** people, for

The ruins of a thermal bath in Italy

they would pass idle time chatting with friends. An unexpected invader, however, added a **dissonant** note to Rome's hygienic way of life: Head lice were common, and without soap, these parasites were hard to control. To **alleviate** this problem, Romans covered their bodies with oil and then scraped themselves clean with an instrument called a *strigil*. Unfortunately, the Romans' hygienic way of life was endangered when barbarians sacked Rome in the fourth century AD. These **bellicose** invaders were not **magnanimous** to their enemies; they destroyed as much of the Roman civilization as possible. **Appalled** by the destruction, Romans fled for their lives, and the highly ordered Roman Empire soon collapsed.

Subsequent centuries in Europe were, hygienically speaking, the **antithesis** of what is prevalent today. The time between AD 500 and AD 1500, **disparaged** as the Dark Ages, was a period when the average life expectancy barely reached into the mid-thirties. Advice about hygiene in the Dark Ages seems almost **droll** today: A Latin proverb from the time warns people that "frequent bathing causes a wasting body." Certainly, sanitation and clean water were lacking in large cities, lice infestation was a constant problem, and diseases spread quickly. The Crusaders, soldiers in Holy Wars, brought soap back from the East, but it was a luxury and not widely used. Authorities issued **edicts** against public bathhouses, fearing their use led to immorality, and many years passed before these orders were **rescinded**. In colder climates, bathing was infrequent because of the lack of heating. Also, in an era of plagues—which killed over a third of Europe's population—many people believed the skin absorbed diseases from water. In the absence of scientific knowledge and with the cause of the terrifying plagues unexplained, people accepted such misinformation. While a full bath would have been an infrequent indulgence, most people did wash their hands and face with some regularity.

The discovery that bacteria caused disease, a revelation that came in the mid-nineteenth

Commonly found in fresh water, these bacteria would have alarmed Medievals.

century, brought about a sea change in hygiene and public health. To control germs, experts said it was **mandatory** to wash hands regularly. In addition, to avoid disease, sewage had to be disposed of safely, and water had to be pure. Meeting these goals, a challenging undertaking, continues to this day. In the quest for better hygiene, science and technology **elucidated** the importance of new and better ways to promote health. Even relatively simple inventions, like the flush toilet and chlorinated water, have probably saved millions of lives. Washing machines and detergents played a big role, too—they helped people clean clothes quickly and thoroughly. In the struggle to prevent bacterial diseases, modern society has clearly gone the extra mile. Hygeia would be pleased, for although she is no longer worshipped as a goddess, people today are cleaner than ever.

Audio

For iWords and audio passages, go to SadlierConnect.com.

Definitions

Note the spelling, pronunciation, part(s) of speech, and definition(s) of each of the following words. Then write the appropriate form of the word in the blank space in the illustrative sentence(s) following.

1. **appall**
   (ə pôl´)

   (*v.*) to fill with dismay or horror
   The assassination of President John F. Kennedy in 1963 _____ the nation and the world.

2. **bellicose**
   (bel´ i kōs)

   (*adj.*) warlike in manner or temperament; quarrelsome
   Teddy Roosevelt's foreign policy was often driven by a rather _____ brand of patriotism.

3. **disparage**
   (dis pâr´ ij)

   (*v.*) to belittle, speak slightingly of; to undervalue
   Don't you think voters are getting awfully tired of listening to politicians _____ their opponents' voting records?

4. **droll**
   (drōl)

   (*adj.*) amusingly odd
   The hero or heroine of a popular sitcom may be surrounded by a cast of _____ eccentrics.

5. **loll**
   (läl)

   (*v.*) to act in a lazy manner; to lounge; to recline, droop
   There is nothing I would rather do on a hot, humid summer afternoon than _____ in a hammock under a tree.

6. **magnanimous**
   (mag nan´ ə məs)

   (*adj.*) generous in forgiving, above small meanness
   The general's victory was so decisive that he could afford to be _____ toward his former enemies.

7. **nondescript**
   (nän də skript´)

   (*adj.*) ordinary, not outstanding; not easily classified
   Fashion critics judged the designer's fall clothing line to be disappointingly _____.

8. **phlegmatic**
   (fleg mat´ ik)

   (*adj.*) slow-moving, sluggish; unemotional
   Sloths are such _____ creatures that they have earned the reputation of being the slowest animals on Earth.

9. rescind
(ri sind′)

(v.) to repeal, cancel

A sitting Congress sometimes _____ statutes passed by its predecessors.

10. whet
(whet)

(v.) to sharpen, put an edge on; to make keen or eager

In most mystery novels, the first chapter is designed to _____ your curiosity to find out "who done it."

Using Context

*For each item, determine whether the **boldface** word from pages 202–203 makes sense in the context of the sentence. Circle the item numbers next to the six sentences in which the words are used correctly.*

1. Who would have thought that one of the city's most expensive restaurants would be located in that modest, **nondescript** building?

2. My friend likes to quote the captions of the **droll** cartoons she sees in the famous magazine *The New Yorker*.

3. Despite the fact that critics are expected to **disparage** the movie as an overwrought mess, audiences are flocking to see it.

4. New technologies are enabling engineers and work crews to build **magnanimous** bridges that span longer distances than ever before.

5. Nothing can **appall** your thirst as well as a glass of plain water.

6. It's very relaxing to just sit outside and listen to the **bellicose** sounds of nature.

7. The contract allows house buyers two weeks to change their mind and **rescind** their offer; after that, they forfeit their deposit if they do not proceed with the sale.

8. The rainy weather provided us with an excuse to just **loll** around the house and catch up on our reading.

9. In spite of the pouring rain, the **phlegmatic** ranch hand plodded on, steadily pounding the fence post into the ground.

10. When you train for a marathon, you learn to pace yourself so that you don't **whet** most of your energy early in the race.

Choosing the Right Word

*Select the **boldface** word that better completes each sentence. You might refer to the passage on pages 200–201 to see how most of these words are used in context. Note that the choices might be related forms of the Unit words.*

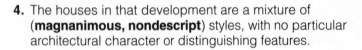

1. The dessert was delicious, but the serving was so small that it did little more than (**disparage, whet**) my appetite.

2. Your relaxed and lackadaisical attitude reveals a (**phlegmatic, droll**) personality, which means that you would not be happy in a fast-moving, high-pressure job.

3. There must be a serious flaw in the character of those who have a constant need to (**whet, disparage**) others.

4. The houses in that development are a mixture of (**magnanimous, nondescript**) styles, with no particular architectural character or distinguishing features.

5. Because of the incidents that occurred during hazing week, the school may (**appall, rescind**) the rules that allow fraternity initiations.

6. Although Americans are not a (**bellicose, phlegmatic**) people, they have proven themselves prepared to defend their nation at any cost.

7. What (**appalled, lolled**) us even more than their fearful living conditions was that the refugees seemed to have lost all hope.

8. Her jokes were actually not too good, but her (**nondescript, droll**) manner of delivering them made a big hit with the audience.

9. Winston Churchill told the British to be resolute in war, defiant in defeat, and (**magnanimous, bellicose**) in victory.

10. Only a truly (**phlegmatic, droll**) person could have remained calm in the face of such provocation.

11. Would you rather (**rescind, loll**) in the back seat of a chauffeured limousine or drive your own convertible?

12. Rather than appear diplomatic, the politician had a (**bellicose, magnanimous**) attitude when confronted with the charges of impropriety.

Completing the Sentence

Choose the word from the word bank that best completes each of the following sentences. Write the correct word or form of the word in the space provided.

appall	disparage	loll	nondescript	rescind
bellicose	droll	magnanimous	phlegmatic	whet

1. I shall never forget your _____ offer to coach me, even though we were competing for the same role in the play.

2. The principal finally _____ the unfair school regulation that prevented new students from trying out for the varsity teams.

3. Even the state troopers, who had been hardened by long experience, were _____ when they came on the scene of the automobile accident.

4. In a time of fast-talking, loud comedians, is there a place for his kind of quiet, _____ humor?

5. She may appear to be _____, but her friends are aware of the strong emotions simmering beneath her quiet exterior.

6. His disposition is so _____ that he is apt to turn a simple difference of opinion into a full-scale donnybrook.

7. I'm usually quite energetic, but there are times when I want to do nothing but _____ about and listen to my favorite music.

8. Unlike you, I have never lived in France, but is that any reason for you to _____ my efforts to speak French?

9. Her enthusiastic and colorful description of the new series on public TV has _____ my desire to see it.

10. Is this _____ little house the "magnificent mansion" that you've been telling us about all these weeks?

Definitions

Note the spelling, pronunciation, part(s) of speech, and definition(s) of each of the following words. Then write the appropriate form of the word in the blank space in the illustrative sentence(s) following.

1. alacrity
(ə lak′ rə tē)

(*n.*) a cheerful readiness; brisk and eager action
Neighbors responded with _____ to the woman's cries for help.

2. alleviate
(ə lē′ vē āt)

(*v.*) to relieve, make more bearable
The doctors and nurses did everything they could to _____ the patient's severe pain.

3. antithesis
(an tith′ ə sis)

(*n.*) the direct opposite, a sharp contrast
Discriminatory practices may be said to constitute the very _____ of our nation's democratic ideals.

4. dissonant
(dis′ ə nənt)

(*adj.*) not in harmony; disagreeing, at odds
The clamor of _____ voices could be heard clearly through the closed doors of the meeting room.

5. edict
(ē′ dikt)

(*n.*) an order issued by someone in authority
Only in fairy tales can human unhappiness and misery be banished forever by royal _____.

6. elucidate
(i lü′ sə dāt)

(*v.*) to clarify, explain
The precise meaning of a passage in *Middlemarch* is sometimes hard to _____.

7. laud
(lôd)

(*v.*) to praise
At the assembly the principal _____ both students and teachers for the schoolwide improvement in reading scores.

8. loquacious
(lō kwā′ shəs)

(*adj.*) talkative, wordy; fond of talking
My dinner companion was so _____ that our conversation quickly turned into a monologue.

9. **mandatory**
(man' də tôr ē)

(*adj.*) required, obligatory
A union contract may stipulate that members are to receive a _____ annual cost-of-living increase.

10. **vivacious**
(və vā' shəs)

(*adj.*) lively, sprightly, full of energy
A _____ individual will certainly never lack for companions.

Using Context

*For each item, determine whether the **boldface** word from pages 206–207 makes sense in the context of the sentence. Circle the item numbers next to the six sentences in which the words are used correctly.*

1. Although this essay is well researched, you took too long to arrive at the **antithesis** of your argument and make your claim.

2. Our **loquacious** tour guide certainly gave us a lot of information, but I wish she had given us time to enjoy the sites in peace.

3. I must **laud** you on your confidence when faced with criticism, as it is not easy to remain composed in that situation.

4. Even at ninety years old, my grandmother still has a **vivacious** personality and is always the life of the party.

5. Our group reached a **dissonant** agreement about who would prepare what materials for the final presentation, with each person's task suited to his or her strengths.

6. Although the class on British literature is not **mandatory**, I decided to take it to broaden my horizons.

7. Although she was still grieving, I could tell from her small smile that being around loved ones was helping to **alleviate** some of her pain.

8. As he tried explaining the topic in more detail to us, he only made it more complicated and **elucidated** the issue further.

9. The **alacrity** and outrage with which he responded to the announcement of the proposed plan showed his opposition toward it.

10. The coach issued an **edict** prohibiting players from altering their uniforms, saying that any violator would be given a one-game suspension.

Choosing the Right Word

*Select the **boldface** word that better completes each sentence. You might refer to the passage on pages 200–201 to see how most of these words are used in context. Note that the choices might be related forms of the Unit words.*

1. In the eyes of such leaders as Martin Luther King, Jr. and Gandhi, violence is the very (**edict, antithesis**) of a civilized society.

2. Do you have any remedies that can (**elucidate, alleviate**) an upset stomach?

3. In the fight against air pollution, many states have made filtering devices (**loquacious, mandatory**) for all cars sold within their borders.

4. Maya pretended to be indifferent about going to the dance, but I noticed that she accepted Joshua's invitation with (**antithesis, alacrity**).

5. By (**lauding, elucidating**) the concept of a pyramid scheme in her opening statement, the attorney hoped to clarify why her client was innocent.

6. It is sometimes said that women are more (**loquacious, dissonant**) than men, but all the men I know do their full share of talking.

7. Her manner of speaking is so (**vivacious, mandatory**) that even her most commonplace remarks seem to suggest charm and excitement.

8. This young man has been (**lauded, alleviated**) by many colleagues and fans as the most creative game designer in the industry.

9. The expression, "What goes up must come down," might be termed an (**alacrity, edict**) of nature.

10. Reporters asked the mayor to (**elucidate, alleviate**) her ambiguous remarks about her plans to seek higher office.

11. Observers doubted that any coalition composed of such (**vivacious, dissonant**) factions could long refrain from petty infighting.

12. I see no reason to (**laud, elucidate**) him in such glowing terms for doing no more than his duty.

Completing the Sentence

Choose the word from the word bank that best completes each of the following sentences. Write the correct word or form of the word in the space provided.

alacrity	antithesis	edict	laud	mandatory
alleviate	dissonant	elucidate	loquacious	vivacious

1. At that dull, stodgy party, her _____ personality was like a breath of fresh air.

2. You can make requests and suggestions if you wish, but please don't issue any _____.

3. Instead of waiting for government help, let's do all we can right now to _____ the sufferings of the flood victims.

4. When the speaker tried to _____ the statement he had just made, I became more confused than ever.

5. Though her friends _____ her many achievements, her enemies ridiculed them.

6. Their sarcastic remarks introduced a(n) _____ note into what had been a harmonious meeting.

7. I would have preferred to enjoy the paintings quietly, without listening to the explanations of the _____ guide.

8. Although in America voting is not _____, every qualified citizen has a duty to go to the polls in every election.

9. In spite of her inexperience as a programmer, she attacked her new job with _____ and made good progress.

10. His idle, pleasure-seeking way of life is the exact _____ of all that his hardworking parents had expected of him.

Synonyms

*Choose the word or form of the word from this Unit that is the same or most nearly the same in meaning as the **boldface** word or expression in the phrase. Write that word on the line. Use a dictionary if necessary.*

1. **hailed** for his good deeds _____
2. known to have a **stolid** temperament _____
3. a **zany** sense of humor _____
4. **lighten** the tax burden _____
5. refused to obey the **directive** _____
6. a truly **commonplace** personality _____
7. **illuminate** fine points of the law _____
8. **lounge** on the couch _____
9. a series of **strident** chords _____
10. skills that are **imperative** for the job _____
11. agreed to the proposal with **dispatch** _____
12. **revoke** the ban on parking in midtown _____
13. joined the **dynamic** group of dancers _____
14. the **complete opposite** of what was intended _____
15. a preview that **arouses** your curiosity _____

Antonyms

*Choose the word or form of the word from this Unit that is most nearly opposite in meaning to the **boldface** word or expression in the phrase. Write that word on the line. Use a dictionary if necessary.*

1. adopted a **conciliatory** attitude _____
2. a **reticent** storyteller _____
3. a **spiteful** gesture _____
4. **extolled** the community leader's ideas _____
5. **exhilarated** by the outcome _____

Writing: Words in Action

Suppose you had the opportunity to enlighten the people of the so-called Dark Ages about the importance of cleanliness. Write a public service announcement explaining why all citizens should wash regularly. Use at least two details from the passage (pages 200–201) and three or more Unit words.

Vocabulary in Context

*Some of the words you have studied in this Unit appear in **boldface** type. Read the passage below, and then circle the letter of the correct answer for each word as it is used in context.*

Many agencies of the federal government have their origins in social or economic problems too large to be handled effectively at a state or local level. Such agencies include the Federal Drug Administration (FDA) and the Centers for Disease Control and Prevention (CDC).

The history of the FDA reaches back to 1906, when Congress passed the Pure Food and Drug Act. This legislation was motivated in great part by Upton Sinclair's best-selling novel of the same year, *The Jungle*. The book was no documentary surveying the **vivacious** nature of the wild. Instead, it was a hard-hitting exposé of the Chicago meatpacking industry. The grotesque violations of hygiene and sanitation did little to **whet** the reader's appetite; on the contrary, Sinclair's novel vastly strengthened the case for **mandatory** reform. Today, the FDA is far from a **phlegmatic** bureaucracy pushing **nondescript** paperwork. The agency actively oversees 25 percent of America's gross domestic product, enforcing strong consumer safeguards and regulations on pharmaceutical products as well as food.

The Centers for Disease Control and Prevention began in 1946 as the Communicable Disease Center, which in turn was an offshoot of the office of Malaria Control in War Areas during World War II. The agency was located in Atlanta, Georgia, because the South was the region with the most malaria transmission. Originally, the CDC focused on malaria, typhus, and other infectious diseases. However, over the years the agency has accepted a broadening mandate with **alacrity.** In recent decades, for example, the CDC has been a global leader in the fight against new diseases such as AIDS, Ebola, and Zika.

---

1. The word **vivacious** most nearly means
   a. precise
   b. dull
   c. lively
   d. protracted

2. If things **whet** your appetite, they
   a. stifle it
   b. identify it
   c. sharpen it
   d. detach it

3. If action is **mandatory**, it is
   a. optional
   b. insignificant
   c. discretionary
   d. required

4. To be **phlegmatic** is to be
   a. excitable
   b. candid
   c. sluggish
   d. whimsical

5. The word **nondescript** most nearly means
   a. ordinary
   b. opinionated
   c. vague
   d. prepossessing

6. To accept with **alacrity** is to accept with
   a. hesitancy
   b. willingness
   c. loyalty
   d. gentility

*Read the following passage, taking note of the **boldface** words and their contexts. These words are among those you will be studying in Unit 15. It may help you to complete the exercises in this Unit if you refer to the way the words are used below.*

World-Famous Dance Troupe Announces First U.S. Tour
<Press Release>

FOR IMMEDIATE RELEASE:

U.S. Tour of Ballets Russes to Launch in New York City

New York, January 3—

The Metropolitan Civic Association is proud to announce its exclusive sponsorship of the first American tour of the celebrated Ballets Russes. The world's most prestigious dance company will kick off its sixteen-city tour of the United States with a performance in New York City. Tickets to opening night will be available at the M.C.A. box office beginning Monday.

The Ballets Russes has enjoyed great success—and provoked considerable controversy—since its inaugural performance seven years ago in Paris. Unique among dance troupes, the Ballets Russes ensures its every production is an artistic collaboration with some of the most notable composers, choreographers, costumers, and set designers of our day. Onstage, its accomplished troupe of thirteen dancers is led by the great Vaslav Nijinsky, rightly hailed as the finest male dancer of his generation.

The company was established in 1909 by the Russian impresario Sergei Diaghilev, whose **zealous** support of modern dance boldly thrust classical dance traditions into the twentieth century. His avant-garde productions offended some early audience members, who were **voluble** in their

Sergei Diaghilev

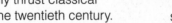

Igor Stravinsky

resistance to the Ballets Russes's break with classical ballet. Most spectators were **receptive** to Diaghilev's ideas, however, and critics now **concur** that any Ballets Russes performance is the epitome of Modernism.

Critical to the company's success has been the music of Russian composer Igor Stravinsky. His contributions to the Ballets Russes have not been without controversy, however. No one familiar with the recent history of this outstanding dance troupe will fail to recall reports of the 1913 **fracas** in Paris, when the composer's *The Rite of Spring* provoked the opening-night audience to near **pandemonium**. An unfamiliar sound on the dance stage, Stravinsky's adventurous music was considered too **abrasive** an accompaniment to ballet. Disparaged as **grotesque**, the Ballets Russes dancers' movements, too, came under fire. Yet lovers of ballet on both sides of the Atlantic have rapidly **acclimated** themselves to change, and by uniting modern movement with modern music, the Ballets Russes has brought a fresh perspective to dance.

A performance of *The Firebird*, Stravinsky's first popular sensation for the Ballets Russes, will inaugurate the American tour. The composer's *Petrushka* will be included in the performance schedule as well. Stravinsky created this work for Nijinsky. The fanciful plot tells the story of Petrushka, a puppet made of straw who comes

Nijinsky and corps in
"L'Apres-midi d'un faune"

to life. A love triangle reaches its climax when Petrushka is slain by his rival. However, the hero then returns to life as a ghost and visits the enemies who have **repressed** him.

The great Nijinsky himself is rumored to be joining the tour later this season. Monsieur Diaghilev, always **reticent**, has refused to comment on the possibility of a performance by Nijinksy in the role of *Petrushka* while the troupe is on these shores. It is therefore with sincere appreciation and high hopes that the M.C.A. commends the Ballets Russes to our friends and supporters.

Tickets to the New York City performances, which begin at the Metropolitan Opera House on January 17, will doubtless be at a premium. So we entreat art lovers not to suffer the **chagrin** of being turned away at the door! Do not **renounce** this rare opportunity to witness one of the most dazzling spectacles of this or any era. No more **vehement** advocate for modern art can be found than Monsieur Diaghilev. Just as a master

chef selects choice ingredients and blends them to create a **savory** meal, Monsieur Diaghilev possesses an uncanny talent to fuse music and dance, whimsy and spectacle. His every production has stirred hitherto **complacent** audiences everywhere the troupe has performed. We have every reason to believe that each U.S. performance by the Ballets Russes will be met with **raucous** applause.

For tickets to the New York performances, please contact the Metropolitan Civic Association at 51 West 11th Street, or telephone Mr. Constantine Z. Schelling or Mrs. Amelie Ziolkowski at REgent 4-2636.

Audio

For iWords and audio passages, go to SadlierConnect.com.

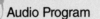

Definitions

Note the spelling, pronunciation, part(s) of speech, and definition(s) of each of the following words. Then write the appropriate form of the word in the blank space in the illustrative sentence(s) following.

1. abrasive
(ə brā′ siv)

(*adj.*) causing irritation, harsh; grinding or wearing down; (*n.*) a substance used to smooth or polish

Within every family there are some relationships that tend to be _____.

Pumice, a natural _____, is a highly porous type of glass that is produced by volcanic eruptions.

2. concur
(kən kər′)

(*v.*) to express agreement, approve

It is indeed rare for eyewitness accounts of an accident to _____ in every detail.

3. defamation
(def ə mā′ shən)

(*n.*) slander or libel

Celebrities sometimes find that they have no choice but to sue tabloids for _____.

4. explicate
(eks′ plə kāt)

(*v.*) to make plain or clear, explain; to interpret

The students listened attentively as the math teacher _____ the geometry theorem.

5. grotesque
(grō tesk′)

(*adj.*) unnatural, distorted; bizarre

Gargoyles, the _____ beasts carved on many Gothic churches, are actually drainage spouts.

6. pandemonium
(pan də mō′ nē əm)

(*n.*) a wild uproar, din, or commotion

The whirl of activity on the floor of a stock exchange often looks and sounds like utter _____.

7. raucous
(rô′ kəs)

(*adj.*) disagreeably harsh-sounding; disorderly

A _____ voice can be a liability for someone wishing to pursue a career in television journalism.

8. repress
(ri pres′)

(*v.*) to hold back; to put down or check by force

As history has repeatedly proved, even the most brutal tyrants cannot forever _____ the human desire for freedom.

9. **savory**
(săv′ ə rē)

(*adj.*) tasty, appetizing; pungent or salty, not sweet; inoffensive, respectable

Some of the characters a reader meets in a detective story are none too _____.

10. **voluble**
(väl′ yə bəl)

(*adj.*) characterized by a ready flow of words; glib, fluent

Reporters never give much credence to tips that they receive from _____ but unreliable informants, however persistent.

Using Context

*For each item, determine whether the **boldface** word from pages 214–215 makes sense in the context of the sentence. Circle the item numbers next to the six sentences in which the words are used correctly.*

1. When you strongly disagree with someone's words, it can be hard to **repress** the urge to speak and express your own views.

2. All the members of a jury must **concur** in order to render a verdict.

3. That lovely wrought iron bench with the vine motif would be a **grotesque** addition to the garden.

4. The **defamation** of an entire group based on the wrongful actions of one individual is both illogical and unfair.

5. The new babysitter was not prepared for the kind of **pandemonium** that the eight children could create on any given day.

6. With the help of powerful tools, the scientists will **explicate** the fossils and pack them up so they can be shipped to a laboratory.

7. The library is a good place to go when you need a comfortable, **raucous** place to read and study.

8. Those little pies have a fruit filling and are sweet, whereas these have a mushroom filling and are **savory**.

9. The air at sea level is more **voluble** than the air at high altitude.

10. Larger, coarser particles, or pieces of grit, make sandpaper more **abrasive**, while smaller, finer pieces make it less so.

Choosing the Right Word

*Select the **boldface** word that better completes each sentence. You might refer to the passage on pages 212–213 to see how most of these words are used in context. Note that the choices might be related forms of the Unit words.*

1. For centuries scholars have argued over how to (**explicate, repress**) certain cryptic passages in Milton's plays and poems.

2. The figures in the surrealistic painting had the (**grotesque, savory**) appearance of characters in a nightmare.

3. He has a good deal of ability, but his (**voluble, abrasive**) personality has prevented him from getting ahead in the business world.

4. Economists have spent years attempting to (**concur, explicate**) the causes of the 1929 stock market collapse and the years of economic depression that followed it.

5. After spending a month in the country, we found the sounds of rush-hour traffic in the big city more (**raucous, grotesque**) than ever.

6. Lacking a positive program of her own, she hoped to gain the support of the voters by (**explicating, defaming**) the other candidates.

7. Rosemary is preferred in this soup due to its (**savory, raucous**) qualities.

8. We all have impulses to violence, but we must learn to (**repress, concur**) them if we are to live in a civilized society.

9. Ms. Sanders is usually a woman of very few words, but she was certainly (**abrasive, voluble**) when we asked her about her operation.

10. (**Pandemonium, Defamation**) erupted when the nervous theater manager announced to the waiting crowd that the rock concert was canceled.

11. Some people seem to relish every (**abrasive, savory**) morsel of gossip that comes their way.

12. After a lot of persuading, our parents (**repressed, concurred**) with our plan to make a bicycle tour of New England.

Completing the Sentence

Choose the word from the word bank that best completes each of the following sentences. Write the correct word or form of the word in the space provided.

abrasive	defamation	grotesque	raucous	savory
concur	explicate	pandemonium	repress	voluble

1. For their art project the children made _____ masks that they planned to use in a play based on some myths they had read.

2. The carpenter used a(n) _____ to remove the old finish from the top of the desk before revarnishing it.

3. The editorial on city government was so unfair and biased that it amounted to _____ of all the elected officials of this community.

4. The library became a scene of _____ when a practical joker released a number of mice.

5. I have great respect for your knowledge of our government, but I really cannot _____ with your opinion about the role of the judiciary.

6. Although I am afraid of the dentist, I must _____ my fears and go for treatment.

7. In an amazingly short time and with only the simplest ingredients, I had a(n) _____ stew simmering on the stove.

8. _____ shouts and boos from the stands will have no effect on a good umpire's decisions.

9. An accountant tried to _____ the new tax legislation to me, but when she had finished, I felt I was even more in the dark than before.

10. The answers that the candidate gave at the press conference were rambling and _____ but contained practically no hard information.

Definitions

Note the spelling, pronunciation, part(s) of speech, and definition(s) of each of the following words. Then write the appropriate form of the word in the blank space in the illustrative sentence(s) following.

1. acclimate (ak′ lə māt)	(*v.*) to adapt to a new climate, environment, or situation You may find it difficult to _____ to a new school if you arrive in the middle of the year.
2. chagrin (shə grin′)	(*n.*) irritation or humiliation caused by disappointment or frustration; (*v.*) to cause such a feeling Much to my _____, I placed a mere fourth in the 100-meter freestyle. The lukewarm reception accorded his first and only opera, *Fidelio*, deeply _____ the composer Ludwig van Beethoven.
3. complacent (kəm plā′ sənt)	(*adj.*) self-satisfied; overly content _____ individuals are, by definition, overly pleased with their lot in life.
4. fracas (frā′ kəs)	(*n.*) a noisy quarrel or brawl Do you think that the _____ on some talk shows are spontaneous or staged?
5. receptive (ri sep′ tiv)	(*adj.*) open and responsive to ideas or suggestions People will generally be _____ to criticism of their work if it is given in a constructive manner.
6. renounce (ri naùns′)	(*v.*) to give up or resign something Throughout history, martyrs have willingly given up their lives rather than _____ their cause.
7. reticent (ret′ ə sənt)	(*adj.*) not inclined to speak; reserved; reluctant She is understandably _____ about discussing her most deeply held beliefs with a group of total strangers.
8. somnolent (säm′ nə lənt)	(*adj.*) sleepy, drowsy; inducing sleep By the end of an enormous Thanksgiving feast, most diners usually feel quite _____.

9. vehement
(vē′ ə mənt)

(*adj.*) intense, forceful, powerful

The defendant's _____ protestations of innocence failed to convince the jurors.

10. zealous
(zel′ əs)

(*adj.*) eager, earnest, devoted

Most members of my family are _____ supporters of our local high school's basketball, baseball, and football teams.

Using Context

*For each item, determine whether the **boldface** word from pages 218–219 makes sense in the context of the sentence. Circle the item numbers next to the six sentences in which the words are used correctly.*

1. Your **zealous** support of my dream to become a lawyer is just the encouragement I need to keep working toward my goal.

2. The professor's **somnolent** tone can make even the most boring subject seem fascinating.

3. Her fear of water means that she is **complacent** when getting on a boat, always wearing a life jacket and bringing plenty of floating devices.

4. When a **fracas** broke out at the concert, we were all grateful that the police were there to put an end to it.

5. Everyone watched as the coach contested the call, and the referee blew the whistle to **renounce** the game.

6. He is happy to talk about anything else but remains **reticent** when asked about his plans for the future.

7. The **chagrin** I felt when my name was announced for the award was reflected on my face in a huge smile.

8. Whenever I visit my grandparents across the country, it takes me a few days to **acclimate** to the time difference.

9. I am **receptive** to the idea of taking a trip this summer, but we'll first need to see when we both have some time.

10. The office manager is **vehement** about making sure his employees are productive and spends more time watching them like a hawk than doing his own work.

Choosing the Right Word

*Select the **boldface** word that better completes each sentence. You might refer to the passage on pages 212–213 to see how most of these words are used in context. Note that the choices might be related forms of the Unit words.*

1. A (**fracas, chagrin**) between rival groups on the floor of the convention was swiftly quelled by security guards.

2. Why is it that some people are so talkative about most things but so (**complacent, reticent**) about their own personal backgrounds?

3. It's not surprising that after so many years of military service, he has found it difficult to become (**acclimated, vehement**) to civilian life.

4. With deep (**chagrin, complacency**), I must confess that I was the one who neglected to hire the orchestra for the class dance.

5. In unforgettable words, the soothsayer called on mankind to (**acclimate, renounce**) the use of armed force.

6. Some politicians are more (**zealous, somnolent**) in promoting their own careers than in seeking to help the people who elected them.

7. The workers were (**vehement, reticent**) to speak about the bank robbery, frightened that the thieves might later seek retaliation.

8. I was startled not so much by your disapproval of my proposal as by the (**fracas, vehemence**) with which you denounced it.

9. Her kind words put me in such a (**receptive, reticent**) frame of mind that I agreed to work on the committee before I knew what I was doing.

10. The (**zealous, complacent**) expression on the antique doll's porcelain face seemed to proclaim, "All's right with the world."

11. Will I ever again sleep as deeply as I did on those deliciously (**receptive, somnolent**) afternoons on that hot, quiet beach?

12. Kim attributed her failure to get the lead role in the play to the director's poor judgment and remained (**receptive, complacent**) about her acting abilities.

Completing the Sentence

Choose the word from the word bank that best completes each of the following sentences. Write the correct word or form of the word in the space provided.

acclimate	complacent	receptive	reticent	vehement
chagrin	fracas	renounce	somnolent	zealous

1. She tried hard to remain awake, but the _____ atmosphere of the warm and cozy parlor was too much for her.

2. When we reached Mexico City, which is over 7,000 feet above sea level, we found it difficult at first to _____ ourselves to the thinner air.

3. The conceited actor was anything but _____ in discussing his innumerable triumphs on the stage, screen, and TV.

4. Both daughters agreed to _____ their claims to their father's estate in favor of their widowed mother.

5. I was confident that after Dad had eaten a good meal, he would be more _____ to my request for the use of the car.

6. You can well imagine my _____ at losing such an important election by so few votes.

7. Since hockey players often crash into each other at high speed, it's not surprising that occasionally a(n) _____ develops.

8. A free people cannot afford to grow _____ but must remain ever vigilant in safeguarding their liberties.

9. He was just an average player when he first joined the team, but everyone admired his _____ efforts to improve his game.

10. We didn't expect such _____ dislike of country-and-western music from a native of Nashville.

Synonyms

*Choose the word or form of the word from this Unit that is the same or most nearly the same in meaning as the **boldface** word or expression in the phrase. Write that word on the line. Use a dictionary if necessary.*

1. willingly **rejected** worldly things _____
2. tried to break up the **melee** _____
3. led to **tumult** on the Senate floor _____
4. need to **clarify** some of the technical language _____
5. made from rich and **delicious** sauces _____
6. able to **adjust** to the arctic winters _____
7. **embarrassment** over their crushing defeat _____
8. grew **self-assured** after 20 years on the job _____
9. **ardent** supporters of the candidate _____
10. a **fierce** debate on a controversial issue _____
11. **stifle** the desire to yell out _____
12. kept awake by the **boisterous** crowd _____
13. a campaign of **mudslinging** _____
14. **heavy-eyed** from studying all night _____
15. twisted into **monstrous** shapes _____

Antonyms

*Choose the word or form of the word from this Unit that is most nearly opposite in meaning to the **boldface** word or expression in the phrase. Write that word on the line. Use a dictionary if necessary.*

1. an extremely **pleasant** manner _____
2. **disagree** on the most important issues _____
3. **quiet** traveling companions _____
4. is **garrulous** when first meeting someone _____
5. **unresponsive** to new ideas _____

Writing: Words in Action

Suppose you attended a performance of the Ballets Russes. In an effort to persuade others to attend a performance by this troupe, write a review, explaining why you recommend the ballet. Use at least two details from the passage (pages 212–213) and three or more Unit words to support your review.

Vocabulary in Context

*Some of the words you have studied in this Unit appear in **boldface** type. Read the passage below, and then circle the letter of the correct answer for each word as it is used in context.*

Until the invention of film and video in the twentieth century, ballet, that least **somnolent** of arts, faced a challenging problem. Bodily movement is the rhythm, melody, and harmony of dance. Yet, unlike musical notation, there was no agreed-upon system to record choreography. For at least 250 years, since French court ballet reached its height under Louis XIV, ballet experts experimented with various systems of notation, many of which were keyed to specific types of dance or ballet styles.

Despite the proliferation of such systems, the key factor in the transmission of choreography from generation to generation was always discipleship. Part creative master and part teacher, choreographers handed on their work to their younger colleagues in the company. Occasionally, these **zealous** students mounted fierce battles as to how best to interpret the master's philosophy or technique. Disagreements, to the **chagrin** of many, sometimes ensued when one set of students saw their rivals' interpretations as little better than **defamation**.

In the twentieth century, the **abrasive** disagreements on how best to **explicate** the intentions of choreographers diminished somewhat with the development of two widely employed systems of dance notation. The first was Labanotation, named for the Hungarian-born dance theorist, Rudolf Laban. In the Laban system, symbols represent components of bodily movement. The system is being continually refined. In Britain, the most highly developed system for recording dance movements was invented by the ballet dancer Joan Benesh. The Benesh movement notation system had the important consequence of enabling choreographers to secure copyright in their creations for the first time, since dance movements were now "fixed in a tangible medium," a crucial requirement for copyright.

---

1. The word **somnolent** most nearly means
   a. dynamic
   b. drowsy
   c. regimented
   d. primitive

2. If people are **zealous,** they are
   a. eager
   b. reluctant
   c. biased
   d. placid

3. If you experience **chagrin,** you feel
   a. proud
   b. perplexed
   c. relaxed
   d. humiliated

4. **Defamation** is
   a. injury
   b. vilification
   c. celebrity
   d. apprehension

5. An **abrasive** disagreement would be
   a. harsh
   b. polished
   c. decisive
   d. judicious

6. The word **explicate** most nearly means
   a. bewilder
   b. elucidate
   c. impersonate
   d. justify

Vocabulary for Comprehension
Part 1

*Read this passage, which contains words in **boldface** that appear in Units 13–15. Then choose the best answer to each question based on what is stated or implied in the passage. You may refer to the passage as often as necessary.*

Questions 1–10 are based on the following passage.

The practice of photographing people when they are unaware that they are being observed is known as "candid photography." Photographers who
(5) specialize in candid photography take pride in their ability to "capture the moment." Capturing the moment may take many forms, but all of them depend on the subject's lack of conscious participation
(10) in the creation of the photograph.

A lot of news photography is candid. Posed photography is **disparaged**. Authenticity and spontaneity are highly **lauded** and **zealously** sought after.
(15) People in the news are believed by the press to be much more true to their emotions when they believe they are in private than when they realize their privacy has been violated by a press
(20) photographer. It is certainly true that they are more uninhibited in their expressions when they believe they are not being watched. They are, however, probably also being perfectly true to their emotions
(25) when they catch sight of the hidden cameraman and express their **antipathy**—there is no doubting the authenticity of people's hostility when they discover that they are being spied upon.

(30)   How can a photographer who conceals his very *presence* from his subjects be referred to as a "candid photographer"? A photographer who violates the privacy of his subjects and shows what he finds
(35) to the public **militates** against candor and the ethics of his art. "Candor" is a virtue. A candid person is honest, open, and frank,

and maintains high ethical standards in his or her dealings with others.
(40)   Many photographers are conscious of the morally questionable nature of some of their activities. They have a "code of ethics" to help them through moments of moral **duress**. They are advised to treat
(45) their subjects with "respect and dignity," and to "intrude on private moments of grief only when the public has an overriding and justifiable need to see." The booklet does not stipulate how
(50) photographers can show respect and dignity to their subjects, or why they should respect the public's "need to see" the results of their intrusions.

The law supports the candid
(55) photographer. People in public places may photograph whatever they like, without permission or consent. Public places include streets, sidewalks, plazas, parks, and beaches. People may be
(60) unaware that shopping malls and many places of worship are open to the public, and so are public places. There is not necessarily **compassion** or privacy in public places even if they are host to
(65) private moments. Only in specific places must personal space be respected.

Ethical behavior, however, is not always best defined within the confines of the law. Ethics and the law are not identical. To
(70) **elucidate** the essential difference: the law states what citizens are prohibited from doing and what they are permitted to do. The law sets the minimum standards of behavior required to maintain civil order,
(75) but it is the mission of ethics to set the standards of **decorum** to which we should aspire.

1. Which choice best summarizes the passage?
   A) It is sometimes necessary to break the law in order to best serve the public interest.
   B) A photographer who invades people's privacy breaks no laws but violates ethical standards.
   C) Photographers are immune to public complaints on the grounds of ethics.
   D) The privacy of the public is protected by codes of ethics, but not by the law.

2. As it is used in line 14, "lauded" most nearly means
   A) praised.
   B) paid.
   C) valued.
   D) skilled.

3. In lines 3–4, the author's use of the term "candid photographer" is meant to be
   A) sarcastic.
   B) admiring.
   C) informative.
   D) amusing.

4. It may reasonably be inferred from the fourth paragraph (lines 40–53) that
   A) photographers are right to conceal themselves because otherwise they will not get authentic photographs.
   B) the best news photographers are the most skilled at concealing themselves.
   C) news photographers must use their own judgment to determine what the public has a "justifiable need to see."
   D) people are sometimes ashamed to expose real emotions in public.

5. The author quotes from the news photographers' code of ethics in order to
   A) show that news photographers are aware that their work presents ethical problems.
   B) indicate the frivolousness of its attitude to problems of professional ethics.
   C) warn the public that they have no right or reason to expect privacy.
   D) demonstrate that candid photographs can reflect the highest ethical standards.

6. As it is used in line 63, "compassion" most nearly means
   A) candidness.
   B) individuality.
   C) sympathy.
   D) impertinence.

7. According to the fifth paragraph (lines 54–66), the author considers that
   A) getting a good photograph is more important than respect for privacy.
   B) even in public places, people have a reasonable expectation of privacy.
   C) news photographers are unethical.
   D) privacy laws are too restrictive.

8. As it is used in line 70, "elucidate" most nearly means
   A) endorse.
   B) underline.
   C) eliminate.
   D) clarify.

9. It can reasonably be inferred from the last paragraph that
   A) ethical codes hold citizens to higher standards of behavior than the law.
   B) the law does not demand that people behave ethically in public places.
   C) the law provides special provisions for those who require privacy in public places.
   D) people who want to avoid news photographers should go somewhere private.

10. Which choice provides the best evidence for the answer to the previous question?
    A) Lines 67–68 ("Ethical…law")
    B) Line 69 ("Ethics ... identical")
    C) Lines 69–72 ("To elucidate...to do")
    D) Lines 73–77 ("The law…aspire")

Vocabulary for Comprehension

Part 2

*Read this passage, which contains words in **boldface** that appear in Units 13–15. Then choose the best answer to each question based on what is stated or implied in the passage. You may refer to the passage as often as necessary.*

Questions 1–10 are based on the following passage.

A quantum leap is a sudden, permanent, and undisputed change. Throughout history quantum leaps have been brought about by an invention that

(5) expands the scope and range of human action, understanding, and aspiration.

The invention of the wheel is impossible to date precisely because it arrived in different places at different times. The

(10) Pyramid of Cheops in Giza, Egypt, constructed around 2500 BCE, is a stupendous feat of engineering, and it was achieved without the wheel. Evidence indicates that the stones were mostly

(15) quarried and cut to shape at sites within 100 miles of Giza, and transported on platforms riding over rollers. Evidence of the introduction of the wheel appears in Egyptian art 900 years later in the form of

(20) swift horse-drawn chariots (which were to revolutionize both personal mobility and the **bellicose** Egyptian's art of war). The wheel was an incomparable **asset**. It allowed for the creation of large goods-

(25) carts that traveled in long-distance caravans, which helped to **alleviate** Egypt's ancient solitude, and created mercantile wealth.

In 1439 a German blacksmith called

(30) Johannes Gutenberg created the first printing press to use moveable type— letters that could be rapidly shifted around, removed, and replaced to make new pages. Before Gutenberg books

(35) were written by hand on parchment (animal skin, scraped thin and dried), which made them expensive to make and slow to reproduce. Literacy was very much an elite accomplishment, and words

(40) were spoken, not written; heard, not read. The printing press made it easy to record and share knowledge as it produced books quickly and cheaply, and for the first time in history, books became

(45) universally available and affordable. People were **receptive** to the change. Populations became more literate and the spoken word found its way on to the page as books came to be published in every

(50) language. Many people had Gutenberg books in their homes. The literature and philosophy of Classical Greece and Rome became part of every European nation's culture. Gutenberg created a quantum

(55) leap in the power of words to determine the course of history. The revival of Classical values was the **ultimatum** that prepared Europe for the Renaissance.

Most people concur that the Internet has

(60) created a transformation so comprehensive and so rapid in the way we communicate that in order to even **acclimate** to it in a useful way, we must be prepared to **renounce** our ideas about the nature of

(65) communication itself. Early Internet pioneers at the Massachusetts Institute of Technology imagined a world in which all information would be available to everybody all the time—for free. The prospect **appalls** some,

(70) but others take to it with **alacrity**. The value of information is unstable and the meaning of freedom is hard to explicate in this era of rapid technological change. The Internet is expanding so fast that it is impossible to

(75) control, predict, or even understand what it is capable of. It is certainly a quantum leap, but it is too early to say where it will land.

1. What point does the author make by including the first paragraph?
   A) The author introduces the idea of a "quantum leap."
   B) The author introduces a passage on social change.
   C) The author introduces the idea that inventions can change the world.
   D) The author provides information on inventions whose impact is ongoing.

2. In the second paragraph, the author claims that the invention of the wheel
   A) improved transportation, which impacted war, trade, and wealth.
   B) allowed for the transport of huge stones over 100 miles.
   C) reduced the necessity of a vast labor force to build the pyramid.
   D) was a stupendous feat of engineering that made the pyramid possible.

3. Which choice provides the best evidence for the answer to the previous question?
   A) Lines 7–9 ("The invention …times")
   B) Lines 9–13 ("The Pyramid...wheel")
   C) Lines 13–17 ("Evidence…rollers")
   D) Lines 17–28 ("Evidence …wealth")

4. As it is used in line 46, "receptive" most nearly means
   A) open.
   B) hostile.
   C) alarmed by.
   D) prepared for.

5. Which choice best summarizes paragraph three (lines 29–58)?
   A) Gutenberg's invention of the printing press was not immediately accepted.
   B) Gutenberg invented the printing press for many reasons.
   C) Gutenberg's invention of the printing press changed how people understood language and books.
   D) The elite classes guarded knowledge from the common people.

6. It can be reasonably inferred from the third paragraph (lines 29–58) that
   A) the availability of affordable books contributed to the coming of the Renaissance.
   B) literacy would have spread through all levels of society with or without Gutenberg's press.
   C) books would not have been possible without Gutenberg's press.
   D) the movable type was more important than the press itself.

7. As it is used in line 62, "acclimate" most nearly means
   A) object.
   B) react.
   C) listen.
   D) adjust.

8. As it is used in line 70, "alacrity" most nearly means
   A) resentment.
   B) spirited readiness.
   C) sensible caution.
   D) astonishment.

9. The tone of the last paragraph may best be described as
   A) pessimistic about the future of the Internet.
   B) confident about the importance of the Internet.
   C) optimistic about the future of the internet.
   D) uncertain about the importance of the Internet.

10. The last paragraph's purpose is
    A) to define the phrase "quantum leap," using examples from history.
    B) to compare the impact of important inventions from different parts of the world.
    C) to prove that the Internet is relatively insignificant compared to other developments.
    D) to argue that the Internet is among the most important inventions in history.

Synonyms

*From the word bank below, choose the word that has the same or nearly the same meaning as the **boldface** word in each sentence and write it on the line. You will not use all of the words.*

antipathy	decorum	loll	raucous
appall	disparage	loquacious	stentorian
bellicose	imbibe	pandemonium	ultimatum
chagrin	laud	prowess	vivacious

1. Now that we have thoroughly cleaned up the living room, we can just **lounge** in it and admire our work. _____

2. There was a moment of **chaos** as the movie star emerged from the car and was immediately surrounded by eager photographers. _____

3. Because of his **thundering** voice, the host is well suited for his job as an announcer at noisy sports events. _____

4. Would it **horrify** you if I ate the berries after they fell on the floor? _____

5. It would be a mistake to **underrate** my opponent's chances of winning, since she has been known to pull off a surprise victory every now and then. _____

6. The Greek gods often interfered in the lives of mortals, granting favors to those they liked and punishing those for whom they felt **hostility**. _____

7. Tybalt is by far the most hot-tempered character in *Romeo and Juliet*, and his **combative** nature helps set the play's tragic events in motion. _____

8. In spite of Spain's great naval **mastery**, its fleet of ships, known as the *Armada*, was defeated by England in 1588. _____

9. The **boisterous** crowd jeered at the disqualified athlete as he exited the deck of the pool. _____

10. Diplomats and other official representatives of a country must show the utmost **propriety** as they perform their duties abroad. _____

11. The **gossipy** author could always be counted on to tell story after story in television interviews and talk show appearances. _____

12. Do you remember what happens in *Alice in Wonderland* after Alice decides to **swallow** the liquid in the bottle marked *DRINK ME*? _____

Two-Word Completions

Select the pair of words that best completes the meaning of each of the following sentences.

1. Though the supply of winter uniforms had done much to _____ the hardship suffered by the troops, the continuing shortage of ammunition and the ominous weather forecast _____ against pressing the attack.
   a. alleviate … militated
   b. whet … elucidated
   c. beset … concurred
   d. acclimate … stipulated

2. I might not be so _____ about suggesting improvements at the office if my boss were more _____ to constructive criticism. But since he seems to resent it, I keep such ideas to myself.
   a. zealous … magnanimous
   b. phlegmatic … implacable
   c. exuberant … compassionate
   d. reticent … receptive

3. Like a Roman emperor of old, the new principal issued a(n) _____ stating that attendance at morning assembly, which had been optional under the old regime, was now _____.
   a. patent … complacent
   b. defamation … sedate
   c. edict … mandatory
   d. facsimile … applicable

4. Alexander the Great was a(n) _____ foe of the Persians as long as they posed a threat to Greek security. But once he had conquered them, he proved to be a(n) _____ and fair ruler.
   a. phlegmatic … nondescript
   b. vehement … repressive
   c. implacable … magnanimous
   d. somnolent … innocuous

5. Edna's _____, offbeat sense of humor proved to be a considerable _____ in the competition for class wit.
   a. droll … asset
   b. savory … fracas
   c. grotesque … antithesis
   d. nondescript … facsimile

6. Though it didn't rule out mild soap, the warranty expressly _____ that _____ cleansers should not be used on the floor because they would damage the tile surface.
   a. rescinded … applicable
   b. stipulated … abrasive
   c. concurred … dissonant
   d. explicated … innocuous

7. "Since the documents are only _____ of the Declaration of Independence," the salesperson said, "the price I'm asking for them is _____ in comparison with what the real thing would cost."
   a. patents … savory
   b. edicts … voluble
   c. antitheses … grotesque
   d. facsimiles … infinitesimal

Idioms

In the passage "World-Famous Dance Troupe Announces First U.S. Tour" (see pages 212–213), the author says that the Ballets Russes dancers' movements "came under fire."

"Came under fire" is an idiom that means "to be criticized." An **idiom** is a common saying that expresses an action or idea in a figurative rather than literal way. Readers cannot always infer the meaning of an idiom; they often have to learn the accepted meaning and usage of each idiom.

Idioms add richness and color to spoken and written language. However, be aware of levels of formality in communication: Like slang, many idioms are informal, appropriate for casual contexts but not for use in formal situations.

Choosing the Right Idiom

*Read each sentence. Use context clues to figure out the meaning of each idiom in **boldface**. Then write the letter of the definition for the idiom in the sentence.*

1. When the lenders discovered that the business plan would cost over a million dollars, they **pulled the plug**. _____

2. When our car ran out of gas, we had to **hoof it** to the nearest gas station. _____

3. Sharon roasted a turkey, mashed the potatoes, and baked a pie—the **whole nine yards**! _____

4. Annie's organic farm proved to be a **cash cow**. _____

5. I had to **bite my tongue** when my sister asked what I thought of her new orange-and-green coat. _____

6. Ann tried to bathe with scented shampoo after she encountered a skunk, but she was just **grasping at straws**. _____

7. The guard must have been **asleep at the wheel** when the thief walked right out the door with the jewels. _____

8. Don't worry about how Malik will handle his success; you know he has his **feet on the ground**. _____

9. When Angela realized that I had been correct all along, she had to **eat crow**. _____

10. I thought I understood the poem, but the class discussion just **muddied the waters**. _____

a. lacking attention; not doing one's job

b. trying to accomplish something that has little chance of being successful

c. avoid saying what you really think

d. admit a mistake or error

e. everything

f. provided additional and confusing information

g. a realistic and sensible approach to life

h. a profitable source of income

i. walk

j. ended something; stopped giving support

Classical Roots

sed, sess, sid—to sit, settle

The root *sed* appears in **sedate** (page 194). The literal meaning is "settled," but the word now means "quiet or calm." Some other words based on the same root are listed below.

assess	**obsessed**	**sediment**	**subsidiary**
dissidence	**residual**	**subside**	**supersede**

From the list of words above, choose the one that corresponds to each of the brief definitions below. Write the word in the blank space in the illustrative sentence below the definition. Use an online or print dictionary if necessary.

1. matter that settles to the bottom of a liquid; lees, dregs

Catfish and snails will help to keep your aquarium free of _____.

2. to estimate the value of; to fix an amount, tax; to determine the importance, value, or size of

A gym or health club may _____ new members a fee at the time they join.

3. to grow less; become less active; to die down (*"to settle down"*)

The candidate could not begin to speak until the uproar _____.

4. furnishing aid or support; of secondary importance; a thing or person that assists or supplements

Evening newscasts generally cover major stories but don't have time to examine _____ issues.

5. remaining; left over

After I pay my monthly bills, I deposit some of the _____ money in my savings account.

6. excessively troubled or preoccupied by

A person who is _____ with the details of a project may have trouble seeing the "big picture."

7. disagreement in opinion or belief; dissent

The nominating convention was disrupted by noisy _____.

8. to displace in favor of another; replace; force out of use

In many homes, streaming video has _____ DVDs, just as music downloads have replaced CDs.

FINAL MASTERY TEST

Synonyms

Select the two words or expressions that are most nearly the same in meaning.

1. **a.** hypocritical   **b.** unfeigned   **c.** contentious   **d.** sincere
2. **a.** opulent   **b.** luxurious   **c.** culinary   **d.** poverty-stricken
3. **a.** wretched   **b.** squalid   **c.** exacting   **d.** healthful
4. **a.** pliable   **b.** vociferous   **c.** subtle   **d.** noisy
5. **a.** fortitude   **b.** asset   **c.** courage   **d.** intelligence
6. **a.** pinnacle   **b.** duplicity   **c.** deceitfulness   **d.** stubbornness
7. **a.** emaciated   **b.** shy   **c.** rude   **d.** diffident
8. **a.** phlegmatic   **b.** complacent   **c.** quarrelsome   **d.** bellicose
9. **a.** threatening   **b.** unexplained   **c.** ominous   **d.** applicable
10. **a.** opposed   **b.** averse   **c.** untrained   **d.** accustomed
11. **a.** indifferent   **b.** malevolent   **c.** spiteful   **d.** copious
12. **a.** pleasant   **b.** early   **c.** inopportune   **d.** inconvenient
13. **a.** rampant   **b.** misconstrue   **c.** dangerous   **d.** misinterpret
14. **a.** elated   **b.** worried   **c.** apprehensive   **d.** unreasonable
15. **a.** study   **b.** ruminate   **c.** relax   **d.** ponder

Antonyms

Select the two words or expressions that are most nearly opposite in meaning.

16. **a.** train   **b.** incite   **c.** quell   **d.** organize
17. **a.** foolish   **b.** palatable   **c.** dangerous   **d.** disagreeable
18. **a.** amicable   **b.** dour   **c.** expected   **d.** youthful
19. **a.** sacrifice   **b.** militate   **c.** support   **d.** fathom
20. **a.** antagonize   **b.** obey   **c.** remain   **d.** placate
21. **a.** charming   **b.** harmless   **c.** virulent   **d.** foreign
22. **a.** embezzle   **b.** profess   **c.** clarify   **d.** deny
23. **a.** colossal   **b.** loquacious   **c.** infinitesimal   **d.** profitable
24. **a.** magnanimous   **b.** disturbed   **c.** intellectual   **d.** petty
25. **a.** glorious   **b.** scrupulous   **c.** cursory   **d.** natural

Two-Word Completions

Select the pair of words that best completes the meaning of each of the following sentences.

26. It is _____ that when some people become famous and successful, they become arrogant and _____ to criticism.
  a. indomitable … nonchalant
  b. endemic … pliable
  c. lamentable … impervious
  d. venal … inclement

27. Although the enemy army was exhausted, it remained as _____ as ever; still, it did not stand a chance against the brave soldiers who felt _____ on the battlefield.
  a. tepid … tentative
  b. nonchalant … rampant
  c. destitute … venial
  d. implacable … invulnerable

28. People decried the clerk's _____ manner and attributed it to his mistaken belief that he was _____.
  a. vehement … loquacious
  b. reticent … diffident
  c. musty … droll
  d. officious … omnipotent

29. It is not wise to _____ another person, because one day, you may regret your _____ words.
  a. renounce … sophomoric
  b. disparage … corrosive
  c. perpetuate … turbulent
  d. coerce … malevolent

30. The brave knight would _____ his lance as he rode forth to prove his _____ in the joust.
  a. brandish … prowess
  b. plod … quandary
  c. waive … reprisal
  d. rescind … rancor

31. The horse's _____ demeanor gave no _____ of the speed that had won many races.
  a. supercilious … ultimatum
  b. nondescript … reparation
  c. placid … intimation
  d. urbane … platitude

32. The pre-Raphaelite painting showed a tragic and _____ young woman floating in a boat down a _____ stream.
  a. acrid … meticulous
  b. crestfallen … limpid
  c. insidious … insuperable
  d. abrasive … disreputable

Supplying Words in Context

To complete each sentence, select the best word from among the choices given. Not all words in the word bank will be used. You may modify the word form as necessary.

conclusive	gibe	somber	temerity
consecrate	guile	stultify	trenchant
dissonant	sedate	suave	vivacious
esteem	solace	suppress	warily

33. The view from his window of the dismal winter landscape put him in a very _____ mood.

34. Let's ignore their vicious _____ and do what we think is right.

35. Her _____ remarks cut right to the heart of the issue under discussion.

36. The fingerprints were regarded as _____ evidence of his guilt.

37. Despite his fearmongering and strict laws, the dictator was unable to _____ the spirit of freedom.

38. He is so _____ that he seems to fit into any social situation without the slightest difficulty.

adversary	facsimile	gnarled	misnomer
compatible	feasible	implicate	multifarious
condolence	finite	inveterate	redress
dearth	garrulous	ironic	tacit

39. Not a word was said, but we had a(n) _____ understanding between us of the plan.

40. With all her _____ activities, it's a wonder she finds time to sleep.

41. The plan was deemed not _____, since we did not have sufficient funds.

42. It would be a(n) _____ to nickname that crook "Honest John."

43. As a(n) _____ concertgoer, my friend Sandra has seen many great musicians perform.

44. I'll have to be at my best on the tennis court to beat a formidable _____ such as Ken.

Word Associations

*Select the word or expression that best completes the meaning of the sentence or answers the question, with particular reference to the meaning of the word in **boldface** type.*

45. You would be most likely to read of **uncanny** events in
- **a.** a detective story
- **b.** a ghost story
- c. a history textbook
- d. a novel of social protest

46. The word **demise** suggests that someone or something has
- **a.** passed out of existence
- **b.** gained final approval
- c. won a prize
- d. failed an examination

47. A nation that is a **belligerent** is engaged in
- **a.** energy conservation
- **b.** land reform
- c. industrialization
- d. war

48. A picture that is **askew** should be
- **a.** straightened
- **b.** dusted
- c. sold to the highest bidder
- d. given a price

49. Which nickname would a **craven** person be most likely to have?
- **a.** Calamity Jane
- **b.** Alibi Ike
- c. Chicken Little
- d. Fancy Dan

50. You would **extol** something that you find
- **a.** crestfallen
- **b.** contentious
- c. commendable
- d. innocuous

51. If people refer to Darryl as **obnoxious**, he should try to
- **a.** behave more agreeably
- **b.** smile more often
- c. speak more clearly
- d. learn to play soccer

52. A movie that is exceptionally **poignant** is likely to
- **a.** put you to sleep
- **b.** fail at the box office
- c. touch your emotions
- d. get a lot of laughs

53. We may apply the word **stately** to
- **a.** a gibe and a grimace
- **b.** a city and a state
- c. a robot and a computer
- d. a duchess and a sailing ship

54. To be **somnolent** implies a desire to
- **a.** exercise
- **b.** sleep
- c. eat
- d. travel

55. To **skulk** out of a room suggests
- **a.** listlessness
- **b.** happiness
- c. haste
- d. sneakiness

56. Which of the following suggests that a team is being **derided**?
- **a.** "You guys are losers!"
- **b.** "Give us a break, umpire!"
- c. "We're number one!"
- d. "Go get 'em!"

FINAL MASTERY TEST

Choosing the Right Meaning

Read each sentence carefully. Then select the item that best completes the statement below the sentence.

57. The sports commentator is as **facile** with words as she was on the playing field.
   The word **facile** most nearly means
   a. unbeatable   **b.** pleasant   **c.** assured   **d.** awkward

58. Marla suggests that we study before going to the game, and I **concur** with that practical plan.
   The best definition for the word **concur** is
   a. disagree   **b.** differ   **c.** agree   **d.** regret

59. I purchased this copy of Dickens's *A Tale of Two Cities* at the bookstore because the difference in price at the store and online was **negligible**.
   The word **negligible** most nearly means
   a. inconsequential   **b.** significant   **c.** expensive   **d.** equal

60. In the chapter on Benedict Arnold in my history book, the author refers to him as a **renegade**.
   The word **renegade** most nearly means
   a. patriot   **b.** heretic   **c.** martyr   **d.** soldier

61. The lawyers argued over a **discrepancy** between what the accused said had happened and what the witness said she saw.
   The word **discrepancy** most nearly means
   a. accusation   **b.** convergence   **c.** argument   **d.** inconsistency

62. I didn't realize how **disheveled** I looked after basketball practice until my mother looked at me and said, "Look what the cat dragged in."
   The word **disheveled** most nearly means
   a. tired   **b.** defeated   **c.** unkempt   **d.** victorious

63. I keep a map in my pocket even though my father claims he has an **infallible** sense of direction.
   The word **infallible** is best defined as
   a. ingenuous   **b.** memorable   **c.** imperfect   **d.** unerring

64. Doctors prescribed a new medicine in the hope that it would **obviate** the effects of the highly contagious virus.
   The word **obviate** most nearly means
   a. remove   **b.** allocate   **c.** repair   **d.** augment

65. Prince Hal, the main character in Shakespeare's play *Henry IV*, is often called a fun-loving **wastrel**.
   The word **wastrel** most nearly means
   a. miser   **b.** childish   **c.** naughty   **d.** good-for-nothing

The following is a list of all the words taught in the Units of this book. The number after each entry indicates the page on which the word is defined.

abhor, 106
abjure, 174
abrasive, 214
accede, 82
acclimate, 218
acquiesce, 146
acrid, 174
adroit, 26
adulterate, 18
adversary, 38
affiliated, 58
alacrity, 206
alienate, 42
alleviate, 206
allocate, 130
allude, 162
allure, 150
altruistic, 70
ambidextrous, 14
amend, 102
amicable, 30
animosity, 114
antipathy, 190
antithesis, 206
apathy, 118
appall, 202
applicable, 194
apprehensive, 114
ardent, 126
artifice, 42
ascertain, 62
askew, 150
assent, 74
asset, 194
assiduous, 130
attainment, 58
augment, 14
august, 170
averse, 30

bellicose, 202
belligerent, 30

benefactor, 70
benevolent, 26
bequeath, 58
bereft, 18
beset, 190
blithe, 146
brandish, 86
brash, 130
buffet, 102

callous, 170
capricious, 126
chagrin, 218
chaos, 106
chastise, 126
chivalrous, 74
clairvoyant, 162
clandestine, 174
clemency, 74
coerce, 38
cogent, 62
commend, 114
commodious, 102
compassion, 190
compatible, 118
complacent, 218
comprise, 82
compunction, 170
conclusive, 158
concur, 214
condolence, 118
conflagration, 170
consecrate, 118
contentious, 150
converge, 62
copious, 130
corrosive, 106
covet, 150
craven, 42
crestfallen, 146
culinary, 38
cursory, 26

dearth, 70
decorum, 194
decrepit, 114
defamation, 214
deft, 82
demise, 38
deploy, 14
deride, 114
destitute, 86
deviate, 126
diffident, 74
discern, 106
discrepancy, 74
disheveled, 146
disparage, 202
disperse, 58
disreputable, 158
dissonant, 206
dour, 18
droll, 202
duplicity, 26
duress, 190

edict, 206
elated, 174
elucidate, 206
emaciated, 130
embark, 70
endemic, 162
esteem, 58
exemplary, 158
exhilarate, 42
explicate, 214
explicit, 86
exponent, 150
expunge, 62
extant, 102
extirpate, 86
extol, 30
exuberant, 194
exult, 130

facile, 70
facsimile, 194
fallow, 38
fathom, 158
feasible, 26
finite, 62
fortitude, 18
fracas, 218

gape, 18
garrulous, 146
gibe, 14
gnarled, 126
grimace, 26
grotesque, 214
guile, 162
guise, 18

harass, 42
holocaust, 26

imbibe, 194
impervious, 30
impetus, 30
implacable, 190
implicate, 102
inclement, 42
indelible, 170
indemnity, 126
indomitable, 74
indulgent, 174
infallible, 70
infinitesimal, 194
ingenuous, 118
inkling, 130
innocuous, 190
inopportune, 82
insidious, 18
insuperable, 150
integrity, 158
inter, 106
intimation, 14
inveterate, 170